ERNEST L. AND RUTH E. NORMAN
Founders and Directors
Unarius Academy of Science

UNARIUS

UNiversal ARticulate Interdimensional
Understanding of Science

BRIDGE TO HEAVEN

Revelations of Ruth Norman

By Ruth Norman

Published By
UNARIUS SCIENCE OF LIFE
145 S. Magnolia Ave.
El Cajon, CA 92020

About the book - and the Author

This book contains a collection of the author's personal psychic experiences, relating her introduction to the Science of Unarius, her efforts and endeavors to achieve enlightenment and a closer relationship with the Infinite. In her Revelations, Mrs. Norman relates in detail personal visions, psychic and spiritual phenomena, some of which are most demonstrative; and to the average layman would be quite incredible or impossible. And, as she writes, many of which would dwarf by far, all previously recorded historical psychic phenomena, such as Moses' Burning Bush . . The Golden Plates of Joseph Smith . . 'The Star' the (so-called) wise men saw, etc., etc. She records how, from the very first day since her contact with the Unariun Moderator (Ernest L. Norman) her life has been filled with wonder, awe, and oftentimes, almost indescribable phenomena; not only of her own personal experiences but by also viewing and witnessing these 'miracles' of other Unariun students as well.

Outstanding among her 'Revelations' Ioshanna relates many memories, flashbacks and workings out of numerous former lifetime experiences, and which, as a result, has lessened her ties and oscillations with the earth-world, making it possible for her to ascend to higher spiritual worlds when leaving the physical —rather than to carry on, as is customary for the earthean in the repetitious returning, again and again to the planet Earth to work out existing karma; and which (karma) with most persons is only intensified or added to, rather than dissipated or lessened. The author portrays from her own personal experiences, proving her great spiritual progress into the future, her wondrous metamorphosis and how man can and does become godlike and live eternally in immortality, through the attainment and conception of the Unarius Interdimensional Science—which the Unariun

Moderator has brought to the Earth people. She describes how this knowledge can and does change one in many ways on all levels of expression for the better, as the Light, Energies and Powers of the Higher Minds are projected unto the aspiring student. The very Master Minds of the Infinite work-through this Channelship—with the sincere Unariun student.

A most interesting part of this book and of their lives lies in the relating of her realizations that she is again walking by the side of the One who was, in Jerusalem, two thousand years ago, the Nazarene (Jesus) and how they were, through these eons of time, again, through the prompting and guidance of their Higher Selves—and due to frequency relationship— brought together whereby she could help this great interplanetary Traveler—Master Mind bring to the Earth people the teachings Jesus was relating and started when his work and life was brought to a halt two thousand years ago. Ruth, for one, knows factually that He has, just as He prophesied He would—'Returned'. She has, through his teachings and never-ending help, found that Kingdom Within, and living much of the time in Inner and Higher Consciousness, experienced indescribable beauty, viewed countless luminous spiritual Beings.

Not only were these psychisms and realizations experienced by herself, but through means of the Spiritual Unariun Brotherhood were all those persons who had to do with the crucifixion two thousand years ago, also brought into this contact whereby they could 'work out' their past negative ties and blocks. They, too were taught how to free themselves of these negations that would, otherwise, tie them for eons of time to this lower Earth world. They, too, were aided by the great Inner Powers of the Spiritual Unariun Brotherhood, that they each one could be freed of their negative past expressions, and to learn the way toward a more progressive evolution. Many of these persons who were then Roman soldiers, etc., have also written (in other Unariun texts: "The Story of the Red Box" book) of their personal flashbacks and realizations, of their releasements and of the great change that has taken place in their lives, as a result!

This book was written especially to point up and prove how factual the science of Unarius is and how definitely it can and does change the dedicated student in so many ways for the better; how, with the inception of the Unariun Principle, man can prepare and condition himself to live in Higher Worlds and planets; how man can become godlike as has the author so proven through her own demonstrative-life-metamorphosis is and which each one must eventually encounter and experience if he is to progress in his evolutionary climb.

It is assured to those who can read carefully, sincerely, and with open mind, the contents of this incredible book, you will indeed experience an awakening not previously realized. Moreover, we are very conscious of the great Power which comes to the reader as he so attunes himself through the reading herein, as with all Unarius texts or messages; the power, Energies and Light, which is the transforming element of the very Infinite, is imbued within the word.

Yes, you, dear reader, can be so transformed as the author of this book relates that she has been transformed; as she now walks (in consciousness) on the Inner with the Angelic Beings of the Infinite. Our hands are ever reaching out to those reaching toward the Light.

Ioshanna (R.N.)

(Because the following notation, written by a sincere dedicatee, Sanosun, serves to further prove how a person can become a channel for the Infinite Powers, it shall be added herein.)

October 11, 1968—Dear Ioshanna: It has been a great privilege to read your pages of triumphant over-coming, and with deepest gratitude, for I know how much this 'Jewel' you add in fulfillment of The Mission will mean to your many students—especially, I speak for myself.

During the time of reading, the wonderful transcendency, the drowsiness, the strong power beams and Lights were experienced as attunement was made and one evening a ray at the top of my head was so intense I decided to close my eyes for a moment, then continue reading. This was shortly after ten. When I opened my eyes again, it was five o'clock in the morning and seemingly no time had transpired!

With these great strides you have made into the future, it is not possible to distinguish the two entities of the Channelship, and I sense only a complete Oneness, a true and perfect polarity with the Infinite.

Your tremendous inner growth is like a great beacon of Light for we who are on that precarious perch and who aspire to that treasured goal when our higher selves, too, shall become the dominating personality of our very being.

Thank you and the Unarius Brotherhood,

Sanosun.

PREFACE

Since time immemorial, man has been greatly concerned with what he calls time. He has used every possible means and expense to try to preserve this time element. His greatest fear is the time he will (what he calls) 'die', as he believes, when he will cease to exist. To the average person, reaching his three score and ten years, finds him dreading each subsequent year which draws him nearer to that day when his 'time' is up.

The following pages serve to prove the complete fallacy of time, as man believes it to be, and convey my true experiences, which prove how man can step off this seemingly endless, time-consuming wheel of karma around which he has been traveling these many past hundreds, yes, thousands of years—and lifetimes! Although this recounting of some of the highlights which have been my great joy—and pain—to experience, portrays but a small part of all that has gone before, it serves to prove that the element called time is only a concept—that man can triumph over time! We learn, rather, that man is simply contacting various points of infinity in his day by day living!

Up to the present, although there have been many articles and books written about the continuity of life called reincarnation or soul metamorphoses, they have all been more or less speculations. None, other than Unarius, has contained factual proof of how man can overcome this all-important concern of time. None of these writings have contained factual portrayals of how man can so accomplish; they have merely talked about other lives, and sensed glimpses or snatched flash memories, yet no one can tell exactly the function of the very scientific evolutionary principles of life from which no person can escape, as does the science of Unarius so adequately teach.

Living and reliving, returning time after time to the earth-world is as natural and certain as is man's nightly need for sleep or for food or any other natural sequences in his earthly life. It is for this reason this book is written—to show how, through understanding, with effort and continuous endeavor, man can gain the knowledge whereby he can desist from further repetitiously reliving, the karmic cyclic earth-life-returning, how he can, through the assimilation of wisdom, learn to sever these ties, the bonds that have held him, lo these many thousands of years, earthbound. My related experiences prove how man can learn to aspire, to unleash himself from his karmic past and to climb up onto the more progressive, regenerative evolution.

Now the average earthman's first thought or reaction to this truth will no doubt be, "How long will it take, how much time?" And, of course, this is dependent entirely upon the person, for no two persons have evolved up to this present point in exactly the same manner. Much would depend upon his dedication, efforts, backsliding, etc. However, any true seeker so desirous can, through his devoted study of the science of Unarius, break these bonds of his past—the earth worlds—and begin his ascent into the Inner Kingdoms, the worlds of Light.

Doubt not my words of Truth, dear seeker; they are factual and convey but one small part of the wonderful, incredible 'resurrection' which I've realized. I've proven in these words how man can emerge from out his animal-like-reactionary existence into a spiritual consciousness whereby it has been made possible that the Light, the Powers and Minds of the Infinite can now so oscillate through this entity unto mankind. This is the goal and purpose for each person eventually; but for the most part, it will take man many thousands of years or lifetimes before he even begins to arrive at the point where the desire to aspire exists, so far has he regressed.

Never has there existed a more opportune time, for we have on earth in the present, the greatest Mind that has ever visited the planet Earth—the Unariun Moderator, Ernest L. Norman, who stands ready to extend unto each one so endeavoring, his Infinite Mind energies that will lift, will help, and which will point the way, through the great Message He has brought. I, for one, along with many students, have proven that his science works! This is the objective of these relatings herein.

This is the Infinite Creative Science of the future. The sincerely dedicated can learn and prove, as have I, that it is just as Jesus also taught, "The Kingdom of Heaven is Within". Now I know, too, what He meant when He said, "My kingdom is not of this world, but of another", for with the help of our Moderator and the Unariun Brothers I, too, have come into this awareness, and time is no longer measured by hours on a clock or months on a calendar but rather, it is accomplishments which makes the difference!

Thus it is, that I have indeed triumphed over time! Our hands are ever reaching out to those reaching toward the Light!

Ioshanna.

IN HEAVEN'S WAY

So Joined am I
    In Heaven's Way replete
All Blessings I have found
    The Stars a carpet for my feet

My Personal Spiritual Metamorphoses

There could be no full biography written of myself, or even a testimonial, extensive or brief, without the constant inclusion of my beloved husband, the Unariun Moderator (Ernest L. Norman) his infinite help, his vast capabilities and expressions, for without Him, his help and efforts and that of the Brotherhood, there would be no testimonial. And so it is with full measure of recognition, of humility, and with a sense of deep appreciation to Him and The Brotherhood which He heads, that I write these events, my memoirs; of the psychisms, experiences, and of the tremendous spiritual progress this entity has realized during this time of inner and physical contact with Him.

In relating the highlights of my life since walking by his side, there are a few experiences that will also be pointed out which took place before our physical contact. However, this would make no difference as far as his help and that of the Brotherhood is concerned; they often work many years in advance of the physical contact. In fact, as I now look back upon my entire life, it is plain to see that He has been working with me from the inner during almost my entire lifetime! Thus, the physical phenomena experienced in the several years previous to our meeting, I realize, were also brought about through the direction and efforts of the Moderator and the Brothers on the Inner.

Thus, dear reader, please bear in mind that the writer is fully cognizant of the truth of Jesus' words, "Of myself I do nothing, but it is the Father (Higher Self) within that doeth all things". Man, in his conscious self, can do nothing to bring about psychic phenomena, healing, etc., as it is ever set in motion and extended from the inner outwardly. So it is, that

1

I, personally, sense no feeling of pride in these countless psychic happenings, and the only help that I, or
any individual could give was due to the fact that I
remained steadfast in my efforts to learn. In fact, I
actually "lost myself" in doing, in working with the
Word the Moderator would bring forth. Self became
unimportant and the work occupied my entire life!
This, frankly, is the only way I, personally, did or
could help, or make possible the incredible and never
before heard of experiences which, in part, I shall
endeavor to relate herein.

One of the very first experiences took place about
four years prior to our meeting. As I slept, a huge circular Ray-Beam, a sort of floodlight was projected into
my face, so brilliant and intense that it awakened me.
I felt that the noonday sun was coming through a
large circular hole in the window shade (and which
was non-existent). So brilliant was this golden light, I
tried to cover my head that the 'sun' be shielded so I
could return to sleep, only to find it was pitch dark
and two o'clock in the morning. Mental thought projections accompanying this Ray-Beam of Light, which
seemed as words, were, "Thou seekest the Holy Grail,
child, and thou shalt find. Go and tell no man!" It
startled and alerted me so that no further sleep was
wanted. I could hardly wait for that evening to come
when, as I usually took several ladies to a meeting on
that night, I could tell them of my wonderful vision;
and which I was told not to tell! One lady realized the
great significance and said, "Oh, Ruth, that is tremendous; it means you are going to take part in some
very important spiritual work in the future." My contact with the Moderator has more than proven how
right she was in this prophecy regarding my vision. I
have since felt that most unusual floodlight was the
Moderator making a first physical contact in that
psychic phenomenal way!

Our Joining

It was a matter of a few days after leaving the desert (taking a house trailer with me) that I met Ernest at a Spiritualist church, one I had never attended before and where a convention was being held. One of the choicest bits of phenomena to us pertained to the three spiritual white-robed, white-haired and bearded, ancient, learned Ones who, as Ernest said, carried about with them huge books. These Ancients (denoting great wisdom) were seen psychically with Ernest during several years prior to this by other clairvoyants who often told him these books represented those which he would one day write. Earlier that very evening, Ernest said, a 'sensitive' told him, "Whenever you are ready, now you can start to write the books." Ernest replied, "I'm ready."

Then here that very evening, we were brought together! After the meeting in a side room, personal readings were given by a few readers. A lovely lady 'sensitive' said to me as she started my reading, "Three Ancients on the inner, wise and learned men with long flowing white robes, with white beards and long white hair, carrying huge books, come to you. There is a wonderful future with you here, everything so luminous and bright! "Oh," she said, "I must read more for you, so many wonderful things here, but now I must speak to another first." At that very moment, Ernest appeared, standing in the arched doorway nearby, leaning against the wall as if waiting! Of course, He knew inwardly and no doubt engineered the entire meeting mentally!

Within moments, Ernest was reading for me. As He came over and sat down by my side, He started telling me of my former husband in spirit, describing him so exactly that I knew here was truth! However, here is my pet joke on myself. I was hesitant to listen to him;

I wanted instead, to hear more from the lady who had told me of the three Wise Men, for that quickened my interests far more than my former husband in spirit. But (laughingly), here was one of the Wise Ones sitting right beside me, in person! We have both had many a good laugh over that incident, all planned so precisely and perfectly!

From that very first moment on, I listened to the most illuminating, revealing, eye-opening and transforming wisdom that has ever been brought to earth! This knowledge, along with the accompanying powers, has changed me so completely that I now know what it is to be, as Jesus said, "In the world but not of it." Former friends, relatives, habits, activities, ties of the past, etc., have all become something of the past; my ties and obsessions with them no longer exist. Friends, within a few months time, became like strangers, so much of the past oscillation with them had been discharged—and which is the very purpose of physical incarnating when one arrives at this point in his evolution—to sever ties with the past in order to conceive the new and higher knowledge and to learn to oscillate instead, more with the Infinite.

However, because I have had continuous, personal help, lived in the Light and Power constantly, having left completely the physical or worldly activities, I have made unusual progress and my life today resembles very little of the person I was before Unarius.

Among the very first readings which Ernest related, (from the past lives of this entity), was the scene of my finding the babe Moses in the bulrushes and raising him. In fact, it was during our second meeting when he saw the king's young daughter tripping down to the waters edge to rescue the infant Moses. He even described the basket in which the babe was found in the water; it was made of reeds and held together with pitch or tar; how the child was placed in the water by an unwed mother who had no way to care for

4

him and put him to drift downstream, hoping someone would rescue and care for him.

He 'saw' how it was the babe's crying which attracted the princess' attention to the river bank and viewed her lifting him up. Some time later, He learned how it was that, only after much persuasion from her to keep the babe, did the old king agree that he could be admitted in, to be raised as one of the family.

This description was not strange to me but all seemed so very familiar in a personal way; however, I did not completely work it out at that time. It was several years later when the movie, "The Ten Commandments", was shown at a nearby theater. As one of their ads, they had built a small replica of this babe Moses scene and displayed it in a street window. As my eye caught this sight, which looked very real and lifelike with the thatched basket of reeds holding the babe among some willow and pampas grass in the water, I became spellbound. It locked me in with the past and there I stood, transfixed, locked in time! I froze.

Soon a sensation of mixed emotions was experienced—the very same feelings the young princess experienced the day of her 'find'—of sorrow for the tiny infant, so cold, alone and forsaken; more than three thousand years in time then became nonexistent and time was bridged as the past and present became as one. Yes, the very compassionate feeling returned as I stood there on the sidewalk gazing back thirty-five hundred years! I was not conscious of how long I was so entranced, but felt the trickle of tears dripping down my face, the 'lock in' or contact with that long-ago past time released. A great sigh of relief, and another block was removed: constant proof that we are but as a living television apparatus, incepting and oscillating outwardly; out-picturing previous inceptions!

This incarnation of 'mothering' Moses was a life-

time which was prior to a life lived as the mother of
Akhnaton—Queen Ti or Tiy—which Ernest 'saw' and
which I worked out later.

I learned of The Moderator—as—the Pharaoh, Akhnaton

It was the first week in March 1954, that we journeyed to San Diego soon after our meeting, Ernest in his car and I in mine, pulling my house trailer. After the second day, He had need to return to Los Angeles for a few days. During the first morning, after He left, I experienced a strange and strong compulsion to go to town, and found myself stopping in an old used-book store—the largest one I have ever seen. It seemed a block long and half as wide; all used books. I had no idea why I was here or what I was looking for, but reading was one thing I had no time for then. However, I walked quickly as though I knew just where I was going; down into the basement to the very back of the shop, stood on tiptoe, reached as high as ever I could and brought down a little magazine. It's title was "Search". I believe it has since been renamed. I was surprised when I saw what my hand held! On the cover was a picture of a very odd and interesting-looking individual called Yada. The face held me spell-bound; it was very oval as was the head and bald, very striking features, eyes slightly slanting upward, large flat ears and he wore a very small distinguished brush beard on the tip of his chin and a colored symbol in the center of his forehead. I could scarcely get into the magazine for the attraction that face held for me.

However, as I read I learned he was a Spiritual Being who, five hundred thousand years ago, incarnated in China as a very wise philosopher. Now, said the article, he worked through or inspired a certain individual there in San Diego while the medium was entranced. In other words, he entered into this medium's (Mark Probert's) body, and spoke through his voice.

Wonders of all! I was on the trail of something, and like a hound dog with the scent, couldn't get off the track until I had found this man, Mark. I hadn't the slightest idea why, but was being 'led'.

The upshot of it was: through the name and address in the magazine, I was able to locate his brother, living in Los Angeles, who furnished Mark's telephone number there in San Diego, right in the town where I was! The book was printed in Illinois! As it came about, Mark was holding one of his regular weekly meetings for his 'sitters' the second day following.

Well, I was really sitting on a hot potato! It would be utterly impossible to convey this tremendous psychic upheaval that continued. The cycle was present and it could not be suppressed, nor could I relate it to Ernest as he was away and could not be reached by telephone for another day. What to do; what to do? The cover picture did not leave my hands; it was as if I were glued to it and I felt surely like the proverbial pullet laying its first egg. I could not relax or become interested in any one of the many things I should have been doing. Inwardly I knew something vital was brewing, but consciously—nothing! So much energy present! No sleep that night!

What a relief when Ernest returned and I could relate it all to him. I met him, not with a normal greeting but with the picture and He, too, knew that here was something important but it didn't 'throw' him as it did me—for it was my objective. The next night we found Mark Probert and sat in his little circle with eight or ten other 'sitters' and soon Yada came in. He entered into Mark's physical and used his vocal chords and, with a slightly broken Chinese accent, Yada told how he had lived in China 500,000 years ago, continuing, "Yes, we know many things. There is one among you here tonight who lived the life of the great teacher and Pharaoh, Akhnaton, who had great wisdom to bring the earthean. I can tell this man these facts and it will not concern him." He knew Ernest was far beyond such information inflating any ego with him. He continued, "This man, even today, carries the scars on his hands of yet another lifetime when he, likewise, endeavored." Then he turned to Ernest and said, "Is this not so, my good Brother?"

Ernest was, of course, rather taken aback at Yada's pronouncement for a moment. He had consciously prepared that others would not learn of his identity at this time; and, of course more than likely, it was He in his Higher Self who helped arrange this important 'miracle' of contact. The others present, of course, wanted to see the scars of the holes in the palms of his hands, and which caused them much concern. They were all greatly moved. This medium, Mark, however, did not possess the very highly developed faculty and ability as is true with the Unariun Moderator, for he permitted the astral entities to enter into his very body and which caused weird distortions not necessarily pleasant to witness. This, too, helped me to appreciate the very highly-developed Infinite Consciousness our Moderator expresses—far removed from these dark séance rooms where a few stray entities come in and obsess the medium! It so happened, however, that this particular spokesman was no ordinary 'lost' entity, but one who truly knew the former lives of the Unariun Moderator, no doubt an advanced Unariun Brother.

Of great interest to me were the lengths to which the Higher Ones went that I be led to this stranger, Yada, who could convey this vital message! (When the Moderator Himself could have related his past, yet, he would not. He would be too humble and, to Him it would be the wrong psychology; but what a wonderful plan and way.) Now I knew why I had the overwhelming urge and great frustration until the contact was made: so that I could, this early in the work, learn who this great Soul was, by whose side I have come to walk. Possibly, too, had He, himself, made such statements, I might not have been able to conceive these facts for there is a natural resistance with most persons; to 'doubt' when another will make such claims about himself. But here, with a complete and total stranger—a spiritual force or Being coming through one who neither of us had met previously—how could one doubt? And the scars in his hands to prove. (However, at this time, I was not conscious that it was Jesus to whom he referred. Later, in my own way, I realized.)

Yes, we know how it is; even now, many will doubt even after they read the "Jose" book. Although they possibly have heard of and expected the return of Jesus, yet they will doubt when they read or hear that it has taken place! Not so? Indeed!

And so, this was our first learning of the true identity of our leader. However, after that particular evening, I doubt very much whether either of us thought of the incident again until the time of this writing, when these memories are again impressed within. For one thing, our consciousness was too filled with so many other activities and expressions, but He, for one, (and myself, as well), would need to have more than any one person's word before it was truth to Him. We do know Yada was correct but Ernest, being the scientist that He is, would have to prove all things in many ways.

And so it was, through the research of the works of Akhnaton, that we proved to ourselves that He did teach much the same as He is teaching today—the same principles. Thus it was, too, at the time when my personal realization took place, of Him living the life of Jesus. He was very reticent to go along, for all things must be proven to Him within his mind. With myself, it was of a different nature. Some may say I'm just gullible, but it is not really that. There is a sense of knowing—a strong, positive knowing that cannot be shaken. Those are the times when the information comes from the inner or higher. Things were happening so rapidly, it was difficult to keep track of time and experiences, date-wise.

Thus it was, from that day hence, one revelation upon another, regarding our own two personal pasts, was realized and revealed by the Moderator. He would view, for instance, some one lifetime in Egypt or Greece, and then we would go to the library to read of these historical events and dates, names, etc., of the queens, kings, or pharaohs. Oh, we both went round and round with the great Temple of Karnak, one of the world wonders which He helped to build and design, for the building was added to more than once. These times and experiences were simply like reading pages from our own personal biographies, so familiar were they; and yet we had never read of them in this present lifetime previously. It was such a revelation to hear Him voice these times, then to find it all there in the encyclopedia or history books. Those weeks were the most outstanding of all in our present life together. The excitement and exuberance was at a very high pitch during these times of relating, of attunement and realizing—then the proving from the printed pages. These past incarnations were, of course, most important to first be freed from—days never to be relived. As luxuriant and glorious as these lives were, in the physical sense, they still existed as ties; oscillations which were created from the physical lives and must be objectified and discharged. All the pieces fitted and jibed.

In several evolutions during this lush Egyptian era, He would view me returning again to help carry on the great dynasty of that epoch. In the one life He lived as Akhnaton, I incarnated as his mother; then, two or three hundred years later, as an offspring of these families in other relationships, as the dynasty wore on but such incarnations were set up, and set in motion from the inner many, many years before the actual expression—all a part of a great Inner Plan of which Unarius is the culmination. (Further mention regarding these lives, later on.) Perhaps some day in the future the Moderator may write his most incredible biography; he will reiterate some of these lives; moreover, after they have been worked out, they cease to be of importance to the individual himself. However, one important note of interest relates to the time of Ernest's reliving and 'work out' with the old priest Caiaphas (who was the one largely responsible for His condemnation to the cross); how, after his contacting him physically that, as He often relates, "I fought the very demons of hell for five days and nights, and sometimes the room was so black with them I couldn't even see the light which was always lit." This psychic battle was beyond imagination and He emerged victorious, but not without scars. Within his hands, were the psychic nail hole scars; the cords were taut, inflamed and near bleeding, so factually physically and psychically was this past relived! At certain times of the year such as Easter, etc., these scars become inflamed and again near bleeding; the finger cords draw up. After many years, this stigma has lessened a little but not a great deal; the disfigurement is still very prominent.

Our Leaving the Business—Social World

As was partially mentioned, upon the very first moment of our joining, Ernest began to read from my past, not only of the present life but of the many lives lived in the distant past. Thus, this viewing He continued and carried on with our every meeting. The many recalls He brought to me were not only interesting, great fun and amusing, but served to discharge each incident as He thus polarized it in consciousness. Before I left the desert, I had a thought that I would possibly go to San Diego, yet when I arrived in Los Angeles, I could not force myself to do so. (I had not yet met Ernest.) But the time was short before we were brought together, a matter of a few days; then to the San Diego area we drove. Previously, I had believed that with the little nest-egg accumulated during the past year from my desert milk venture, I could possibly purchase a small flower shop, but when arriving in San Diego, this plan was quickly dismissed. Ernest mentioned that he felt he could write a book if I would be interested in helping to get it published, etc. Well, of course, I was eager, even though I knew absolutely nothing about books, publishing, or the like. The decision was made and very quickly his words began to flow. Any former thoughts I had entertained regarding my activity in the business world were never again considered. We were going to print his books.

At the time, I doubt if He was conscious of the particular material to be used, but happily, he need not have to be! When the work started, it flowed like water and each dissertation was a new and wondrous revelation. A new and tremendously interesting life was entered into.

I am afraid had I known, during my just previous months of endeavors in the desert, soliciting new accounts, keeping the books, etc., what lay in store for me, that I would likely have been unable to do a very thorough job with the work at hand, so excited would I have been. But Spirit is all-wise. These events, happenings and expressions unfolded quite naturally, each in due and proper time and cycle.

Ever since I was brought in contact with the Moderator (Ernest), my life has been filled with revelations, with psychic experiences, with a new understanding of life which has explained to me all the heretofore unexplainables! Life has become meaningful and purposeful; far removed from the robot life previously lived! Although for twelve years previous to our meeting, I had been seeking quite extensively and seriously all the metaphysical schools and fields of thought, I could never feel satisfied with any, or that they held the true answers to life. Viewing these past endeavors now, they were simply a step removed from the more orthodox religion itself and not a true science of life. It was a matter of unlearning them, and which took place quite naturally, probably because I was not really a believer in them anyway.

Since our very first contact in the church in February, 1954, Ernest has portrayed a great and unlimited scope of wisdom and knowledge of an infinite variety. The complete magnitude of his Mind has never been realized or conceived, nor could it be by any, other than one with like development, and which exists not on earth. There have never been questions for which He could not supply the answers. If He is not at the moment conscious of the answer, instantly He attunes unto his Inner or Higher Self, and there it is! His is part of the Infinite Creative Mind.

14

There was one interesting experience after another; spiritual Beings would come to me as huge luminous balls of oscillating Radiant Light. At first, in the formative years, these Lights would appear as pinpoints, then gradually as I progressed in consciousness, they seemed larger, until at the present time, the Higher Ones appear larger than the common basketball! There were transcending experiences that would take me literally and figuratively out of my body, and which would happen with each contact of the Luminaries, especially with the very large infusions of Light.

Now, at the present, nearly fifteen years of Unarius' physical contact and working with, I believe I shall not have to return to earth because of the ties which for so many lifetimes have bound me—as is common with all eartheans. If another return does take place, it will simply be from the desire to help the earthean, not from the subconscious tie which so commonly binds man to it. Thus it has been thoroughly proven beyond any possible doubt, that man can and does become a spiritual being; he can change from his robot, animal-like, homosapien existence, to become an oscillating entity with the Infinite—one who functions not from subconscious compulsions, but rather, from (and by choice) mental oscillation. He then experiences that which he selects to so experience in his future!

My 2,000-Year Flashback

During these formative years, there were several places we visited which held for me an immediate flash-back or re-attunement with the past, but the most important reliving or 'workout'—the one of greatest value—was the great log-jam removal when my attunement was made with Jerusalem. This rug-jerking—earth-shaking—experience has been told in the "Little Red Box" booklet, but for the sake of those who have not read it, I will repeat briefly.

It was only a few weeks after we met and went to San Diego to live that we drove to a nearby little lake, surrounded with small hills, huge rocks and boulders. This similarity to Jerusalem two thousand years ago served to tune me back, as it were, and especially so when Ernest happened to step away a few yards out of my sight. When I did not see him, I experienced the sickening feeling, "Oh, He's gone. They have taken Him!" That did it! Instantly, I literally fell apart and all connections to the various parts of my body seemed nonexistent. I seemed to become rubber-legged, dizzy-headed and lacked any coordination necessary to manipulate the body, and I crumpled to the ground. As quickly as Ernest stepped back into the picture and saw my distressed condition, I told Him, "I thought you had gone—thought they had taken you away!" So complete and thorough was the attunement, the reliving with that past, it seemed as if it were taking place right then and there!

Only with his physical help did we manage to get my limp body up the hill that we had just descended shortly before. He had quite a struggle to help push this physical as I was almost completely out of the body, more like jelly than flesh! During the strenuous climb that took everything I had to make it, we were both sensitive to the few people nearby who likely thought me inebriated. Little did they know the two-thousand-year span back to Jerusalem which had just been bridged!

Ernest was somewhat relieved when he could finally shove the body into the seat of the car and make the wild dash necessary to the nearest equipped service station. Fortunately, it was only two blocks distant, but how I ever lasted those few moments, I will never know. A voluminous purging of black liquid followed! All the negative debris of those two-thousand-years duration was thusly discharged and I felt more dead than alive. A major crisis was this reliving, so thorough was the re-attunement. He then drove home where, upon my bed, I passed out for several hours.

The repercussions of this workout lasted not only these few hours but for ten entire days and nights following! I was more out of the body than in it, and about all I could do was sit or lie about and await my return. When I finally 'came back' completely and the psychic work being accomplished on the inner was, for then, finished, all things were different with me. The sensitivity had been so stepped up that normal sounds seemed deafening. Nerve ends such as the tips of my fingers were so sensitive to the touch and I seemed to feel so 'out-of-place'; I seemed to be a stranger to all things! An awareness existed of many things which, for a large part, were to take place in the future; normal people on the streets looked peculiar, unfamiliar. I had been reborn of the Spirit! I felt many pounds lighter in weight! And I was 'seeing' the world for the first time!

It was during this time of rebirth that the realization came to me who this person really was that I had so recently met, and by whose side I now walked; that He was re-establishing on earth the mission of Jesus, and that it was He, the Nazarene, Himself, returned!

17

Words could never convey the many happenings of those ten days, but suffice it to say upon returning to the body, all things were different. My physical world was no more; I had been robbed, but good, and loving every instant of it! Now, only one interest consumed my consciousness (using 'consumed' in every sense of the word)—that of the mission, the work He had just begun. The complete change and progress, the difference noticed in my entire being—physical, mental, and every other way—could not be evaluated in earth terms, but many, many lifetimes were then cancelled out, ties severed; and due, of course, to previous preparation on the inner and the existing need of the Moderator in his mission to have a compatible polarity with Him, the great projection into the future was being accomplished.

As He has often said, "It was similar in effect to being shot from a cannon into the future!" I call that 'lost week' (ten days), my 'Rocket into the Future'—lost so far as the world was concerned; but no greater benefits or accomplishments have ever been realized in so short a time or in any one lifetime, of that we feel sure!

A few years after our meeting, there appeared in my left hand a knot—the cords and tendons of the second finger drawn. The intensity was not as great as exists in Ernest's hands, but at the center end of the drawing was what appeared as a psychic nail-hole scar. Interestingly enough, of late and since the "Jose" book and the recovery of his red chest (box), this defect has disappeared. In my case, it was no doubt due to the rapport or viewing of Jesus, although fortunately, I was spared the viewing of the actual attaching of Jesus to the cross. With Him, the physical (psychic) scars are still vivid and deep.

During my entire present lifetime prior to this 're-living' of the Jerusalem hill climb, I had never been able to walk up any hill, not even the slightest grade.

I would puff and pant, become exhausted and out of breath with just a few steps up! I was not conscious why; only thought it a deficiency with me, and because of this inability, missed out on many picnics in the canyons the children often attended during school. However, after my recuperation from the 'lost week', from that day on, hill-climbing was no different than level walking. The healing was complete with the realization of the emotion, the frustration experienced as they 'took' Jesus two thousand years ago, and as I, in my great fear, anxiety and love for Him, attempted to climb that Hill Golgotha; but which was too late! Then, here at the little reservoir lake, as He stepped aside out of view, this momentary absence served to do the trick, and I have never been the same since! I stepped two thousand years into the future!

The Moderator has said more than once, "Never on this earth has there been the like take place, and to such lengths and with such benefits—never!" But it was most purposeful, the need existed and, with the Infinite, there are no impossibilities! Time was short to bring about all that was to be accomplished for mankind. He had a great mission to fulfill and needed all the help I could extend; first of all, a more compatible frequency was necessary. Surely, the great accomplishments of the present would not have been possible had not this great sluffing-off process taken place—the rebirth; for the opposition of existing oscillations from all my many earth lives would have been too great for such a Being to endure.

Strong, negative obsessions too, had to be removed and overcome; accumulations and encrustations of many lifetimes and eons past needed to be met, faced and worked out. Certain of these can be done—and are, by the Inner and Higher Minds, but man must ever accept and assume his personal responsibilities for what he has incurred in these many previous lifetimes and all this cannot be done easily, quickly or painlessly! Most vital is it for one to learn self-exor-cism—not an easy trick or act to learn, yet once learn-ed, it becomes an important part of our daily expres-sion to keep our 'self' separated from these impinging gremlins of the past and from the astral forces; some most destructive and strong. And I must admit it did take me several years to finally overcome these terri-ble interferences which must have given our Beloved One great trial and difficulty in so coping with—yet the only way was to do it myself. This is the most im-portant lesson any person can learn in these earth life incarnations! However, now these past influences, acquaintances, etc., can no longer live through this one—they shall not pass! I have learned—as the Bro-thers used to laughingly joke—'to keep the cellar door down' on the one from the past! Of course I am most regretful for every moment that I was unaware of how to use this principle! But most glad and thankful that the lesson has been learned!

The average earthean would be quite surprised were he able to actually see how much he is influenc-ed by the astral forces, by friends and relatives, etc., who (as he believes) have died.

Yet, even with all this, there was much that still had to be overcome in a personal, conscious way with me for several years into the future. Man must always work toward his own overcoming and progress, other-wise life would hold no purpose, no meaning or goal, for always it is the experience that conveys the less-ons, the progress. 'Tis a never-ending endeavor—this progressive evolution!

The poetry had already begun to flow from his Mind; the Venus book was also started, and we were on the way! Of great interest to me it was, how some mornings, upon awakening, the Moderator would have within his consciousness dissertations that just could not wait! The feelings with Him were, He said, as if He would explode if He did not voice them immediately.

So intense was the Power, the Energies that accompanied the discourses, He would just have to give them birth, often even before he could drink his morning cup of coffee. Thus, the earthly emergence of Unarius had begun to take place, and for me, new and, at that time, incredible and unheard-of experiences.

The continuation of Jesus' mission, from which He had been so abruptly and forcibly stopped two thousand years ago, was now being re-established. The Light, which only such an advanced and developed Being could project, shines again upon the earth to illumine the hearts and minds of those receptive—those who have prepared for this, their advent. The great cycles of time evolve that which the Infinite Minds have so set in motion. Man cannot destroy; he can deter his own evolution in his destructive efforts, but the Infinite is infallible, is eternally Infinite and cannot be contaminated or harmed; for always will these great illumined and creative Minds find the way, the plan, and the time to so accomplish and to help the earth-bound animal-like homosapien (man); yes, even in spite of himself, for these great cycles move in perfection in all ways and in all things; and just as Jesus told in that long-ago era, "I shall return," indeed, He has, for the Infinite would never set any expression in motion and permit it to become dormant or deteriorate due to influences or interferences of the entities of the underworlds. Thus, the Infinite is being effective in helping to change the direction of those persons who previously endeavored to block and to destroy—the true meaning of 'turning the other cheek'!

Yes, it is up to man to learn to become receptive to this inner and higher guidance—guidance which is ever present and but awaits for man to 'ready' himself for this, his opportunity to begin to sever his bonds of the past and step upon the more progressive, regenerative, evolutionary pathway.

The Mission in Progress

Always as the Moderator would voice his illumined Message of Truth, great Powers were present, often so intense were the frequencies, the Rays so potent, I would become so transcended, it was most difficult to remain awake; the Beam would just project me right out of the physical at times! And with each dissertation He brought was a new revelation; more and greater Truths of the Higher Worlds were added; day, after day, after day. He would let the Light shine and the Word and Power flow! Often, as He voiced and described the scenes on the inner—Venus in particular—did I also view these happenings. At one time, I recall I saw my brother, in spirit, as the Moderator was describing the line of plebians just passing through the great flames or fountains of Light-Energies, and I said, after He had finished, "Danny was in that group of emerging entities!" He said, "Yes, the fourth from the end." Thus, much of the time I traveled in consciousness through these many visitations to higher worlds and which, of course, could never have been possible without the great discharge, the release of the many earth negations and ties which existed a short time previously.

Always were the teachings and transmissions in the wonderfully perfect continuity of word and sentence structure, far removed from the manner and ways the earthman writes a book. Instead, He would simply sit down and begin to dictate, either to myself, to write it down in longhand or to the tape recorder. Unarius' works have been printed just as He voiced them, word for word, with no rearranging or editing necessary, other than my typing errors, in all that He gave, so perfect has it all been with Him—and He not a college student; which serves to prove He brought the great Infinite Wisdom with him as He came into the world! Yes, the enthusiasm, the excitement, the wonder of it all was overpowering. He was actually bridging two worlds! He was bringing Heaven right down to earth—the two wedded in one. Those never to be forgotten days and years! And very likely, never to be repeated; however, to those so likewise ready, this Infinite Power, the life-changing Rays and Light are presently existing in the Unariun curriculum for whoever will so devote and dedicate himself to his personal development. Thus can these persons also experience growth, change and progress.

To those who may be interested, we state that this great illuminating Light, the energies have also been interjected and oscillated into the very printing of the Word and into the binding of the very books themselves, as we have worked in 'consciousness' with these individuals so involved that the works may be so imbued! All so concerned, having to do with these works, have been polarized with this Radiant Energy in order that you, the reader, may be aided in every possible way to receive the fullest measure of benefits. I could tell of the time when speaking on the phone to one in charge of the printing plant when the Higher Ones were polarizing the work there, the plant people, etc., how one man, Marvin, said, "What's the matter with me? Here I am, shaking all over! I've got to get some coffee." I had to smile for I realized he was not accustomed to these Ray Beams and electrical Charges from the Inner that are projected, but it really startled him. Little did he know, the very Light of Heaven had descended!

Boiled Alive!—In Cheese!

A very interesting phenomenon was experienced by us just a few weeks after the mission got underway in San Diego. A Mrs. Day, who had heard of the rare psychic diagnostic work of the Moderator, brought her little daughter to see him. The girl was about ten years old and had experienced a very rough life due to physical problems. She was puny and would not become interested in school. She could not adjust to this earth or people and experienced the strange peculiarity, every time she would attempt to put her hands in slightly warm water—to wash the dishes, etc.—of becoming ill; feeling faint. If she sat before a fire in the fireplace she would also feel faint. Her mother often tried to get her to drink milk, believing it could give her strength but it made her deathly ill. The parents, her father a chiropractor, had spent large sums on doctor bills in their effort to help her, but no help could be found. It was plain to see, the child was in a very bad way. Some had even told the mother she should not expect to raise the girl and the constant worry was ruining all their lives. It was such a very peculiar case, the doctors would have no way of knowing the cause of her troubles.

It took no time for the Moderator to tune in and locate what caused all her difficulties. He saw the child in a former lifetime as a young woman sincerely in love with her husband, who as his livelihood, operated a large cheese factory in Switzerland. It so happened the husband was in love with another woman. The wife came to the factory one day unexpectedly and found him and the other woman embracing. Ernest saw an enormous vat of boiling cheese cooking, being mechanically stirred. After some argumentative words, a fight ensued; the husband began chas-

24

ing her around the cat-walk (a ledge about the big cheese vat); and, catching up with her in his pursuit and in a fit of anger at being caught, he pushed her down into the boiling cheese. Of course this caused her immediate termination after some horrible suffering. Now in her present life the girl carried over great and strong fears—the resentment for milk, heat, the man, etc. It was a wonder she had life at all. As she sat in front of the fire-place, the heat would set in motion the oscillation of the former boiling cheese and the same with drinking milk or even anything warm near her! The same negative fears would be set in motion as she placed her hands in warm water.

Well, Mildred was a most fortunate girl to have been brought to the Moderator for help, for it is entirely likely that there is no one else on earth who could have helped her. But oddly enough, through the ensuing several years—about eight or nine—every time little Mildred would get near the fire or experience a re-attunement with that past, the negation would be set up with Ernest! We both could smell the cheese on Ernest's mouth! It was a most unpleasant odor; it smelled just like an infant's soured burpings or like spoiled cottage cheese. Because of her youth, she not knowing how to work with the science mentally, being unfamiliar with these karmic principles of reliving the past, it was with Him so long. But the time finally came when He no longer experienced it and we knew she had been completely healed.

Yes, letters from her mother came telling how well she was and how very thankful they all were that her life had been saved and health had been restored —but not before Ernest had endured many hours, and years, of working with her on the inner! This was the only case I recall which remained with us for any length of time. Ordinarily, it is a matter of attunement or tuning into the past, and that's it! All other work is done on the inner and in the higher states.

Twice Saved from Death

One important experience that took place during the time we lived in Pasadena, during the first year of Unarius, served as a wonderful lesson to me but nearly cost the Moderator his life. We had made an acquaintance with a little lady named Mary Stark, who operated a small sweet shop, earning a modest living but who had a real 'rat' for a husband. I say this in the strictest sense of the word, for he tried in many ways to kill this sweet little soul. We did not go into details about their differences nor would it be of importance other than the fact that they owned together, although they lived apart, a duplex home; she living on one side and he on the other. He was constantly thinking up mean tricks to worry her and cause her harm. He would attach wires about her place when she was absent which would make weird sounds at night to frighten her; but far worse, he would plant poison around that could prove fatal to her! On one occasion, the Moderator viewed psychically how he was placing bits of arsenic on her silverware and we called to warn her to be sure to wash it thoroughly before using.

However, she was so far under his trance control that she did not even remember our call of warning. She went ahead, used this contaminated silverware and ate with it. We received a phone call from her at the hospital that she was deathly ill and needed help. The call came shortly after Ernest had taken seriously ill himself. His fever rose beyond the danger point, his face was flushed, and perspiration was pouring from him. We wrapped him in an electric blanket and he went to bed. This was during the very same moments that Mary was undergoing the effects of the arsenic which she had eaten. He had actually taken on her poison in order that she could live! He suffered it psychically, and only because of this did Mary pull through! Well I remember how he shook and quivered while he underwent this ordeal in her place —or instead of her physical body experiencing it— and, although she was very ill, she did live.

It was about two hours before the fever broke with Him, then quickly he returned to normalcy. Only because he knew what it was and how to deal with the situation did he overcome it so quickly although as a rule, these psychic healings remain with us in consciousness but a few seconds. However, this was a most unusual and critical case; all the powers that could be extended to her were needed and the psychic of Him took on the negation, even to the point of physical distress.

Mary, too, received rapid healing. This, to me, was a tremendous proof of how such Advanced Personalities can and do take on others' conditions—even to the point of death!

Still, all this did not serve as a sufficient lesson to her, for it was only a few weeks later that Ernest viewed psychically, her husband placing a black-widow spider in her bed. When I phoned to tell her, she immediately went to her bed to look; I waited on the phone until she inspected the bed and she said, "Why, yes, between the sheets there was a large spider and, after killing it, found it to be one of the black widows!" Strange as it may seem, yet with all of this and much, much more, Mary still took back her husband into her heart and home. We believed, however, that he had such a strong, hypnotic control over her and, with his lower astral forces, she was helpless.

Had Mary been a devout student, things would have been different; she would have had much more help; but self-help is most important too! However, she had not at that time reached the point of taking seriously the study and will simply have to wait until such time. This is something one cannot force, each one has his choice of which direction he wishes to proceed. I have always had a sense of compassion for the girl when passing by her place but the relationship of the two probably was a continuation from previous lifetimes. Thus, it is doubly difficult to sever.

The above experiences took place over thirteen years ago, and now just recently, through a friend of hers, she came across one of the Unarius books and immediately wrote to tell us how she had finally made her break, that she was freed of that terrible influence, and now was very happy; in fact, she said, "I have never been so happy in my life!" Thus the energies which were directed to her during those trying times continued to regenerate and were the 'saving grace' for her; otherwise, she would no doubt have regressed and reverted in her evolution further and further down and backwards! Again, it was the Catholic religion which played a large part in binding her, but when she freed herself of that negative influence, things began to get better with her on all levels of living. Mary can be most thankful to the Unariun Brothers for her deliverance; it is difficult to believe anyone could have been in worsened straits!

Past . . . Present . . . Future — As One

It was during the very first year of Unarius' mission on earth that the Moderator gave a few lectures in Monrovia and, at the close of the sessions, He would give the various students personal readings, psychic diagnoses, or whatever the particular individual needed. This was the very first of his public work of this nature I had witnessed and I was fascinated at his most unique ability. He would pass from one to another without any preparatory efforts or need for any adjustment on his part, but would move right from the consciousness of one into the next, recalling their childhood activities, things that were responsible for their present conditions or emotions and, of course, for the most part, he would tune back into their previous life-times. For instance: one lady would be seen in some European country in say, five to six-hundred years ago; then He would jump to the man beside her who he would view in perhaps two thousand years past, or even in Atlantis or Lemuria, one hundred and fifty-thousand years ago; each time with the perfection and accuracy that would discharge the individual's problem, whatever the circumstance was, at the time, responsible for the negation.

To prove it to the person, He would explain to them the particular reaction he would experience in viewing some scene or area. For instance: if he saw in his 'reading' the individual in a shipwreck, He would know the person would retain a fear of water, boats, and of the many things involved in such a happening; and when the student would be questioned as to his reaction to the particular situation, always, and without fail, would the answer be of the positive nature. With the Moderator's inner or Higher Self, he would attune the person to the scene or experience so the individual could, in the viewing or relating, discharge the negation, and healing of whatever the condition or fear was, would result.

This particular work is, to me, the most valuable of all his vast and infinite accomplishments. Of course, there is not enough of Him to go around to reach the countless thousands in such personal need, but such psychic diagnoses will or could, in time, make it possible to dispense with hospitals, prisons, mental institutions, etc., for all causes would thus be located in this manner and the patient, himself, taught how to deal with it and to heal himself, whether it be mental, physical, or whatever the problem.

During the first couple of years of the mission, the Moderator gave quite a few personal past-life readings and, although we did not keep in touch physically, with the persons for whom He read, (time simply did not permit), this collection of readings can serve to point up these very vital principles and exactly how the diagnosing in this psychic manner works. It shall be one of my future endeavors to get together these (about two-hundred) past-life readings and install them in a book (possibly a book with student testimonials), to help point up and show this very vitally-important and scientific manner of locating the originating cause for any condition of the human; and, as He often says, they most always stem from previous lives lived.

And so, Unarius is digging the postholes for the science of the future. Seeds are being planted and the ground is being tilled that your grandchildren and their children's children will be taught this science in their academic schools. This is one reason why I marvel at this great and learned Being who has descended into this pit or earthworld—and to Him it is the lowest of the astral pits of hell—to bring to mankind wisdom that can change the entire world for the better in time. For He is not alone in his great and unmatched endeavors; He has with him on the inner, working ever close by, thousands of Advanced Spiritual Beings, scientists, doctors, psychologists, philosophers, teachers of every conceivable manner and means, and many inconceivable! Thus it is, the earth is most fortunate at this time and era to have this great soul again extend unto it the great Wisdom, the Infinite Creative Light that can lead mankind out of the pits into which he has strayed and fallen, and to lead him up into infinite and higher reaches or dimensions, or as Jesus termed them, 'Many Mansions'!

Thus, dear reader, if you are most wise, you will spend every possible waking moment in effort to conceive the science the Moderator has prepared for you, and you, yourself, will prove the authenticity of his words through the change, the improvement, the greater peace of mind you will experience as you travel closely to the Infinite Creative Light.

Physical Phenomena

This relating was truly a real phenomenon. It took place during the first few months we were in San Diego (our first year together). I had parked the car for the night, as usual, by the curb. Our house was on a rather steep hill. I had gone inside and passed the night and, when we came out in the morning, the car was gone! Within a few seconds, our eyes focused on the car down the hill a few houses and standing right in the middle of the road and the middle of the hill! How could this be! Whatever could have stopped it from rolling on down to the bottom of the hill and crashing into other parked cars? Questions crossed my mind but fast, when suddenly we both knew at the same time! Ernest had psychokinetically, in the night, as the car lost its compression and started rolling downhill, stopped it with his mind energies! As we approached it, he touched it with his finger to prove it, then it started to roll. He jumped in and applied the brakes and we realized this was an outright miracle!

Strangely enough, the car had no lights on nor were there any street lights, yet no one had driven into it! It took me quite some time to get over that one, as it was not one of the smaller cars but an older, heavy, clunky Cadillac and which, if it had smashed into another, would have done great damage; yet, here the Rays from His mind had stopped it right in the middle of the sloping hillside!

This did not teach me the needed lesson about parking on hills, however. It was several years later, when we moved to Los Angeles and again on a hill, an even steeper one, in my many activities and dashing about, I was careless about my putting the 'park' lock on and the emergency brake did not hold well; but I should have turned the wheels into the curb, which I failed to do, and within a few moments after I left the car and stepped inside the house, I saw through the window, the car start to roll away from the curb down the hill; it was aimed at the house kitty-corner from us and gaining momentum. We both had spied it and ran outside but were helpless to do anything, we were so far behind it. I wanted to cover my face before I saw it crash into the house of the neighbors, but as we ran there, to our great amazement, it had stopped just about three inches short of the wall of the house! I could not believe this—just couldn't, even after I had seen! The owner came out raving mad, and I blamed him not. I apologized profusely, for the tires did flatten some small rose-bushes, but there was no damage, really, although I returned home very sheepish, to say the least. All I could do was shake my head in amazement, but did not wonder 'how' this time—we knew! Wonderful psychokinetics, it surely saved my day!

She Never Knew!

Again speaking of the first year in San Diego, there was a small cafe where Ernest and I used to visit as a change for me from my daily cooking. We noticed the young waitress limping severely as she served us, and all of a sudden, she walked out of the restaurant, leaving the owner to fulfill our needs. As it seemed strange, we asked this owner, and she said, "Oh, that poor girl has the strangest condition in her feet; she will be working and, for no apparent reason, her feet will give out on her and she will have to dash home and off the feet! It is most inconvenient for us both, and painful for her." She continued to state, "Sad as it is, I'm afraid I will just have to let her go, and she's such a fine girl."

We had not spoken to the lady herself about her condition, only the casual remarks one makes while being served a meal. A few weeks later, we went purposely into the place to see how she was, to hear from the owner she had not had one spell since we were there, and previously they occurred often. We waited about another month and returned to make sure, and she had indeed experienced her healing. The owner, we never did learn their names, secretly came to our table. She was so happy to say, "She's never had another, even slight, twinge of her trouble since the day you people were here!" No, the girl never knew from whence came her healing! This of course would be true in countless cases wherein not even a physical contact was made—for where e'er is placed Consciousness of such a Developed and Advanced Being—there flows the Power—the Light! Thus it is true: everyone who comes in contact with this Inner Consciousness —is helped in some way and degree—whether it be via the mails or otherwise! Infinite Consciousness carries the creative healing Rays!

Another interesting experience took place about the same time in a larger cafe not distant from the above-mentioned place, during one of the weekly meals we would have there. During the times the lady owner of the cafe placed our food before us, Ernest would pass on to her comments about herself, her family, and many things which only she knew. She seemed to take it all in stride with little or no reaction, and we continued to return a few subsequent times. Always Ernest would enter into the Higher Consciousness while there. Every chance he would get when she came near, He would relate some particular experience about which He knew no other person was necessarily aware. He was, of course, endeavoring to prove to her this wonderful power of the mind and of the continuity of life. Whatever it was he brought to her, she would agree it was correct; many things about her young son who had some severe problems. But these things did not seem important to her, nor did they 'ring the bell', so to speak.

However, it happened one day as He was bringing to her, her grandfather who had been in spirit many years. He showed how this old man used to have an apple orchard and liked only the apples with the long stems on them. Well, we thought she would jump right out of her skin. That did it! She became so excited, she ran about her place telling her girls to go talk to 'that man', he is wonderful! She related how Ernest proved to her that her grandfather continued to live on in spirit. Seldom does one really get so emotional with these relatings, but she was really on cloud nine. All the Light and Energy he had previously projected into her seemed suddenly to become a part of her! (She had let down the resistance—healing effected.)

We have sort of made our own little joke about 'long stems on apples'. Here she had received countless testings and provings far more important and wonderful than the grandfather, but it was the long stems on apples that 'did it' for her. Of course, since our first contact with her, she had been 'in touch' on the inner, and as her body slept, she was taken—as are all sincere students—to higher planets to school, there to learn; then it can mean something to them in the conscious mind. So any more, when one has difficulty in believing or relating to what is brought, then some little thing will mean much, we say, "That's 'long stems on apples' for her!"

From that day on, as we would enter the place, several waitresses would immediately gather about and beg to be told 'something'. Thus, we soon avoided going there; we did not wish to attract any undue attention, and which would be most easy to do.

My personal 'long stems on apples'? Indeed, I have had one—many, but one in particular has meant so much; in fact, there have been many thousands of these testings He has brought to me, but the first one which, as they say, I really 'dug' was one morning as we met at breakfast, he said, "The last letter you wrote last night, second page, fourth line down, you misspelled a word; you typed a 't' instead of the 'l' you intended to write. It was a five-letter word."

The study where I worked at the time and often typed until one or two in the morning (or later, if necessary) was in another wing of the huge house, away from the one in which he slept so I would not disturb his important sleep with the sound of the typewriter and the even noisier Varityper machine. Ernest had not been in this workroom for days, but I knew if He 'saw' such, it just had to be there; but I went upstairs and opened the sealed envelope. Sure enough, I had typed 'tegal' instead of 'legal'. This was my 'long stems on apples'! I thought that was just tremendous; yet, when we conceive principle, no one vision or sighting is any easier or more difficult, nor is it more or less miraculous than another. When we conceive that all things are energy creations and it is a matter of attunement to that specific energy vortex then we get a slight idea of principle. But to do it—that is another thing! His is such a perfected state and He has worked at this perfecting so many, many eons of time that He just does not err.

It should not be omitted either, of the several previous wonderful demonstrations manifest; for instance, with our very first house purchase, after we had spent a year or so in mother's old home (due to insufficient funds to purchase at the time). As soon as the neighborhood became, as it has so often, so noisy, our desire to leave and to buy existed but we lacked the necessary funds. I felt that what little income existed at that early stage should be used to set in motion at least the book He had just dictated. I felt, too, it should be a rather large house, first due to the noisy Varityper machine which I was using to set type for the books, and the stapler which jarred the entire house when putting together the lessons. Ready cash was scant, but I began looking in the newspaper for houses for sale.

On the second day came the prompting; I sensed it as the ad was read, and when inspecting the house, I could hardly wait to have Ernest see it, for it would indeed serve our needs and was a very large one with, of all things, a room or second story in the garage for my noisy work! The street seemed very quiet, peaceful and was tree-lined. Upon his inspection, He agreed we should make the effort to obtain it; but how? I did, however, as the strong, positive knowing was present, quickly put an ad in the paper for a small home I had and rented out in Manhattan Beach—one I had kept many years. The day the ad appeared, of all things, a Real Estate lady phoned me; she had already seen the place and, over the phone, and on the first call, agreed to purchase it! In fact, and this I had a difficult time to believe myself, the next day in the mail came a note from her saying, "If you want the money in advance, I will mail it to you so you will not have to await the close of escrow!"—and which she did. She, no doubt, planned to resell it herself later, but to offer payment outside of escrow in such a manner is truly unheard of, but send it she did! That, to me, was an incredible demonstration. Then I 'just happened' to think about a few cemetery lots I had purchased at one time, many years ago when in Real Estate, just for a small investment and had forgotten all about them, but now I came across the deeds. Quickly I inserted a small ad and there was the buyer—happy to buy the lots for three times what I paid for them! It was not a great deal, but at this point, every few hundred counted to secure the home in Eagle Rock. It took but a few moments at the cemetery to pick up her check for the plots, but the lady buying them said something that still makes us smile when thinking of it. She said to her family who were present, after accepting the deeds, "Now we'll all have someplace to go," and looking at Ernest and me with a pitiful glance said, "Now you folks have no place to go!" Frankly, I could scarcely wait until we got out of earshot before bursting into laughter, for of course to us, going into such a place as the ground is inconceivable and should be to any logical mind as well; the body, yes, the person, indeed not!

Then there was some value in my house trailer, which I didn't know why I had ever brought along from the desert. An ad in the local paper again brought a buyer, a naval officer who was most happy to buy the trailer as he was going on an extensive vacation. Within the hour, he was towing it off; he had exchanged it for the thousand which added up to more than our need to make the down payment on our first home. The little beach home, the lots, and the trailer more than sufficed after selling them and which took place all within a few days time! Thus, our first home was started in escrow but as was true in each move, we did not have to await the normal time for the closing; we moved in immediately. This, too was all fore-planning from the Inner. The place served us well until that fateful day when a neighbor rented out his home to a large family of noisy ruffians. The negative forces always on our trail—so off we must go to re-locate again.

This moving, however, the various areas in which we have located up and down the coast, has served a dual purpose, for now these areas have been prop-erly polarized with the Higher-Inner energies for a later time when, very likely, Centers of Light shall be erected!

The sale of this first house we bought in Eagle Rock was quite demonstrative, all factors known. Al-though we were glad to find and obtain it at the time, when the neighbors made our move necessary, with just one ad in the local paper, quickly came not only one, but two parties at one time—two who wanted it and were almost quarreling over who would get it. Surely Spirit arranged this meeting! It was a very old house and shouldn't have been in demand, but so it was and we were very glad to leave that noisy area. The school teacher who bought it was equally as glad to have so much room for his several kiddies. Always, the ever-existing guidance was present, with one dem-onstration after another!

I am sure some Real Estate people would appre-ciate such guidance yet, were they spiritually devel-oped to that point to conceive guidance, they would no longer be concerned about accumulating material gain or wealth. They would realize the true values exist only in the spiritual—the eternal.

Distance No Barrier

Another interesting proof of this viewing at great distances, for instance: two student brothers, John and Leonard Nero, lived in Cleveland, Ohio, when Ernest made a phone call to them. (He has never been to their state.) During the conversation, I heard Ernest say to John, as John was planning on doing some house improvements, "You boys have quite a bit of dry rot in your lower floor under the kitchen. If you will go down to the basement and look up in the right front corner, you start digging out some of the wood in the corner there and you will see a large area of dry rot." He said, "After you find it, call and let me know so I can get off the hook with it."

They did so immediately and the next day, John related to Ernest on the phone, "We found the dry rot you told us about, exactly where you pointed it out. My, but there is a lot of it; we will have to do a great deal of work to replace all that decayed wood!" And as most always, he finished with, "How do you do that?"

Of course, during Ernest's life, and especially the past thirty to thirty-five years, there have been countless demonstrations similar, and which to Him has been his normal way of functioning. He did not have to learn it, but it was a development He came to earth with, in fact, which has been a part of Him for many eons in the past.

Another student, Louis Spiegel, had just purchased a new home in Boston, Massachusetts, a state Ernest has never visited either; but as Louis had come to California on business, we had invited him for a visit as I felt he may take part in placing books in shops and libraries, etc., and thought a contact could be helpful in his efforts. (This visit, however was some time before we found it necessary to call a moratorium on personal counseling.) During his short stay, the Moderator told Louis, "Now, when you get back to Boston to the house which you have just signed up to purchase, get a ladder and climb up on the roof in front of the house on the left side. Take a good look at the metal valley where the gable rests; you will find there a need for repair. It is torn up and in need of fixing; the rain could enter."

Upon his return to Boston, the first thing Louis did was to get up on the roof and examine the described area. A long-distance call from him related to Ernest, "It is exactly as you said it would be; the roof in that area does need quite extensive repair, and I will get it fixed right away—but how do you do this?"

Before Louis hung up the phone, Ernest said, "Now go into the hall, about halfway down and about a foot in from the wall, and you will find a nail sticking up in the floor. After you remove it, look at it and you will see that it is quite crooked. I'll wait here while you go find it." Louis did—it was! The nail was sticking up exactly where Ernest had pointed it out to him, and it was indeed a bent one! Louis was actually speechless; he was flabbergasted and confounded, but this is the Moderator's normal way of oscillating from the Higher Self, rather than, as does the earthman, from his subconscious. Time or distance makes absolutely no difference—ten miles, a hundred or ten thousand miles or years is of no consequence when it comes to his 'seeing', relating happenings or situations.

'Strangers Become Transcended'

Interestingly enough, most folks do not become surprised when they hear things that He views because of the transcendency that is ever present at the time. Anyone in His company is transcended. Most often they are not aware, but it does exist. The great and strong force field within which we walk simply lifts the person out of his normal frequency oscillation into the higher. For instance, I can seldom if ever go into a store or shop without the clerk fumbling or muffing the transaction. Although they may express these same deeds all day long, when they come in touch with this force field, they become flustered, incoherent at times, and unable to function properly. I have seen one lady make three attempts to count back the change to me and simply could not do it. They forget to give us the parcel we have just bought, or any one of a number of slipups. I have heard some say, "What is the matter with me, I can't do anything right here."

Another never-before heard-of phenomenon is the heat wave, the ray beam that is sensed as strong heat that is projected. Sometimes it is for our protection, other times for help to the person; but it does become so intense, the person will perspire profusely. It can be a cold day, yet if the person has a virus or is in need of healing, or either of us is in need of some special protection, in comes the heat. I have seen many take off their sweaters upon my approach when it is, in fact, a cold day!

One lady insisted, with Ernest, that her airconditioner was out of order, so potent was the heat ray, the power beam of healing for her, and when Ernest replied, "Oh, is it too strong for you? I'll turn it off." What was her reaction? She became fearful! Yes, people fear that which they do not understand.

I have gone into a food-mart on more than one occasion and sensed the checker to have a headache. Upon mentioning it to her, asking, "Do you have a headache?" the reaction was "How do you know?" Then as I would turn to leave, my reply, "Well, you won't have it long!" One lady called to me before I had taken a few steps away, "Say, it is gone already!" But spirit knows no separation, no limitations. Where e're our consciousness is projected, there extends the Power, and where e'er we direct our thoughts, so do the Higher Minds add theirs, when the need exists!

The Mission of Unarius Started
Over 150,000 Years Ago

It should be noted that the effort to bring this vast accumulation of wisdom, of teaching, etc., of this infinite nature was started not only in Jerusalem two thousand years ago, but even unto the time of Atlantis and beyond; over one hundred and fifty thousand years ago, unto the time of Lemuria. Yes, in Lemuria, where He, (the present Moderator of Unarius), then Captain of the crew of twelve interplanetary travelers, came from the spiritual planet, Lemuria, in suspended animation via spaceship to the earth to try to teach the aboriginal earthean the basic principles of life. But earthman is slow to want to change, to learn.

Thus it is, and reasonably so, that we two do sense feelings of fulfillment, of accomplishment after endeavoring, lo these many eons of time; for the various texts, books, lessons and recorded taped Messages have all been distributed throughout the country, not only to individuals but many have been placed by sincere students in libraries, in shops and stores, in colleges, whereby they shall live for posterity! The demons of hell shall not again deter or prevent man from receiving that which this Emissary and the Infinite Creative Minds have endeavored to teach the earthman for such a great length of time; yea, even unto and before the time of Noah! (And that too, regarding Noah, is but one of the many 'tall tales' and fables.) Unarius has been thoroughly established so that man shall not again destroy that which the Infinite has set in motion. However, due to the advanced science that Unarius is, for the most part, the earthean will not be ready for this understanding of life— the very science of creation—until many years into the future.

But to those who have had the conditioning and can accept and conceive, they can experience their rebirth, the leaving of the past and incepting the creative principles for their future. True it is, with the vast and Infinite Knowledge He has given, of such scope and magnitude, topics of an infinite variety, suffices to change any person who will so devote and dedicate himself to his personal development. Yet, the Moderator states that even with all this, it is as but one small grain of sand compared to all that could be brought; all that He could give to man were man ready to accept; were he capable of conceiving; for such is the infinite nature of Infinity and of the developed Infinite Creative Mind which oscillates in attunement and in harmony with the Infinite Creative Intelligence!

Via Frequency!

On the lighter side, thinking back about three months after we moved to San Diego, Ernest and I had been surveying the San Diego area, searching for a desirable location for our home. A Real Estate lady showed us a house which she said had belonged to Carrie Jacobs Bond, a very lovely place, but too dark for us. Within a few days after this mental contact of Carrie's vibration, she evidentially prompted me with her thoughts. Early one morning at sunup, I felt the urge to take a writing tablet and go outside and sit on the grass, which I did; in a few moments, thoughts began coming which I wrote down. It did please me greatly! Everything to which I would place consciousness, a tree, boulder, an old shack or whatever, there would come lines about this particular object. I wrote and scribbled, wondering from whence this intelligence came. Oh, I was having fun! Quite a few poems found expression through my pen and it was a delightful experience—the first, and up to now, the only poetry.

As I questioned Ernest about it, he said, "Because we had made Carrie's contact, via her house, she no doubt came through, in a way, with her thoughts," and it made her happy, too, she said.

Of course, the writing was not the majestic, wondrous poetry our Moderator has written, but it was meaningful and intelligent, and I was happy about it, hoping, of course, to become better attuned whereby there shall be no obstructions that compatible Infinite Contact may be experienced, should a need exist in the future, however, we do have, in the Moderator, this perfected channel who so expresses so infinitely, thus, no need for myself to do similarly; yet I am sure, when He leaves the flesh, I shall, due to our great preparation, conditioning, etc., be able to be receptive to any necessary inspiration, promptings or writings that may be necessary to be brought through; however, whatever may be so expressed, in some future time, after his arrival (back) into the Worlds of Light, would very likely be more specifically done as further proof —to prove the principle of attunement, consciousness and the oneness of all Infinity.

Reliving Through Attunement

The following, although not the most outstanding experience, serves to show how the symbolic attunement of a mere name or word can serve to re-attune one to some past experience, to be relived and worked out. As the tune, "Yellow Bird" is being played on the radio, it reminds me of the incident. This particular melody has always fascinated me in a peculiar sort of way. I liked it, yet it gave me a sad feeling at the same time—a sad-happy feeling! Finally, the scene from the past popped into view. The Moderator saw me dressed as a yellow bird, feathers and all and, as was the belief and custom of the people at that time and place, when the volcano erupted, the only way, they thought, to stop it was to satisfy the 'fire god' by offering up one of the loveliest of the virgin maidens. He saw me walk up the petal-strewn hill, to the brim of the volcano, and, as the rising lava spewed its inferno of destruction, I plunged down into the glowing coals!

As is the wonderful ability with the Moderator, his words and descriptions often are visible to the listener; his words create the picture. Thus it was that I saw the 'yellow bird' girl (myself) take her death plunge, which was supposed to be a privilege, to be sacrificed to their god! Thus, here was my strange attraction, yet weird repulsion, to the "Yellow Bird" melody. Working with principle in recognition, the negative oscillation is then changed to an out-of-phase relationship with the present, thus the tie of the past was broken, discharged, and again I had been robbed; the "Yellow Bird" melody became no different, as far as reactions were concerned, than any other tune. Principle proven!

Dear Reader, as you will note, quite extensive lengths have been entered into in the various aspects of my countless experiences. This was not done merely to take up space but especially to show you, too, by being conscious or observant of this ever-present function or action—the oscillation from the subconscious (or past)—can begin to realize that everything to which you are drawn, either as a repulsion or a distasteful (fearful) reaction, or the opposite, feelings of attachment or the liking for some person, place or thing, you can begin this severance action. You can start to discharge the countless ties that bind more tightly than any bars of steel, to the past. Thus, work with it, begin to objectify, as is so definitely demonstrated in several mentions made through these pages; such as the tune, "Yellow Bird", remaining with me as a negative oscillation with the past. It is through observance, analyzing and viewing one's emotions and reactions that the individual can start himself on that upward climb out of the past and onto that forward motion in a more progressive oscillation—the regenerative evolution.

However, this youthful death was but a reliving of a previous lifetime, for many years ago in my sleep, I viewed myself running down a lava-covered hillside where the volcano of Mt. Vesuvius was erupting (and which killed so many thousands of persons). The scene came very clearly; as I ran, I saw wide separations in the ground where the very earth was opening up, splitting in two parts. I was running, jumping in between rivers of lava and coals when the very ground in front of me opened up and as I tried to jump over the large crack, I slipped down in between the walls of earth which popped me like a pea in a pod! That was a sudden death, but it left its mark, sufficiently so, that I was evidently attracted to the area now called Hawaii again to repeat the afore-noted happening.

And speaking of workouts, comes to mind several recalls of the various animals contacted in the past which the television movies have brought into our home, enabling me to free myself from their effects from previous lifetimes. For instance, when I would see a snake, even though caged, it would cause me to cringe, and fear existed. However, with the travelogues viewed and in working with principle, these former deaths were all worked out. Snakes and vipers had been a large part of many religious rituals in the past ages, even to the point of worshipping them, and I had been bitten, poisoned and killed more than once in the past from snakes. Also, venom from a poisonous viper had been spewed into my eyes and once blinded me.

Especially did I experience a strong and most beneficial 'work-out' with one of the huge cobras. As was the custom in India in that long ago—and they still use this practice in some areas—to prove her powers, that she could hypnotize and overcome the huge reptiles mentally, the priestess was forced to seek out and run down one of the enormous giant-sized cobras. With her hands tied behind her, she would, after locating one of them, use her mental prowess to quiet it and as it stood upright, often taller than a person, she would have to kiss the snake atop its head! Of course, many were killed by the snake in their efforts. But as I viewed this actual happening on television, I was enraptured! I was reliving indeed. I realized it and at the same time, Ernest spoke out, "You did that too, at one time." But I was already experiencing the flashback and cancellation. Another negative tie 'down the drain'.

During one of the old-time war pictures, as the warriors poured hot oil upon the invading armies who attempted to climb up the walls of their castle, this scene on television also served to re-attune me to a lifetime in which that particular experience happened to me, and which was partially responsible for an eye problem in the present life. However, this eye trouble was a most complicated situation, for so many things have happened to the eyes of this entity in the past— anything from a red hot poker being jabbed into them in the Reformation days; one lifetime in the South, the eye was shot out, and along with the snake venom and boiling oil, destructive ray-beams from a space ship, the psychic of the eye had been quite shocked, although no physical effects are visible. In fact, the opticians say there is nothing wrong with it; thus, I recognize it to be psychic. Even though I see very little from one eye, it seems unimportant to me, for it is hoped that in the next dimensions where I shall express when leaving here, there will be no need for the physical eye (or body)—and this is what 'yours truly' is striving toward!—and I trust I shall not need to return to earth again.

My Saucer Contact

In another vein entirely, mention should be made about the spaceship that once came into my view. It happened a few months after our San Diego move. Ernest was writing the Mars booklet when he was, mentally, carrying on a conversation with two space travelers. They said they would make a contact in just two months from then at one o'clock in the morning. Of course, I was quite taken up with this news and highly interested. Then, a few days prior to the mentioned date, we spoke of their promised visit but did not place too much importance on it; however, the time arrived. Ernest went to bed and to sleep, but my mind was quickened.

I was lying in bed with my chin cupped in hand, leaning on my elbow just contemplating, waiting. I felt rather drifting in consciousness, but still not lying down. Suddenly it happened! There appeared directly above me a huge dome-shaped, chrome-looking object, appearing about the size of a small house. The shape was quite similar to the common waffle iron with three extended appendages. I could see windows around the sides. Strange as it may sound, I viewed the top, the bottom, and the sides at the same time although it seemed larger than the house in which I was living. I could see it distinctly. It seemed to hover directly overhead. Then the craft turned into a rosy hue, almost like a hot coal; then a third change in appearance took place; I viewed it as a translucent object and could see right through it! The structure was now clear and the interior was visible and so scientific-looking. I saw no persons aboard, possibly it was operated from a mother ship. I was having a grand time observing; everything seemed so shiny and sparkly. It was most difficult to tell, in such a 'conscious' state, as to time. It was not that I experienced only a mere quick glance, but it did hover quite a while.

Then suddenly my arm, upon which I was leaning the weight of my head shifted and slipped. I moved and broke the contact. I have always felt had I not done so, I might have taken the trip with them. This is only speculation, however. That night held no sleep for me! I wanted so much to awaken Ernest to relate it all to him, but knew it would be unwise, for He does much important work as his body sleeps teaching the students who are likewise asleep.

The following three days were filled with questions galore to Ernest, and for which He always had the answers. It was quite a frustrating experience for me to realize how it was, that I could see the entire saucer or spaceship, top and bottom, as I lay inside the house! Yet, this was the way it was, and the ship hovered above. It was eventually resolved within me and I knew, but it did take a great deal of doing on His part. I have never seen one since; no purpose, I guess, but I learned much from that psychism. Especially, I learned how very real and seemingly solid things can seem on the inner. After all, that world of the inner is just as real and just as solid to them as is ours to us—all frequency and frequency relationship attunement!

He Knew — Fifteen Years Before We Met

Upon more than one occasion Ernest told me how He had searched for me for over fifteen years—said how He would often tell others in his company and describe the brown-eyed gal He knew He would find one day. I suppose the reason He repeated it was that He knew I hadn't believed it—and I hadn't! I thought He was just kidding, trying to make me feel good. Not until years later, when He entered the fact in one of his writings and I read it after it was published in the book form did that truth come home to me! And when I did realize it as fact, I had a little cry. Yes, He described me to many people in the Los Angeles area, He said, many years before we met, telling them there was one woman on this earth who could understand him and his science and would help him bring about the great work He had come to teach.

And so, we came, we met, and we accomplished! This 'finding each other' in this great world with its masses of people does, in itself, serve to prove the principle of harmonic frequency; otherwise, how could it happen—two entities descending from the Inner spiritual worlds unto earth with the billions of people and seeking each other out among such numbers! Only through understanding of the energy concepts can such otherwise 'seeming' incredulities become commonplace.

The same would hold true with the many students who have been likewise attracted to obtain the teachings—although there have been but few we have met personally—we work with many via the mails, the contact had been set up from the inner that they could begin their start upon the more progressive evolution. Invariably, when some student is contacted who has had much preparation and is most ready for the teachings, they will write—after reading only our advertisement literature sent—words to this effect, "Oh, this is just what I've been waiting for these many years," and quite often they will add, "Please rush my order, I want to get started quickly."

But the complete or full measure of accomplishment of the mission will not be known by any man for ages to come; and then, only through the personal experience, the understanding and conceiving of Principle which He teaches, can one factually realize the magnitude of these Infinite Creative Principles of life. Only when man becomes, likewise, an oscillating polarity with the Infinite Intelligence will he be able to conceive the great magnitude, not only of the Science involved, the printed Word which the reincarnate Nazarene (the Unariun Moderator) has given to the earthman, but even far more important, the never-ending projections of Radiant Energies which He steps down from Higher Dimensions to project into the minds of the receptive eartheans, and which are life-changing. Thus, dear friends, the Light, Power and Energies so projected shall continue to regenerate creatively eternally!

I say with all sincerity and fact: were one to combine all the greatness, the accomplishments and benefits which have been so expressed by the so-called greats of all time on earth, they would not begin to compare in value and importance with the benefits and help so contained in the expressions of this One Infinite Mind, the Unariun Moderator, and the combined constant help from many thousands of likewise Advanced Beings on the inner. This is not said with any effort to boast or brag. The Moderator has far surpassed any such need—it is simply fact. However, there are no words that could adequately and completely describe or convey even one small part of this great and indescribable achievement; possible, because He is an interdimensional Traveler—a Being, just as He was when the Nazarene—from a Higher Spiritual Planet.

My wish for each one who may be upon the path of Truth is, that you, too, may conceive, understand and realize even one small part of his Interdimensional science. He will be working with and aiding each one who so endeavors to seek, as shall myself and the entire Brotherhood!

Tut's Daughter—Hatshepsut

Another lifetime the Moderator viewed for me was one in which I incarnated in Egypt as the daughter (Hatshepsut) of the Pharaoh Thutmose I, and although he had two sons, one who took the rule for a very short time, it was Hatshepsut who assumed rulership for many years. The Moderator viewed her going through a ritual which symbolically changed her sex to that of a male. He saw her lying on the couch, a priest in attendance, undergoing this symbolic ceremony as she donned the beard of the male, thusly did she rule as the Pharaoh; possibly the people being unaware, as she was the only female ever to rule as a Pharaoh. This was all viewed and described by Ernest to me but which seemed not at all strange; and when the research was made in history books and the encyclopedia, his reading was, of course, all found to be fact!

This strong desire to express in ways of strength and ability to prove the masculine superiority, which I, no doubt, subconsciously felt, showed up in the present life, as I have so endeavored in various ways. Years ago, I was evidently trying to prove, as I often said, "Anything a man can do, I can do better!" Yes, even to the laying of stonework, cement slab, painting the outside of a huge building—and silver yet—trying to duplicate the great temples, buildings of ages past. Yes, I even built a stone wall and patio floor and barbecue, even though there were men nearby who offered to help or to do it for me. But no, I had to prove I was strong and capable. These things, too, were all reminiscent of a great temple which I had had built in Egypt and in which time the ego was running pretty high. For instance, when this entity built an obelisk in her honor, she—Hat, as I called her—built the very tallest one ever erected. (It still remains intact.) And that is a pretty strong ego, and had to be all worked out; but that is what living some of those lives of royalty help create of one unless he has Infinite Intelligence, and for the most part, the men of great wisdom do not incarnate as rulers; only very rarely.

Akhnaton, however, was the one exception, for he was the most wise and infinitely inspired of all rulers, but he did not wish to be a ruler; He only wished to be one among the people, to teach them of the great wisdom he came to bring them. He has never, nor does he wish now to be erected upon some pedestal, to be worshipped but rather, his one wish and endeavor is to try to get people to understand; to place importance upon the principle he brings, that they may learn to live better lives.

During the lengthy reign of Queen Hatshepsut as Pharaoh, she built one of the largest temples of that era called Tel-el-Amarna; it was built up against the mountain, using, in part, the stone of the hillside as the background, in a three-tiered structure. For years, I have been aware of this structure, and when viewed in magazines or movies, a sense of sadness overcame me—it was home to me. I was aware of a long tunnel through the mountain connecting another temple, a secret passage, and it was during this long trek through the not-too-wide passageway that the carrier, or palanquin, would get jarred or bumped against the sides—bumps that still existed within me as small fears, as it jarred me as I was carried. I was quite subconscious of all this, and in his descriptions, Ernest brought it more firmly into focus. Then later, we would read it all in the encyclopedia. One thing they have found only recently, and which I knew, is that this queen's body was buried there behind the second temple, the secret structure. All this seemed as real to me as something that happened yesterday. I would be far more at home and familiar with Egypt, Greece,

Rome, etc., than do I feel here now in the United States of America although I have never been there in this lifetime.

As Ernest would view some of these various past happenings, he would describe the many things to which I would be relative or would have liked, and always, He was correct; memories of those ancient times such as He would see—the four tall black slaves carrying me on a palanquin, so common in that time, and what a memory I retained of that! In fact, one of those slaves incarnated in the present lifetime as my brother, although he is not colored (no colored blood in our family), yet he retained the inferiority and great timidity with me.

We two, Chuck and I, as youngsters, actually work-ed out this 'carrying me' on the palanquin, for I would ask him to carry my feet, and he would place one foot underneath his armpit and walk back and forth with it (as I lie down)—and for which I would pay him pen-nies! Just about as close to actually re-living as one could get! He even used to tell people when a young-ster, "My sister makes me carry her foot around be-cause I can't carry all of her (laughingly)!" Of course, then I did not know why, but thought it just a game. My brother's name at that Egyptian time was Oskaar —a name he brought through, for mother named him Oscar, a name which he disliked, so he changed it to Charles. I guess it reminded him of that lifetime, one, possibly not too pleasant as a slave.

An experience which took place several years be-fore my physical meeting with Ernest served to prove that incarnation. I was living at one of the beach towns and phoned this brother Charles, who I had not seen for about three years, to come down to visit me, that I had something for him. I had purchased a diamond ring, something he had wanted for a long time. His wife had a bracelet, a family heirloom and he had wished she would break it up so that he could have two or three of the stones put in a large ring for himself, but she was not willing. I thought, "I'll buy him such a ring for a present to give him a little joy." Although I was not, at the time, necessarily able to be this extravagant, it seemed I just must, the impulse was so strong.

He came, and I took him to a little restaurant nearby. When I presented the ring to him and he opened the box and viewed it, he burst out in a hard cry! He cried and cried and cried! No matter what I did, I just could not stop his seeming heartbreak! Fortunately, it was an off hour and no one else was in the cafe, for which I was thankful, for it would have been most embarrassing had others heard this man crying so uninhibitedly, although as thoroughly shaken, so emotional as he was, it may not have concerned him had the place been filled! I would try to get him to put the box aside and eat, but all he would do would be to take another peek at his ring, and off he would go again into another sobbing, grieving spell! Finally he said, "Sis, I can't take it." I simply thought that he felt it too costly, but it was far deeper than that. I was greatly disappointed, for I had so much wanted to please him. Although he did take it with him, I learned that he never wore it; and with reason enough, after I learned why.

At that time, I was not conscious of this 'reliving' principle, but years later when Ernest was reading from some pages of my past during one of the several Egyptian lives this entity has lived, he saw this brother, Charles, as one of my personal black slaves— one who helped to carry the queen on her palanquin, and who was sort of a special bodyguard to her; one who was with her for her duration; one, he said, who thought a great deal of his queen and took it very hard when she died. Due to his great loyalty and devotion to her, she left to him upon her death, her finger-ring which this present one symbolized! So here I was, causing my dear brother to relive again my dying and his great loss; the ring served to re-attune him to that time. Little wonder that in a short time, Charles had the stones put into a Masonic ring, one of his own purchase! No, I have never told him, for like so many, he knows nothing of this continuity of life.

Yes, this reliving and objectifying can be most interesting and beneficial.

I Floated—Seemingly.

An interesting memory of weightlessness—one which was quite different than most transcendent times: it was about two months past the year that we had gone to San Diego at the time that my divorce was made final, when upon our return to Los Angeles, and as we walked down the short aisle to be married, the feeling was one of floating. I still do not believe my feet touched the floor! Surely, the Higher Ones used this time as opportunity to extend their Powers.

Of course, in the Higher Worlds these symbologies or ceremonies are not carried on; this marrying is but the earthman's way. On Higher worlds it is all attunement, consciousness and oscillation, or frequency. It was—no doubt—that they were putting me through some initiation on the inner, such was the feeling experienced at the little Self-Realization Church—the least orthodox we knew!

Mowed Down—via Rays of a Space Ship

Once again the television has served (in 1957) to give re-attunement or flashback of a former life, as it projected the movie of a strange phenomenon which the scientists still cannot figure out. The movie was a showing of an area in Bolivia on a high plateau of the many wide strips of dark color crossing and criss-crossing roadway appearances in the desert sand. These areas of the odd-colored sand were from forty to fifty feet wide and extended over many miles distance. This phenomenon had been searched and researched and examined by many scientists throughout the ages, but still they did not come up with satisfactory or factual answers to how this oddity could have been caused. It looked as though the very ground had been changed, sort of crystallized and molded together, and throughout the many years, it has not blown away or changed one bit in the precise pattern; burned some way, they thought, but how?

At the very moment these wide roadways of darkened color appeared on the screen, I went into a state of shock. I screamed and began to stutter, "Oh, my god, oh, my god!" I just could not control myself. My entire side seemed paralyzed for a time. I was locked in with that former past. But Ernest, with his great wisdom and ability to 'tune in' to anything he wishes, and/or unto his Higher Self, who knows all things, instantly knew what it all was. He explained to me that these crisscrossing patterns in the sand were the result of spaceships as they spewed the ground with the rays unknown to the earthmen many years ago. The ray beams from their guns were devastating and thousands were killed, many maimed and, of course, death was far better than some of the terrible effects which many experienced.

63

My reaction to seeing this was, of course, a subconscious memory, as I was one among the many who were mowed down by their death rays. So potent and effective were they, that they actually burned or seared and welded together the earth particles which, even until this day, remain weirdly scorched or crystallized and to the scientist—a great puzzle. Another negation went down the drain! The reaction here had been more severe and critical than have most. I was actually scared speechless!—the same reaction sensed as that which was experienced as the ships came over that fateful day. Within several moments, things returned to normal with me, but is it not food for thought to wonder how many persons may be continuing to relive such pasts, not knowing what it is with them? With such an experience it would be difficult to know how many thousands of years such effects may last—even now some reaction is sensed occasionally along one leg from this radiation. Does the world need this science!

Other Death Flashback-Attunements

I must relate a time when we two were house hunting, an excellent example of how we can be prompted to seek out ways to 'work out' the past! Oh, quite a bit of our time had thusly been spent in moving, but not by choice. The following incidents took place in San Diego in 1954, just a few months after our joining. As we scanned the newspaper for rentals, a broker showed us a large redwood house atop a hill. It seems we were always looking for a hilltop house—this present one, I guess! After a short time looking about, Ernest had a most unusual rapport or feeling with the interior of this house, but soon He became ill and said, "I've got to get out of here quickly!" We rushed to the car but not before He had made his attunement with, of all things, the way the boards were applied in the living room! It attuned him unto a time when he evidently died or was killed in some prison, for he became very psychically ill.

By the time I got him home, He was nearly out. At that time, I was not yet accustomed to these flashbacks or re-attunements of the past and thought He was really dying! Very little consciousness remained with Him as I tried to shake him and bring him to. He even said, "I'm going." This, no doubt, was the complete reliving of the previous death. After about fifteen minutes, He began snapping out of it and soon was back to normal and began analyzing. He realized in his wonderful ability to objectify that it was the boards of the house, the manner in which they were applied that brought about the attunement, and because they were redwood. But I did have a few moments of great concern. I had believed He was dying, and inwardly knew we had a great work to accomplish and which only He could bring!

He could hardly wait until the next day to return there to see if any reaction remained, for he wanted to be rid of it all. Well, the unexpected often happens and this time was no exception. The hilltop redwood house served again—but for myself this time! Ernest was outside speaking with the owner and I wandered inside looking about; trying to see how it might fill our needs, when I noted a very small step down. The floor was one of the old Spanish floors and at the end of the living room was a low, two or three-inch step, down to another room. As I walked toward it, I seemed to know I was going to fall but felt helpless to avoid it. I went head-first, down upon the stone floor and there I lay, half out, trying to scream and crying, but no one answered. Ernest was out of earshot. I could not get up and felt as though I were dying, sure! Imagine such a tiny low step, but it did serve to tune me back to a time when I had been thrown over a parapet into a dungeon several stories below. As I lay there, I felt as if every bone in my body was broken. Finally, Ernest came inside. There I lay, barely able to mumble and unable to walk, telling how, "I can't make it, I'm done for!" And just the day after He had had his 'death' reliving, one during the Reformation! After He helped to get me to the car and home, I was still very ill; every bone in my body ached and I felt like they had all been broken. I just knew I would never survive!

To bed I went, and the Brothers took me out of the body, immediately after one of the Indian spiritual helpers came and rubbed me all over with what they called 'bear grease', and it did smell like it! That psychic smell was so strong it stunk up the entire house for days. It was about two P.M. when I fell, and I slept all through the rest of that day and evening, through the entire night without stirring, so far away was I taken!

66

During the night I saw myself as it really happened. The huge castle was one of the brick type with the parapets atop and I saw myself thrown down from several stories into a dungeon. I could sense that every bone in the body was broken; this is what I relived so realistically. I can still see that picture of the crumpled, broken body lying far below.

Came morning and no sign of pain or hurt, and we had a hearty laugh over it all—but at the time, it was no laughing matter! Oh, I have really had it! Ernest had very little of this sort of reliving, for He has not been an earthean, as have the rest of us. He has lived on higher spiritual planets far removed from earth; however, the comparatively few times He has returned have not left fond memories, for often have the negative and destructive earthmen brought his life to a conclusion, even as He labored to bring man words of wisdom that would make his life a better one.

Think on this, fellow seeker, and you will know why the Interspace Travelers do not stop here! Man always tries to destroy that which he does not understand, and it has happened to Him more than once. However, in the present, the Powers and Forces of Light shall be victorious. We have taken great caution that our whereabouts be unknown and have lived very secretly that the negative factions shall not again block, deter and waylay the great and infinite Message which He has brought mankind. Vastly have the teachings been distributed, not only throughout the many States but to foreign countries as well. Truth as He has so abundantly given shall not die and Unarius shall live on eternally, possibly under different names, but the science has been thoroughly interjected into the world. Thus, if we both feel a sense of satisfaction, it is because of the many, many years, of lifetimes, yes, of the eons of time this vast program and endeavor has been underway. We have overcome and indeed accomplished!

And now it is up to each one so prepared to overcome his own personal past, to study and to conceive of the great wisdom which this Infinite Mind has again descended to earth to deliver—his Message of Truth, of Light; and along with the Word is projected the very Energies that will aid man in his never-ending struggle and upward climb.

During my youth and growing up years, hats were a hobby with me. I never could buy just one hat; always must there be two or three at one time, and as I look back, they all resembled crowns! Moreover, they were never worn more than a few moments at a time, for I could not stand anything on my head. Plain to see why; the crowns of the ages past were most often very heavy and clumsy. One felt top-heavy with them and at the first opportunity, the wearer would most often remove them as soon as he was out of sight of the public. And this is the way I would wear these many crown-like hats off they would come and into the back seat of the car they would get tossed. We don't get very far away from our past, not until the severance has been consciously started as the science of living is learned.

On more than one occasion in years gone by in the present life, I have sent to India or Persia for incense in large quantities, only to hear the Moderator relate how, in the lifetime of the Pharaohs, Queen Hatshepsut sent a fleet of boats to these different countries for cargoes of such things. This experience was quite a vivid memory as He told of it, and I could have even drawn a sketch of the odd-shaped boats used at that time. Yes, it is all there within, and so exists with each person—all that he has been and lived in the many, many lifetimes of the past. Truth is, indeed, stranger than fiction!

The following mention will be related simply to show how the very most minute detail can serve to reattune one. A certain student, Leonard, from an eastern state, came to California for the summer to help in what ways he could in a clerical capacity. Leonard, as a hobby, repaired watches and was very good at it. I had a watch for many years which I had taken to several shops but they could not make the stem hold. Leonard was successful, and as he handed it back to me repaired, he did not dangle it on his finger (as it was a bracelet watch) but took his two hands and held it up in the circle coming toward me with the raised jeweled front facing me. As he approached I cried. Just this simple act of seeing the circlet—looked to my subconscious as would a crown being brought to be placed upon the head. There were several other students standing about in a semi-circle which served to fill out the picture of what such ceremony would also appear like. They even seemed to be 'waiting for something to happen'! Could you believe it if I related too, how some of them also shed the tear—they were reliving! None knew why, until it came to me in consciousness, of just why the reactions. Then it was comical. So you see it takes a very slight symbology sometimes to recall ones past experiences. In fact man is, from day to day in his hourly living, reliving his past but so slow the change, he is not conscious of it. Unarius teaches the short-cut!

The Negative Forces Had Me 'Bagged'

This relating brings to mind a similar happening which took place in San Diego just a few weeks after we two had met. While I slept, a very negative force overtook and awakened me but I could not arouse my body. It seemed I tried to call out but no voice would come; I tried to open the window to call to Ernest (who slept in the house trailer in the yard), but evidently I was at the window in my astral body and not the physical, for I could not open it. The pull and horrible feeling that this 'thing' was engulfing me was most terrible and I tried to open the door so Ernest could hear my call, but again, I found I could not open the door. This effort continued for some time, when evidently I finally broke loose from the hold of this horrid 'thing' and screamed out. I awakened Ernest and he ran into the house to find out what was wrong. He stayed for a few moments until the influence subsided, then went back out to bed.

He had not gone far when the entity returned; (but I knew I could not keep Ernest awake all night fighting my horrible obsession). It was such a miserable and unpleasant feeling when he would be close; my entire body would experience a strange and awful shaking vibration. After a few attempts to go back to sleep, I found that I had to remain awake. I burned all the lights and started typing, thinking if I could keep my consciousness on this higher frequency, he could not get to me. Well, it was my saving grace! So long as I did this—kept consciousness in the texts—I was safe, but the moment I relaxed, even a second, back he would come and it was a terribly fearful thing I would experience.

All night long I had to remain at the work. Even

worse—it kept up all the next day and on into the night. At times during the day when Ernest would be very close by, I was freed of this terrible influence, but for the most part, my entire psychic shook if I did not hold to the higher consciousness. All through the second night did I have to fight, and fight I did! Ernest told me that it was something I had to overcome and work out—that this destructive monster was a powerful old priest who had taken the lower path. At one time many, many years ago, in another lifetime, I had made a vow to him and he was holding me to it. Ernest would not mention his name, for he knew were I to think of it, it would only attract him to me. I was told that the only way to win out over this negative force was to fight with everything I had, and this would be a 'first step' in my personal overcoming and development. Fortunately, I am no quitter. Had I been, I would have sunk with the boat then. I had only begun to fight!

The battle was not an easy one to win, but only through this constant and never letting up, keeping attuned with the teachings, the Infinite Words, infinitely inspired did they serve to lift me in consciousness to where this lower force was unable to reach me. He could not aspire to such a state. Thus, after the third day, on into the late evening was when I experienced one of the most wonderful visitations ever!

This was my first contact with the Higher Self of the man Jesus and He came through our Moderator to me and said, "You are having great difficulty but you are making headway. We can see that you shall be successful in your overcoming which is most important to you. We shall be with you, but it is you who must complete this severance of the lower powers to gain victory, for it will mean victory over self—Selah." Oh, the Light, the Power and great sense of oneness, of Infinite Love that I sensed with this Presence cannot be put into words—but it was wonderful. Needless to say, the 'going' from that moment on was far less difficult and, late that evening, my great battle was completed and won. This was the third night without sleep and I was completely exhausted! I, too, know what it is to be ensnarled in the vicious tentacles of the destructive forces of evil. I had become victorious and what a sense of relief and peace that filled my being.

There have been many times since that I have worked on the books either most of the night or even on occasions, no sleep was wanted, so interested and anxious was I to complete what was being expressed; I felt no loss of sleep as the Power and Energies were constantly being interjected and morning found me not wanting for rest—which, too, was a wonderful demonstration. But here, with this great Battle of Armageddon I had begun, it was all different. I had to do it for the most part myself, and this also helped give me greater strength and knowledge for the future. There have been many times since that it was needed and used!

The horrible and predominating feeling with this great negative time was that he had a huge bag or sack and the moment I would relax, he would throw it over my head. Upon relating this feeling to Ernest, he said, "That's about what happens; his negative energies formed such a container or restricter." But that old astral energy 'bag' did cause my entire psychic to shake and quiver in a most miserable way and I was more than happy to be freed of this past contact as I emerged victorious! Surely the lesson gained in this overcoming has been invaluable, and without which I would never have been able to make the progress which has so been experienced since then.

Of Heavenly Hosts

Were the very most profound of all the countless experiences that have been realized by this entity mentioned in their entirety, they would be inconceivable to the average person; at least, until such person himself had likewise psychically experienced. Words fall very short to convey fully a true psychic happening; however, to name another: this incident took place one afternoon in the summer of 1959, as I sat on the lawn of our Santa Barbara home. Suddenly, with no sense of warning, seemingly from out of the 'blue' I slipped out of consciousness with the physical and saw within, a host of Angelic Beings! Oh, it was the most beautiful sight! These Higher Beings—heaven only knows how many but seemingly many hundreds —all with the loveliest faces whose hue seemed so soft and radiant, it was as if the heavens opened up and there were the countless Unariun Brothers and Sisters, so happy-appearing, smiling! Especially was I conscious of the great white Light that emanated from the entire gathering; there seemed to be a backdrop of soft, luminous cloudlike formations. Even in the still-suspended state which existed, I went quickly into the house to relate the phenomenon to Ernest, but when I got there, I was so transcended with it all that I could scarcely speak. But He saw and knew something very wonderful had taken place—I was in a state of blissful euphoria!

The beautiful cloud on which this experience left me floating was a most memorable experience. There was the feeling that I just did not wish to speak lest the spell be broken. The wondrous vision lasted, no doubt, but a few seconds but its glorious effects endured for nearly five days and all with whom I came in contact also sensed this new spiritual radiation! The sensation was one of complete buoyancy—almost as if I could walk about without touching the floor. Ernest would meet me in the morning with, "Oh she's still on cloud nine!" This was, indeed, the most heavenly time I ever had! The predominating feeling that continued to remain was a desire to encompass the whole world with arms of infinite love; this, of course, due to the great Light and spiritual Oneness projected from the Angelic Hosts! Indescribable and most memorable! Such beautiful, radiant, heavenly faces that gave forth from their Minds rays of creative, regenerative oscillations.

Two days following this heavenly peek, I telephoned to one student to relate my vision to her. She said tears flowed as it was told, due to the higher energies which were transcending her, even over the phone! When another student, Bess, passed me by, she said she got all 'duck bumps' and her skin just crawled with the power! Yes, wonders upon wonders! Of the many unique and uplifting experiences this entity has, through the years experienced, surely this was among the most tremendous and memorable.

The following several relatings pertain to times previous to our personal meeting, but which I'm sure would make no difference as to the inner help extended from the Moderator and the Brothers on the Inner; for as I have mentioned and realize, Their help has existed with me since my entrance into the world; these (B.U.), before Unarius, previous experiences and psychisms were possible only due to His and and Their bringing them about. I, personally take no credit nor make any claims but was simply preconditioned and receptive that they could be brought through to me. That we two had not as yet met physically was of no consequence—regarding His Inner help and workings with me on the inner.

One of the First Relivings

The year was about 1949 when, after a visit to a beauty shop, I found that the various procedures the operator used on my hair caused it to all break off to within an inch of the head. It took a bit of time on my part for I did not realize the seriousness of it instantly but the more she fussed with it the more broke off until very little remained and that—only an inch, or less, long! As I sat in front of the mirror, I noted tears streaming down my cheek for I became quite emotional with it—unlike myself.

The operator of the shop, Patricia, happened to belong to the metaphysical school which I was attending and we were familiar with the process of metamorphosis. When Pat realized what she had done, she became very upset, fearful and panicky; she, too, was crying. Within a few moments after the first shock subsided with us both, we began to analyze the situation. I said, "Pat, this removal of my hair has to do with having my head shaved or burned, during an initiation of joining, in some temple ceremony of the past." Burning seemed right, for here too, it was due to too much heat in the permanent wave machine.

"Yes," she blubbered, "I know, I did it before." Pat, too, was a little clairvoyant and realized the entire reliving. She said, "I was the priest who forced you to have your lovely hair cut off and, when you refused, I ordered it burned off instructing, 'Mind not if you burn the scalp as well!' Your hair was especially beautiful; long, thick and auburn. This was done especially, as you were rather proud of it, to make you more humble—a sort of punishment; however, it was the custom when women took the vows. You grieved much over the loss."

75

No wonder we both had repercussions and no wonder I sought her out, of all the many shops to repeatedly do my hair, until that particular cycle swung about—to repeat the past! I had to wear a scarf to cover the head for several months as it looked so unsightly, for I was nearly bald. We were both happy when it all grew out; now we can laugh over it all, but that is the life-continuity; daily we prove this never-ending, reliving our past.

My Severed Finger—Grew Back

I shall relate 'one for the book' here, which to some may be unbelievable; but no matter, it was fact and did happen. About five years prior to the start of the Unarius mission on earth, I was operating a cafe. A specialty at this little beach cafe was French Dips. It was noontime, and I was busier than the customers could be properly served. In my haste, I was careless in using the huge, sharp French knife in cutting the hard French roll, and instead of the knife passing through, it slid off the side of the roll, cutting off the end of my finger instead! It was, fortunately, the next to the little finger (the ring finger) but there remained intact a bit of flesh at the corner of the nail—about one-fourth inch attached.

I did not wish to attract the attention of those present and just flipped the end back in place and pushed on it, wrapping it quickly; no one knew of my mishap. I did not remove the bandage for several days, but when I did, to my delight, the end had begun to grow back! Now the scar remains all around the end, like a thread about it, but again, spirit worked a miracle. I did not lose the feeling in it, and use it just as any other!

The 'First' Psychism

I could relate that one of the very first inner sightings or visions experienced, happened to me at a time least expected. I had just come home and sat down on the swing in the patio to remove my shoes when, looking down at the feet, the green grass seemed to have a radiating aura. It was colorful and lovely, looking like many jewels. As I lifted my glance, the trees also appeared with a surrounding radiation. Oh, it was most beautiful to behold. Although this took place before my meeting with Ernest, I did realize it was the life aura of the growing things. The awareness held me spellbound; shrubs, flowers, every growing thing to which I'd turn my attention was gloriously colorful, radiating, oscillating in seemingly rapid motion. The nearest it could be described: a Christmas tree covered with multicolored neon lights, then a slight haze or fog in between the tree and the viewer. As I peered closely at the tiny tendrils of grass, each shoot or blade was surrounded with this emanating, radiating luminosity. We could compare the sight slightly with the rays coming from a bright, artificial light globe as it appears at times under certain light conditions.

The most interesting part was the lovely, alive feeling it gave me. I felt a beautiful rapport with all this greenery, never before sensed—a sort of oneness. Some may call it love that went out to this beautiful, colorful oscillation. It was not only the colorful emanation surrounding the plants, etc., but seemed to extend in all directions from all sides—long, colorful rays reaching out in all directions, causing, for instance, a tree to appear far larger than its size. All colors of the rainbow were existent, plus a few added, and oddly enough, green was not a predominating color, and which serves to prove what the Moderator teaches: we do not see color as it exists. For instance, the green in a leaf is color not absorbed by the leaf, but is reflected. Thus, my seeing (truly) into the inner or psychic body of the greenery as all other color except green would serve to substantiate his facts.

I sat in transcended amazement quietly, fearful that if I moved I would lose it, but not so. This viewing of the psychic anatomy of the growing things lasted as long as I remained to absorb it, until dusk, which left me with a new respect for the green, growing life; a never to be forgotten experience. It was a definite contact with the psychic or spiritual plants and trees, with absolutely no forethought whatsoever. No conscious effort was needed, nor can such effort aid in any way. Neither the Moderator nor myself have ever so indulged ourselves in meditation etc., but rather, have looked for the workings of the Infinite in all things ever about us.

My Psychic Surgery

An interesting phenomenon took place during the time I attended Dr. Bailes' metaphysical class in 1949. Not that I feel he had anything to do with it, for I know that only through the workings of the Higher Spiritual Unariuns could such experiences take place. However, I was glad that I did seek out all these various schools of thought, for now I know how very advanced Unarius is compared to all others! These 'so called' 'New Thought' schools were but a step removed from the orthodox religions, and even one step from that is improvement, but is a far cry from the all-creative Infinite Science of Unarius.

One evening as I was sitting quietly contemplating, suddenly I sensed a sensation underneath one eye, a rapid vibration, a tingling effect which I recognized to be psychic. It continued moving up and down in distances of about one-half inch and around from one side of the eye to the other side. It felt as if a needle was sewing, yet there was no pain. Then the other eye received the same treatment to the far-too-loose skin underneath the eye. Psychically, I knew They were giving me face surgery—a face-lifting treatment spiritually! I had thought of having it done, yet the price was prohibitive. Now here I was, receiving one without pain, scars, or fee! Then the work started at one side of the neck, another area which needed the slack taken up. The rapid vibrating sensation moved slowly all around the front of the neck, just as would a sewing machine. I could hardly wait until the work was completed to look in the mirror to see the results, but the wait was no more than about ten minutes. And yes, the mirror did show the difference! The slack was gone, the loose skin that just a few minutes before draped in wrinkles, was now smooth flesh, and I was so delighted!

The first person to see me was my agnostic daughter, who soon came over, with the words, "Well, what happened to you? You look like you had your face lifted!" And how right she was. I merely said, "Oh?" 'Twas my little secret! She'd never have believed in psychic surgery, for she is one who will have to wait a few more lifetimes, no doubt, before she begins to 'wake up', bless her heart.

A Prophetic Vision

A short time later during this Bailes' school session cycle, a tremendous body-shaking experience took place, a prophetic vision that shook my body similar to an earthquake, and which has since begun to be proven true. Again it happened during my sleep that I was awakened with a start and the vivid realization of a tremendously important vision was present. There appeared in my line of inner sight a huge white square, similar to a large sheet, perhaps the size of a huge building, and the (then) teacher, Dr. Bailes, was holding one corner of it, the president (then Eisenhower) held the second corner, and I had in hand the third corner of this great white square; but the fourth corner was dangling, hanging loose, no one to hold it up. I had not yet met the Voice of Unarius, who later would be holding the fourth corner of the square which would 'cover the world'. Underneath this white square was the globe or the earth!

I recognized this was indeed a most important prophetic vision, but the even greater phenomenon was how tremendously shaken up I was; the energy seemed as if I was on a vibrating floor. So intense was this force field that I was unable to do anything that entire day except walk about to try to walk it off or that it would subside. It was a feeling as if I would explode until I could relate it to someone. Well, the only person I seemed prompted to relate it to was Dr. Bailes, and who was quite impossible to reach.

I'll never know how I lasted that day out until class time. I thought perhaps it would relieve me if I related it to Mrs. Bailes, but not so; she said, "Better tell him". But what to do, how to see him! I was frantic. Suddenly I knew. He took a three-minute break between the three-hour session and I would catch him before he began to speak. Perhaps this sounds very foolish to think of 'stopping' a lecturer before one hundred and fifty people to relate a vision but believe me, it was no ordinary vision; it was a seething, dynamic thing within, and it seemed I would simply explode if I did not let off some of the tremendous oscillating energy, and which I felt relating it to the right person would relieve. This I did! Just as Dr. Bailes stepped back upon the podium to begin his talk, I popped up in front of him with my back to the class and said, "Sorry to stop you, but I just must tell you this vision!" And very quickly it came out. He said, "Very interesting, very interesting!" and continued on with his lecture.

As I removed myself and returned to my seat, the tears poured. With cheeks soaking, I sobbed as if my heart would break, so intense had been the energy buildup, but I was relieved. The few to whom I related it later knew it must be something tremendously big and important for the future and which Unarius has since proven, for it was this mission to which the prophecy related. The phenomenon of the very potent energy within, proves to me it was the Unariun Brothers beginning their preparation with me—truly, a most memorable happening!

The great significance and symbology of the vision was, of course, concerning the great Light, that would, eventually, 'cover the world' and which has been more than started with the Unariun mission of which I, at that time, was unaware but which did indeed become manifest as the Moderator has, without a doubt, brought to the world the wisdom, the power and the Light—Energy that is and shall extend throughout the world, in time.

For the most part, the peoples are not ready to wish to change; but those who have come with their 'lamps filled', who are found ready and receptive, their lives begin to change as the Light of Unarius begins to infiltrate into their consciousness and as they endeavor to understand the great Infinite Science of Living the Moderator has prepared Wisdom he has brought from these Inner Worlds of Light.

(Note: Of course the entire vision was symbolic and did not necessarily infer that Ike himself would take part; his personality was simply symbolized to portray the vital importance of the vision. This revelation was one of the most vital, and was, as said, most earth shaking of all others that have, in the subsequent years, followed.)

Flashbacks—Former Lives

Comes to mind one of the earlier workouts. About three years before our meeting in the physical, after a metaphysical meeting, I stopped by another student's home and her television was turned on showing a large close-up of the organist, the Indian boy, Korla Pandit. On a few previous occasions, I had seen him play and was fascinated for some reason could not keep my eyes from him; but at the very first glance this time, I burst into a hard and loud cry. My hostess said, "What's the matter, Ruth? Something I've said or done?" I just blubbered, "I don't know!" This wash-out lasted for some moments, then lessened and oh, but I did feel better after it subsided.

We two never did know why, but later, after I met Ernest and the mission had actually been started, I learned. It happened one day as I was speaking to a Unariun student, Velma. Suddenly, a picture flashed into my consciousness, and an inner knowing, and I saw the young Indian boy, Korla, about sixteen years of age, slip from one of my elephants (I had, in India, in one lifetime, a line of one-hundred white elephants), and he, a mahout—my favorite. As he lost balance and slid off the elephant's head, he plunged head first under the foot of the animal which accidentally crushed the boy's head and he died. Now, Korla seems no different than any other entertainer to view. These flashbacks are so very real at the time, and these happenings and experiences are such perfect examples of proving principle.

'Framed in Light'

One very profound and unusual phenomenon took place in these few former years. Early one morning, long before the sun was up sufficiently to shine into the house, my little granddaughter, then about eight years old, viewed it first, as she saw the materialization, saying, "Oh, Grammy, look at Jesus' picture!" A drawing of Him which hung on my bedroom wall was surrounded with a circular frame of intensely brilliant golden Light. The Ray was about five inches in diameter and shone nowhere else, nor did it extend onto the picture but was projected in an exact frame all around the picture! Thus it remained for three hours. Even my daughter (who is in no way sensitive or psychic) saw it and remarked, "Well, how come? That's real weird!" And which served to prove to me that it was a physical manifestation or a materialization and not a vision viewed only from the mental—a real phenomenon! I am sure these various experiences were brought about to help condition me for all that was to be.

Who Held the Axle Together?

The following relating you will have difficulty in believing, but this, too, is factual. This bit of real phenomenon happened during the year I lived in the mountains at Big Bear Lake. The weather was lovely as I left the 7,000-foot elevation but, before long, I drove down into a terrible snowstorm! So fast was the snow coming down, the windshield wipers could not keep the windshield free of the heavy layer of the white blanket. The narrow road was so winding, I was unable to tell which side of the road I was on and I was terrified. I promised myself that if I ever made it to the bottom, I would never return again, even though I lived at the mountaintop. The car actually froze up at one point and stalled. I didn't know at the time why or how, after standing a while—and which would normally have become all the more frozen—the engine started when I made the attempt. A mystery then, but I have since learned from whence came my aid! But that was not the greater miracle.

I had remembered, about half way down the steep hill, hearing a loud bump, as if something underneath the car had hit a huge boulder, invisible due to the heavy snow, and which was exactly what must have happened, for when I eventually made it to the bottom and to the nearby town, I drove into a garage (due to prompting) to have the car checked as a safety measure. After looking it over, the mechanic said, "Where is the tow car that brought you in?" I told him there was no tow car, I had driven in, when he said, "But lady, you could not possibly have driven this car. Look at your axle! It's broken completely in two; there's nothing to hold the car together!" When I looked at the break, I was indeed amazed but gave up trying to convince him that it was driven just that way. He only called the other two men over saying, "Look, this woman is trying to tell me she drove this car in here!" They laughed as though I was joking with them; but it was no joke to me! I realized the great wonder of it all and knew supernatural endeavors brought me down safely; I could say, psychokinetics. But surely, the Higher Ones rode my shoulders that terrible trip. I am sure it is difficult to conceive how this heavy iron axle could have, through spiritual or psychic means, been temporarily welded or held together to the extent of pulling that heavy vehicle—an old-time Oldsmobile, about the heaviest that is made; yet, how else could it have been wheeled down that steep, rough, winding, snowy road to deliver me safely? This happening I'd say, was one of the most profound of all my many experiences.

Time Nonexistent

On one occasion during a time I was operating a small, lunch-fountain cafe in San Pedro, about six years B.U. (before Unarius Mission was started on earth) the need existed I felt, for a short vacation. Carlos, the former husband—the man Ernest first saw in spirit when we two first met—and I, took a trip to the mountaintop at Big Bear Lake for a week. Driving into the town we passed a large lodge, consisting of sixteen cabins scattered between tall pines past, a strong inner knowing overcame me, "This is ours," I told Carlos, "I am going to purchase that camp!" Knowing how things worked in such manners with me at times, he said, "Well, if you say you are going to get it, you doubtless will do so!" Although we had come for but a vacation—our first visit to the area and with but a glance at the property—I felt as though I had already bought the place not even knowing if it was on the market.

We did not stop but kept traveling; we were headed for a small lake nearby we had heard about and after enjoying the beauty of this lovely small lake, called Bartlet's Lake—an area used frequently by movie people to photograph the wild outdoors—we met a gentleman there who 'just happened' to own the lodge which I so suddenly sensed was to be mine. It seemed foolish to ask him about it for in my mind I had already bought the place! After speaking to Mr. Bartlet, we learned that it could be purchased, he had placed it on the market although no visible signs existed on the property.

This will be to some, difficult to believe, but within the hour I had signed papers, the contract to purchase the property and only having looked into but two of the cottages. So strongly and positively was I locked in with the future I couldn't have done otherwise. Having done all possible for the time we forgot all about our vacation and dashed back down the mountain road to San Pedro, so that I could set in motion the wheels that would turn some holdings into cash, and began to attain necessary funds to consummate the deal. I really had no idea how I would ever acquire sufficient for the very large down payment necessary, but start we did. We did have two smaller properties of far less value but most often it takes time to sell such real estate. The average home or apartments sell after about 7-8 months, to a year, on the market.

When the ten-day period was up for the initial payment, I had received the necessary large sum and when the thirty-day time had lapsed for the balance of down payment, all funds were on hand—a truly incredible demonstration! I had sold the two separate properties which netted far more than I had anticipated, making the transactions personally, I turned the cafe over to my daughter, packed and drove up the mountain again to take over and operate the lodge; an operation which I had never previously experienced. But it all worked out so quickly and smoothly without a hitch or even any real 'conscious' effort on my part. The point being made here is the inner knowing, even before entering the houses, as if it had already taken place! This guidance was not a rare function but wherever any important moves were needed etc., it was existent and only when I would not heed the guidance, would I go wrong. It was only eighteen months later that I sold the place for one-third more than I had paid for it; so here spirit was helping, endeavoring to build funds for the future, that Unarius could get underway.

Later, with this accumulation, however, I went wrong. I acted without the guidance and instead of waiting until it was present, went off 'reactionary' on

90

my own and bought a 'dead horse', so to speak, and a great loss was experienced. When I acquiesced to purchase the cafe in Glendale, however, it was with a sad feeling. I actually was depressed with the idea, I did know I was doing wrong, yet did not heed; but lessons were gained in making the error too! Any more I could not go against guidance—I have learned that lesson well. There would be too great a resistance. A subsequent cycle was again encountered with the more positive realization and back on the right track, in a more positive expressing.

However, after but another year with much inner help I was removed from that cafe of negation to start upon another cycle and which a little later did prove successful as you have read of my desert adventure with the milk routes.

Spirit Pushed

To show how very exacting our past lives are re-lived, and most often in minute detail: before meeting this person, George, with whom existed a brief cycle of karma to be worked out, I lived at the beach, some twenty miles distant from Los Angeles. One Saturday evening early, I had a sudden prompting to go to a certain dance pavilion in Los Angeles. After asking permission to take time off from work, the pharmacy owner refused, as it was their busy night. I told him, "If you won't give me permission to leave, then I'll just have to quit my job and go, for it is important." (I didn't tell him why or he would have thought me 'touched'). Of course, he then told me to go ahead if it meant that much to me.

At the time I did not know why, but just went and there at the dance, met George who I married within a few weeks. I questioned my actions, wondering why I would want to marry him, when there was nothing about him I liked unless, perhaps, that he was some-what interested in metaphysics. The upshot of it all was that we went to the desert, started house-to-house milk route deliveries, adding month by month other trucks and doing exceedingly well.

Likewise, it was quite miraculous when on the des-ert after striving less than the one year soliciting new customers (we had started from scratch) that, by the time I was ready to leave the desert, sufficient custo-mers had been obtained that now it took five trucks to serve them their milk, so quickly was the business built up! Truly not the normal manner of business growth!

The house on that property in Lancaster too was an inner prompting. As we drove past it, just the year before, I said to George, "Stop the car. There's our house." The sign on the lot seemed to "tug" at me. As we looked about the place, I still knew it was the one. I even took a chair we had in the car trunk and placed it on the porch and said, "This is my 'hex' sign—now it's ours!" But as we were just starting out in a new business, George was doubtful and had not the where-withal, but I persisted, saying, "Don't worry, it is ours; somehow it will work out." It so happened one of George's sons was a World War II veteran and could buy a house with his certificate with almost nothing down—which he did for us, but I knew surely just as it was first viewed. With that positive inner knowing, we're never wrong.

The house, being a part of the property on which the milk dock was built, made it a very attractive package deal to the buyer at the end of the year when we sold. Only with that higher help do things work out so precisely and perfectly just beautiful to watch.

It was just a little over a year (after our settling in the desert) when suddenly I heard the bell ring. The prompting was there! All things were settled within a few hours time, and I left with no repercussions.

When George heard, as I told him after his asking, where I was going and what I was going to do, "I am going to help build a church," and, after being questioned with whom and where I met the man, (but I had not really met Ernest yet, not in the physical), "I met a fine soul at a church, giving a lecture, and we have a big work to do;" thus, he was willing that I enter, as he put it, "into God's work". (Of course Unarius is not a church or a religion, but this was the best way possible to impress George, that he would understand.)

The interesting and prophetic part of that conclusion was when the discussion arose of how to work it out with the business, the home, debts, holdings, etc., it all worked out within moments. As I proposed a plan, he agreed, "But," he said, "Who would buy the

93

business?" Evidently the Higher Self came in, or possibly the Moderator, for the words that came out of my mouth were true and factual predictions of exactly all that took place the next day! They were, "The man from whom we purchase our products will buy it." Of course, George wanted to know if I had talked to him, but I had not; the thoughts had not even crossed my mind, it all took place so quickly. I continued with the prediction, "He will pay so and so for the entire business, and he will even buy the house, too." Frankly, I had heard of others prophesying the future but was unaware that I was, even temporarily, so capable. It turned out exactly that way, and within twenty-four hours.

There existed, I remember well, strong, positive feelings, as if I knew; as these remarks were made, a feeling of assuredness, and which I have since come to know as the Inner Self. Later, I learned from Ernest that this delivering milk to desert people was symbolic and a reliving of the time when I as Mohammed's wife, Khadijah, who owned a string of camels, sold them to start Mohammed's work on the Islam book, the Koran. Thus it was, the milk delivery trucks were symbolic of the camels who worked crossing the desert to carry water to the thirsty people; and the reenactment of selling the (iron camels), trucks, to help get Unarius under way!

After my quick departure from the desert, I soon met Ernest, and it was these incoming, periodic sums that enabled us to retire from the business world and to start getting the existing Unariun Library together. However, it was not until some time later, when the Moderator 'read' for me of the tie-up in a past cycle which had brought George and I together again in the present—a life, said the reading, in which George, then a slave-master, stole me from a palace garden and took me as one of his several slaves, all chained together, we were forced to cross the desert in the heat of the day barefoot. A cruel slave-master he was.

So here was my way of working out this life, as his slave, even to going to the desert itself! In Ernest's viewing, He saw me slip away in the dark of the night as the slave-master slept, and as I repeated this time, in case he would change his mind by morning! In the former lifetime, it was seen that after my escape, a king found me and took me in to become part of the family (similar to the place from where I had been stolen). Of interest, too, the several truck drivers all spoke of George as their 'slave driver'. Yes, truth is far more interesting, and stranger than fiction! Yes, we are chained to our past with energy ties far stronger than any chain of iron or steel—until we learn the vital principles of thus discharging these past negations. Thus with recognition and realization, the shadows of the past receded into the past and I was no longer bound.

It was a profound 'feeling of freedom' that I experienced as I drove away from my slave-master of old—after that brief cycle in Lancaster and no wonder! However, little did I know that important history was henceforth in the making, in which I would be enacting a vital role. Had I known, I doubt whether a car could have taken me fast enough!

Backtracking here about a year, the following 'revelation' took place during the very first few days after our arrival at this desert venture and should be included due to the proof of just how far spirit will go, will prompt and inspire when we can be receptive and cooperative. Surely great religious movements have been started on far less grounds and proof or revealings than this truth I will here relate, yet it seemed so very natural to me.

As has been said, this particular enterprise was a completely new experience and adventure to me. There existed the need, as I learned, for the several routes and drivers thereof, a very exacting and detailed manner of setting up the bookkeeping system; especially so, because some products had to be tallied in fractions of cents, etc. The owners of the large dairy from whom the milk was purchased agreed to teach me their 'system' for, as they said, it was vital to the success of the business. Well, I took them at their word and spent two mornings with their bookkeeper, to begin to learn their necessary processes and which, to me, seemed very complicated, laborious and elaborate. It was soon discerned by myself, that their methods were most intricate and entailed far too much of that very precious 'time' element, necessitating one person's nearly full time to tab, tally, recopy and carry out in their manner, the complete records of their daily purchases, sales, of the several routes which they too, operated in another city.

Contemplating the situation I mused with it all and realized that I would indeed be quite tied down with that work alone—leaving me no time for the even more important soliciting of new customers. Finally when I relaxed with it all, it happened. Suddenly spirit prompted, and in a flash I knew the complete answer. Instantly I became aware, the revelations and vision of the entire plan and procedure, the picture of the 'work sheets' was viewed, and the entire layout was shown which seemed more exacting and was a far more rapid way to arrive at the desired ends. I was shown psychically within, just how to set up the large, lined sheets specifying the various routes, drivers, products, costs, etc. The entire procedure was quite simplified, uncomplicated and could be kept daily in approximately one-third the allotted time via their methods! Mind you, I was one who was a high school 'drop-out', and math was the main reason; I loathed anything to do with numbers; arithmetic and algebra floored me completely!

I quickly shopped for the particular large, lined sheets (that I had psychically sensed); there they were, exactly as I had viewed them within. After completing the 'setting up', the system proved to be foolproof and it also proved to be a great time-saver! When I failed to show up for my third day's instruction at the dairy, Mr. M. phoned to learn why, and when I related that I had learned a much better way, far simpler and quicker, of course he wished to learn about it—and well, the up-shot of it all was: their company immediately discarded their entire former system entailing the many huge books, and adopted my (psychic vision) one sheet shortcut method! These two businessmen were quite nonplussed for they had used their former methods for many years, paying their bookkeeper a high salary. In fact, they both were, for a time, speechless when they saw my set up sheets, they stood staring at each other rather foolishly. Finally one brother exclaimed, "Well, I'll be!"—the other, with hands on his hips, slowly shaking his head in a negative motion, silent! What confounded them so thoroughly, they said, "that it was so completely simple yet rapid, and why didn't we think of that!" And I dared not relate my source of revealing! But they did not have this wonderful Brotherhood to work with.

Thus, it was proven to me that the higher self and the Brothers do work through in all manners and ways. I felt very happy about my 'find'; it did work out well for me and served throughout the duration of that adventure. I have learned indeed that there are 'no limitations' with we who live from the Inner; and as has been previously mentioned, the Moderator was, without a doubt, working with me on the Inner throughout most of this lifetime, even though I had not met him until 1954. And so we can say as we often do, "Never underestimate the Powers of spirit!"

A Physical-psychic Phenomena

To go back in time, a little over a year before, a most noteworthy phenomenon took place soon after George and I met—(and which was about a year previous to the meeting of Ernest and myself). Although I am quite conscious of the 'normal' reaction to relating such as here will be pointed up, nevertheless, it will be included for those who can appreciate and who realize the infinite and limitless powers of spirit. An average reaction to the following would be, "Oh, it was only their imagination," or the like, but you who are reading these lines are above-average persons, otherwise you would not be a Unariun!

The experience to which I refer took place in an alfalfa field in Lancaster, California with George Marian, the one with whom I had the cycle to work out and whom I married for the one year duration. This was my last cycle just before I heard the 'call' which the Moderator sent to come to Los Angeles. George was also interested in metaphysics and we had gone to the desert to look for a location for a home and a business, as we had planned to marry. On the way, we spied a beautiful new green alfalfa field where we took our packed lunch and sat down to read our metaphysical lessons before eating. Almost immediately we were both prompted to 'look up' into the sky, as we sat, back to back on the greens. From out the very clouds began to pop into view, sculptured faces; heads and shoulders of the twelve disciples! I would name one as he came into view, George the next, and so on. They were not the consistency of the regular cloud formation, but looked as if they were factually sculptured marble of the whitest white! During our viewing, we seemed not surprised nor stupefied as

98

one after another would appear with his long, flowing, white hair, most with white beards, and the expression on each face was most natural and perfect. This continued appearance remained until all were in view. There they were; all twelve, large, distinct, beautiful faces, a truly glorious sight and we were transcended. We lowered our heads as our necks became cramped from being upturned so long and when we looked again, they were gone. The disappearance took place as quickly as the first arrival. What a sight we had witnessed! The display had lasted several minutes.

We were too impressed to speak—with such an experience, words seemed too harsh to utter. We picked up our lunch and started to walk to the car when the owner of the ranch came out shouting, "Get out of there! This is no place for picnicking. Clear out!" We did so, but little did he know the unforgettable memory we took with us. The drive to the city was made in silence.

This was a rare situation, for customarily a vision is an inner or mental experience seen only by the one individual, but here we both viewed exactly alike and knew who each man was as his marble-like, 'live' statue appeared. I have never realized exactly the reason for this, other than perhaps to begin to help clear the channel. However, now since the "Life of Jesus" book has made its appearance, it is reasonable to objectify the previous rapport with these men in Jerusalem. During the time of the 'viewing', it all seemed so perfectly natural and normal but later on, we became aware of the truly phenomenal experience that it was, and then we became quite dumbfounded! Thus, in case some reader may wonder how this came about, I would say the phenomenon was mentally projected into both our minds at the same time from the inner but which actually did seem physical.

My Instant Healing

It was in 1949, during my first visit and attendance at a lecture of the psychic (who was Jesus' true mother) I will call her Rose, that I experienced a wonderful healing of the spine. During the early thirties, I worked at a large and busy cafe in Hollywood. Someone had dropped a piece of butter on the floor, and in my dashing about, my heel hit the grease which acted like a skate and I landed on the end of my spine. Only with great difficulty could I get up and the back gave frequent trouble; mainly, the entire lower area would get numb if I sat for long periods of time. This condition came and went for several years, with the numbness progressively increasing. If I sat for an hour or two, it would require help to lift me up, to get me moving again.

Then I heard Rose was holding a meeting in Los Angeles, and I had wanted for many months to hear what she taught. It was only a short time after her lecture began that I sensed an electric shock shoot up my spine, starting at the affected area at the base, going right on up to the neck. It was severe and lasted only an instant. I whispered to the lady next to me, who took me there, "I have had a healing on my spine. I know it is going to be well now!" And, would you believe me, it was! I could hardly wait for the talk to end to test my spine in walking. Yes, the healing was complete. I arose with no difficulty, the pain and stiffness never to return.

No, I did not credit Rose with this miracle, but know the Brothers with whom we now work were present, possibly Rose included, served as a polarity whereby the Brothers could extend this electric shock-ray so needed. This, no doubt, was one of the inner contacts of the Unarius Moderator, as He worked to aid me in those former years previous to our physical meeting.

Proof of Astral Travel—and Healing

A most demonstrative phenomenal healing was projected for my aged mother during the year I lived in Lancaster, just prior to my meeting Ernest, during my preparatory stage and, doubtless, the Moderator was largely responsible. Mother was pulling weeds in her yard and slipped on the slick dry stems and fell, unable to get up. A neighbor heard her cries of pain and ran out to help, but she could do nothing except call a doctor, who hospitalized her immediately, as she had broken her hip. The family was informed there was little hope for her recovery due to her age of eighty-three, let alone ever to walk again, and which, of course, threw a cloud of gloom over the household. (They were not familiar with the life-continuity principle.)

Living in the desert as I was, they informed me by wire of her accident, but I knew that anything I could do to help could be done where I was—on the inner—and it was impossible to leave at the time. I simply turned it over to the Higher Self and the Infinite, and knew there was nothing in the physical way I could do. I did not know at the time but mother told me afterwards that she kept thinking and wishing, "Oh, if I could only get hold of Ruth's hands, I know I would be all right." Then, she said I appeared to her. In her words, she said, "Then you came and stood at the head of my bed in back of me and reached your hands down, took hold of my hands. It was then that I knew I would be all right!"

What a miraculous healing she experienced! Even in spite of her age, when bones are so brittle and do not heal easily, the doctors claimed the broken hip healed to the point whereby they could not even distinguish where the break had been! No scar remained where the knitting took place, and in record time, less than thirty days! Needless to say, the doctors were confounded and marveled much. One even kiddingly remarked, "Someone up there must really like you!"

Although they were not aware of subsequent happenings, as she never went back to them, it was just two weeks after hospitalization that she came to the desert to stay with me for a time and, after just one week walking about with the help of the walker (a metal framework), she wondered whether she would walk with a limp, and I told her, "Go ahead and try." She released the walker without hesitancy and stepped out with no sign of a limp, never to use the walker again! Her walk was as steady as before the accident—and which the doctors said she would never do. There were no resulting after effects!

No doubt this fall was a reliving of some former lifetime, for she was always afraid someone was going to fall. Up until the time she died, several years later from another condition, she still believed I was there with her in the flesh. It was impossible to convince her otherwise. To further point up how perfect and complete was the healing even in her consciousness, she never spoke of it as most elderly people are wont to talk of their operations other than to mention, when another spoke of it, "Just as soon as I got to hold Ruth's hands, I was all right," and always, "Boy, was I glad you came, Ruthie." The real helping hands (Minds) was the Spiritual Unarius organization, of course!

Speaking of my mother, another note of interest took place some years later, about five, I believe. I had not seen her during this time as she had been placed in a home for senile persons, and I just did not wish to become saddened by viewing these poor souls. I remained away, feeling the Moderator needed my more positive state. Suddenly one day, I sensed a prompting to go to her, so I drove there to find her in a state of coma, which she had been in for some time. She could not recognize me but I spoke to her, telling her to go on out into the Higher Worlds of Light, to step out of that body that was binding her, causing so much misery, and I quickly left. Before nightfall the message came that she did just that! The severance was accomplished! I was glad that the change took place, that now she was freed. Possibly she needed that higher energy to help sever the bonds of the earth, however, it was a definite demonstration of spirit, (so-called) death within a few hours.

Psychic Diagnosis

The following incident took place several years before Mom died, and it can serve as a good example of psychic diagnosis about which the doctors know nothing. The Moderator could teach them much, were the doctors, psychiatrists, etc., ready to listen and heed, but they have their very tall, self-erected pedestals and believe unless one obtains his knowledge from their particular academic book-learnings, they know nothing! What a sad awakening they have in store! Incidentally, the sightings, prophecies, healings, etc., etc., which have transpired via this great Mind of our Moderator would fill several books were they enumerated, and we trust this, too, shall be recorded at least in part. His biography would indeed be the most incredible that one could ever imagine.

The diagnosis which is referred to here is similar in principle to one the psychiatrists use today, as they endeavor to trace back into early life for causes of existing conditions. However, for the most part, the originating causes usually lie in some distant past lifetime, and to our Emissary, a thousand or ten thousand years in the past makes no difference with his abilities to 'see' or contact.

In a contact made visiting my mother in Pasadena one day just a couple of weeks or so after we first met, we noted that she had many long, deep scratches over her face across both cheeks. They looked as if she had been clawed. My brothers with whom she lived, were quite perturbed as the doctors did not know the cause of this disfiguring and could offer no help for her. The Moderator made an instant attunement with his Higher Self and 'saw' the cause. He asked her, "Have you ever had chickens that gave you fright?" Mom went into great lengths to tell how very frightened she had been so many times, that forty years before, when the chickens which dad kept would get out of their pens and fight! They were prize show birds, had long spurs, would fight to the death, if permitted, and she would get a severe scolding from dad. So here on her face were the claw marks—her fear! Ernest asked her what kind of pillows she used and, of course, they were feather! He advised her to remove them, to get another type, which we did that day and within twenty-four hours the scratches disappeared. The feathers in the pillows set up an oscillation and triggered her fear of the chickens, a perfect proof of principle in action and of the Moderator's unique ability to attune unto anything he chooses. Past, present or future hold no barriers with him. As he always says, "No limitations!" This is why the doctors have such a small percent of healings; they know not this science of attunement to the past.

An Indian Spirit Motivated her Body!

Another definite example of an interesting phenomenon happened one evening some years back. I had just finished helping my aged mother into the bathtub, as she was too deep in her senile condition to motivate her limbs in such activities and had to be carried into and out of the tub. I had left her there to splash about when suddenly I heard Ernest calling to me. When I arrived at the room where he was sitting, I found my sister (in spirit) in contact with him and he—very transcended. My sister was making a few remarks to me through Ernest's voice about the teachings that were being brought, etc. When I began to be concerned about mother, wondering if she might have slipped beneath the water, I asked my sister (who could see from the inner), "How is mother?" She said, "Do you wish to go see?" Of course, I ran in to check, but to my great surprise, Mom was gone! How could that be!? She could not possibly climb out of the tub! I rushed about the house searching when, of all things, I found her tucked in her bed!

Upon my return to resume my spiritual visit with sister Esther, through Ernest's voice, I learned that the big Indian, White Feather, had slipped into Mom's body, dried it off, then walked it into her bed and left. Well, to say the least, I was dumbfounded! But I have learned never to underestimate the powers of spirit. Just anything is possible, and with us, it surely has been!

Returning again to the subject of my mother—and not that she or anyone of my family was especially close to me—they weren't; but spirit worked through her, an interesting demonstration for us.

As has been said, in her later years mom slipped

into senility and her memory was very poor; but she, like most older people, became accustomed to certain surroundings, such as a home or rooms, feeling lost when separated from certain little areas.

To accommodate both mother and ourselves, we two shared her old house for a time—about a year, it seems—the place she had spent over forty years; thus, she had become practically a part of the place. As usual, the neighborhood became too noisy and the need to move existed. We were concerned as to how mom would survive a move wondering if she could accustom herself to another place. As there was no one to care for her there alone, we had to take her along. Happily, it worked out just fine, evidence that she had previously prepared (from the inner) for it was quite plain.

Our stay in the next house was about two years and mom had come to just love her new room, similar to a child loving its doll. This was our home in Eagle Rock, where we had to run from the hot-rodders who moved in. By this time, so numerous were my needs and deeds, so great were the variety of expressions, services, etc., that I realized I must put Ernest and the mission foremost in mind and put mother in a 'care' home. All of my brothers had always opposed the thought before, but no one could take her so it was the only thing to do, although I did have strong inhibitions with the thought. I felt like I let her down.

Soon we found our next place of location—Santa Cruz, and realized mom couldn't go along and it was decided. Believe it or not, spirit worked it out so very wonderfully that neither mother nor I had one moment's qualms or sadness! In fact, a week before I took her to her new care home, she began saying repeatedly, "I want to go home; when are they coming for me?" Just the day before our leaving town, there was the ad in the local paper for the vacancy for her. I drove her there, she went right in and immediately became acquainted. When the lady in charge came in, mother grabbed her, of all things, and hugged her as if she were a long-lost daughter but they had never physically met before! Moreover, mom was not an emotional or expressive person, which proved beyond any shadow of doubt, spirit had made them acquainted on the inner long before—in preparation!

They got along so well, the lady said mother always wanted to kiss her goodnight—something she had been completely adverse to—expression of affection! Yes, I had a tremendous demonstration and could leave her in Ruth's care (as was her name), with no regret or sadness in the doing. Oh, what a load from my concern! Spirit—nothing like it! I did want to cry for joy!

As I walked out the door, having turned mother over to Ruth's care, an inner realization was sensed, "I'll not see her again, this is goodbye to mother for this, her earth life." And so it was not until five years later when she was in her death coma did I see her, but she was so suspended, little remained and she knew me not; but she has come to me in consciousness, and as I write these lines of the dear soul, she's right close by, happy. No mother ever was a more devoted one to her flock, bless her soul.

Lazarus' Resuscitation Viewed—Psychically

Because these memoirs are not in any sense a month by month biography but rather, the effort here is simply to point up happenings and experiences that may serve to aid the reader as he enters into his personal metamorphoses in the future. The recalls and notations are being listed as they are again tuned in to the present, just as I remember them.

The Bible story of Lazarus' resurrection was a very real memory to me of that incident. During my youth, my sleep had been disturbed many nights with the exact scene—Lazarus lying covered over with the sheet, (as in death), myself and another lady nearby while others were, seemingly, waiting in the background. In my frequent visions of this, I would then see him 'sit up' after they had thought him dead! I had no conscious memory of any relationship with him at that time, only the vivid memory and repeated night vision of the experience itself; and which was more than a tale to me, for it was a reality. However, what the Bible does not tell is that he was only in a state of coma and was not dead. Due to the power and energies radiated from the force field of Jesus, he was snapped back into consciousness and into the body, from which he had been projected, but he had not severed contact.

In 1964, when a former student, Helen (Reis), came to California, she and I had a very familiar rapport; we both experienced the realization of being sisters in Jerusalem and that Lazarus was our father. Earlier, she became aware that she was Martha, Mary's sister. She was quite conscious of his being brought back from his suspended state. However, it was not until the 'Jose' book that all the pieces fitted together, all perfectly dovetailed, resulting in even greater release-

110

ments with me.

I had known, as was mentioned, since 1955, that I had walked by the side of Jesus in Jerusalem, that there existed a closeness and personal feeling of love toward Him, but it was not until the 'Jose' book was revealed that the complete and entire truth fell into place. It verified in all ways my inner visions and findings and explained the feeling toward Him in a manner of something more than mere respect and admiration for His works and teachings.

The Past Never Dies

The following relating served in a working out and flashback with a little lady student named Velma, and myself. Velma had been an unusually fine seamstress and a real artist with needlework in the present life. On one occasion, as she read a certain poem the Moderator wrote entitled, "The Seed", which she liked so much, she embroidered the entire verse on cloth for a wall hanging—a real work of art. The Moderator had seen her in former lives as she wove cloth and did very fine handwork. She brought her talent through the many past lifetimes.

Velma had mentioned to me several years before about a certain piece of pure silk she was keeping and promised, "One day I will show it to you." I had forgotten about it, then one day three years later as I went to the Unarius Annex where she lived, she brought out her beloved yardage to show me a piece about four yards long of the loveliest, softest, multicolored, pure silk I had ever seen. It was easy to see it meant a great deal to her; but before I left, she was telling me, "Now I think I can turn it over to you, as it is meant for you." Of course, I didn't want to take away something of which she seemed so fond, but she insisted, although in tears, so much did she hate to see it go! Well, I told her I would take it home and look at it. The colors in the cloth were many and sort of run together, as one would dip cloth in dye while knotted —exquisite!

As I laid it out on my bed to observe and wonder about her strong tie-up with it, came the picture and the words. She had been a famous weaver of fine silks in a lifetime in Persia. This entity was, at the time, in the position of a Princess, and I had ordered her to

112

make for me a silk with the blue of the midnight sky, the red and orange of the summer sunset, the green of the Nile, the silver of the moon and the ochre of the seashell; on and on went the description by which she was to weave this very fine silk! The time involved in the making was the exact time she withheld and could not show it. I called her on the phone to relate my vision and she had a good cry—a releasement. Then the cloth was no different to her than any other. But no wonder she had come to love it—her labor of love!

As a note of interest, to demonstrate intuitive powers, or whatever one wishes to term them, during the couple of years my daughter, Peggy, and her husband, Paul, worked with me in the cafes. I would let them take one shift and I the other. They had great fun in seeing if I could tell them how much (or little) business they did on their shifts. All days varied, and they would not turn over the cash bag until I would play that game. Most often I would hit it, not only in the dollar amount, but in the cents column as well. Occasionally, they would do twice the average amount and feel sure they would fool me, yet always did I seem to know! I would just speak out the first thought that came and invariably it was right. In fact, so much so, they finally said, "Oh, no use trying to fool Mom; she always knows!" They didn't like it, so then I realized it was more fun for them if I would guess wrong, so I played it their way a few times, but it was a good demonstration of the intuitive faculty. Less in perfection, perhaps, than the Inner or Higher attunement the Moderator expresses—It is the greatest; but serves a good purpose.

A Prompting of a 'Dead' Husband

The following recall is a definite proof of how our loved ones in spirit can and do influence us when they wish and there's a need, or that it is purposeful. In this case, no doubt, the entity was endeavoring to prove to me his own personal continuity of life.

This incident took place two years after a former husband, Carlos, passed into spirit. I had kept myself so busy that I scarcely ever thought of him, for I tried to block the past from consciousness to try to prevent any loneliness, as we did have a very compatible rapport. Carlos, by the way, was the one who brought through to Ernest the many tests, the phenomena with the odors as he was undergoing training on the astral; and fond are these many memories!

I was attending a dance at one of the beach towns quite distant from where Carlos and I had lived; in fact, he had never been to this town of Manhattan Beach, and as I danced with a certain gentleman, the question of the time of day came up. This man, Jake, —as he told me was his name—said during the one dance, "Oh, I don't know, I don't have a watch." With that, I experienced a strong desire to dash home and get a watch for him that (my deceased) Carlos had owned. Mind you, I had just two or three minutes before met Jake. I said, "I have a watch you can have if you will come home with me to get it; I will drive you right back down here," and which he did. As I went into the house to get my little strong box, in which I kept Carlos' watch, there came over me a strong urge and hurry-hurry feeling. I couldn't get the box opened quickly enough and, instead of unlocking it, I broke open the lock with a hammer, so strong were the emotions to get it for him!

As I handed the watch to Jake, he said, "Oh, you don't want to give this to me." "Yes," I said, "I do, I must!" Well, as he admired it, he experienced a strange feeling; he walked back and forth across the room looking at it, and as we talked of Carlos, Jake said, "Well, he must have been a pretty fine fellow that you think so much of him." I happened to remember a picture of Carlos I had handy, and upon viewing it, Jake said, "Wait a minute—I know this fellow!" Of course, I thought he was just trying to make me feel good that I had given the watch to one Carlos had known and I laughed. But then he began describing Carlos, what he did, and how they both worked at the San Pedro shipyards where they called Carlos 'Spike'. When he mentioned the name Spike, I knew! He told how Carlos loved to shoot craps (which was his hobby) and how they used to play in the hold of the ship while someone would be a 'lookout' during working hours! Other things he related proved he had been a close friend of Carlos; but the interesting way Carlos prompted me to go to that dance where Jake would attend, etc., was indeed all the proof anyone should need. As Jake realized the entire situation, his eyes watered, for he was fond of Carlos, as were all who knew him. That, quite a revelation, indeed; so strong was the urge with me that I had to chop the box open! Wonderful Spirit! Evidently, Carlos had liked this fellow Jake and it was his way of getting his watch to someone who would enjoy it. It did serve to prove a point to me, and I recognized instantly! The thing that impressed me so was the intense feeling of urgency present; the strong 'push' involved! There's no doubt but that Carlos has made good headway on the inner with all the help received from the Moderator from this side of life.

We Walked the Two Worlds

The following several mentions should be of interest and do prove the psychic joining of the two worlds and of the workings from the inner when a compatible relationship has been formed, and by a trained Mind.

As was mentioned earlier in these recalls, a former husband, Carlos, had died a few years previously, and it was with him who Ernest made the first contact at our meeting in the church. Evidently Carlos had set it up on the inner before his last incarnation to work with the Brotherhood and we two, for during the first, almost two years, Carlos was in contact several times a day. I am sure the efforts were most purposeful, for Carlos would, from his side of life, prompt and relate to Ernest countless things that took place during our (Carlos' and my) approximately eight years of marriage. Whether Ernest would be driving or having a meal, or just contemplating, Carlos would come to him and relate some scene, some happening or event that took place throughout these years of our togetherness. Sometimes mere descriptions of certain artifacts, of furnishings of the house, or at other times, he would relate happenings which occurred as we operated the businesses.

On one occasion, Ernest said, "What in the world is this? I see a head, a bald one upside down on a counter. The top of a man's head is sitting like a football on the counter!" This did tickle me, for there was a young man, a plumber, who used to visit our cafe who had learned to stand on his head—no hands, just on the round of the top of his head. Then someone would place a small glass of liquid into his mouth and he would drink it. It was his 'gimmick' and always whoever was in the place, got quite a kick out of his stunt. This was what Ernest was seeing, and upon his first viewing, it did seem queer. But how right he was —as always!

These various scenes Carlos would depict or project were infinite, and many of the happenings he would bring to Ernest, I had even forgotten until hearing of them. Well I recall, the great difficulty I had to locate a correct tie, as Carlos, when on earth, wanted a certain kind with specific-sized polkadots, and the back-ground had to be a certain shade of blue. Well, I think I bought four ties in my efforts to get the one he had in mind. Either the dots proved too large or too small, or the dots were reversed in color to that he wanted; yet, he wanted me to get it for him, and which I know now was a definite memory from a former life when I had placed certain colors about his neck as he represented the family in some fete or games. But this mixup with the tie business kept Ernest busy off and on for several days until it was all cleared up and Carlos got his message through loud and clear, then he was pleased. I had a good laugh over this but didn't laugh before when the pesky ties almost drove me crazy!

On and on went these testings and provings. Carlos and I had made over the last cafe we operated into a farm-like place during which time all the neighbors brought in the various implements they had, to decorate, and it was these various harnesses, etc., that Carlos mentally projected to Ernest: checkered cloths, kerosene lamps, etc., the whole bit. In fact, Ernest lived practically the eight years of Carlos' and my life together through Carlos' projected thoughts and pictures. Week after week this work continued; there were no secrets between us three, and I am sure it was most beneficial and purposeful in my preparation and in the clearing of my channel for future work.

A most interesting phase which all three of us enjoyed during these two years was pertaining to certain energies. Carlos said he was working with chemicals and would be working with us in the healing later on, but at that time he was in training with chemicals and fragrances. Carlos would show Ernest an article (mentally), such as a rose, violets, soap, a certain object with a fragrance, then he would project the smell into my consciousness and I would have to guess or voice what it was, as Ernest saw (mentally and psychically) the object with which Carlos would be testing. Of course, I would always call it correctly because the smell was so definite and clear. Most often, the object would be pleasant, such as perfume, lotions, flowers, bread cooking, but occasionally, he would play a trick on us and project a horrid smell of a rat, and another time, a skunk, and always were these smells exactly as if the object were right under my nose! Ernest, at times, would go into the next room to see if it made any difference but no, he could 'see' and I could sense equally as well. This went on for such a long time, we began to wonder if it would ever come to an end. It was indeed a most interesting game. I recall at one time he left the pot of 'boiling strawberries' smelling for more than an hour. I thought it was going to boil over, so factual was the realization! Shoe polish was one that I didn't care to smell, then his favorite English Lavender face lotion. But most every time he would come in, he would not forget the lovely gardenia fragrance.

When he was still on earth, Carlos used to purchase a gardenia for me the first of every month—our anniversary! And here in spirit, he carried on with this thoughtfulness. This did please me; and so perfect were his projections, never did I relate the wrong fragrance as Ernest would view what he was demonstrating. Then one day, I awoke and felt very sad. It was quite a deep depression and I could not understand why. Soon, my sister came in and, through mental projection with Ernest, said to me, "You were wondering why you were sad this morning. It was because Carlos went away. He was taken to another part of the Universe to study and you bade him farewell, for he will not be in touch any more for many years." Of course, this made me feel better after the psychic adjustment, and soon, normalcy was regained, nor have we contacted him again. Our attachment with each other was quite strong and needed to be severed—not an easy accomplishment!

How Realistic Psychic Contact—Can Be!

Although it may not be drawing a very beautiful mental picture for you, I could relate an experience which both Ernest and I underwent as the Eros book was being dictated. As you read it, you will find, when da Vinci was in control of the mental projections, he mentions about visiting the mental cases receiving treatment; obsessions being removed, etc. In fact, he warned Ernest that it would not be a pleasant viewing and, if he chose, not to visit that area, during his psychic visit on the planet Eros.

Of course, Ernest being the scientist he is, wanted to see all possible, and although this may be difficult for some to realize, we both (He and I) became nauseated as our Higher Selves viewed the cases. Our stomachs took a flip-flop! The methods being used to help these poor souls were wonderful to conceive. After we returned to physical consciousness, in a short time we made necessary psychic adjustments, etc., but it was a very physical reaction as we viewed the leech-like creatures being pulled from the auras and psychic bodies of these poor mental derelicts. Quite a shaking experience to say the least and, could the earthmen realize or see such efforts being expressed, necessary to aid such persons, they would live different lives! They would be far more careful not to incur such obsessing influences and hindrances. What a lesson I had gained in that Eros visitation— lessons mere words could never describe. Only through personal experience can one truly conceive these things and of the vast and eternal help extended by these great Infinite Minds living on higher planets.

To gain understanding of Principle is the greatest of all (so-called) miracles; it is in the conceiving of the very science itself, the great wisdom of the Unarius curriculum which accomplishes the change. 'Concept' is the very element of change, of growth and progress; it is in making the wisdom one's personal knowledge that makes the difference. It is this information (energy) so oscillating within the psychic of the individual that brings about the change—slowly but surely. However, with Unarius this change is stepped up many, many times normal development.

We Walked Heaven's Way

During subsequent years, it seemed all things were being expressed very naturally and normally; neither of us seemed surprised nor perplexed, not really, as one dissertation after another, book after book, lessons, all came about when certain cycles were right. It was with the very first work, the book, "The Elysium", as He was voicing these beautiful verses I wondered from whence it all came. Then one day, during my ten-day 'lost week', as Ernest stepped to the store, came my reply. It came not in any word forms but suddenly, the great and huge Being, Elisha, appeared to me. He was enormous! With the Presence, came the realization of knowing that it was He (among others) who was aiding in these heavenly poems. The Light and Power was so potent He brought, I just sat and, in heavenly ecstasy, tears flowed down my cheeks as more debris was sluffed off and another higher state realized. When Ernest returned, he saw my transcended state and was glad for me, as He, too, knew of my great Visitor.

Speaking of Elisha reminds me of the time (as Ernest has related), when he was in one of the Los Angeles Unity churches, he said that Elisha appeared to Him and seemed so huge that he filled the entire ceiling area. He told, too, how very transcended it caused him to become, for he could scarcely walk out of the building when the time arrived to do so! He related how all physical surroundings suddenly became nonexistent and there, in stark relief, was this great Spiritual Being. Elisha's mental words to him were, "Yea, my son, thy voice shall be as one-hundred voices; yea, one-hundred times one-hundred." This experience meant a great deal to him at the time—

years previous to our contact. Yes, He walked the Two Worlds, throughout his entire earth life!

Our Work Was Laid Out For Us

The Moderator, so completely dedicated in his mission, knew his work was monumental and unequalled on earth and, with each dissertation, I learned much. Growth became a natural consequence as I would either take down his words in longhand or transcribe them from the tapes. As naturally as it was all expressed, looking back now, it was an exceedingly phenomenal accomplishment, but with spirit, all things are possible—and were!

Of course, this contact with the inner worlds was possible partly because we had completely shut ourselves out from the physical world. The more normal oscillations with it became nonexistent (normal to eartheans). It was necessary to leave behind this former physical world in order to live in these higher and constantly more progressively higher states. Our greatest difficulty was in locating the quietness so vitally necessary; the efforts from the opposing or negative forces were ever present to distract, deter and block; yes, even as far as to project distraction through the constant bark of dogs, did these forces of evil use such means!

Even though a neighborhood would seem quite adequate at the time we would move in, it would soon become so noisy we would have to sell and relocate— and which always entailed several months time to properly polarize from higher energies. Thus, the twelve moves in ten years shows the great effort and opposition set in motion from the lower negative forces to try to prevent this great Light from being brought to the earth world; however, as difficult as it was to find necessary quiet—and which was never really accomplished—still the work progressed in spite of all opposition, proving that only a Master Mind could so accomplish. Such a move in this case would take more energies from Him than would a dozen books! Much more than a mere household move was entailed, for we always carried with us the book stock, office equipment, etc., which was a major undertaking.

So with the many interferences, obstructions and oppositions, it was always a special joy when our Moderator would tune himself into his Infinite Mind and bring forth another discourse—another part of this multitudinous accumulation of wisdom which has now become the Unariun curriculum. And so, dear brothers and sisters, when you read and study the various Unariun texts, remember, they are not mere words, but Infinite Creations, brought about through eons of blood, sweat and tears, for as history so reveals, Jerusalem was not the first or only time this great Being paid with his very life as He endeavored to teach to the earthman a better way of life. As was mentioned previously, how the strong, opposing and evil forces brought about his early termination when he lived the life of Anaxagoras he had to flee for his very life to succumb in a cave, where he strove to write the final chapters of his teachings, and which have also become thoroughly distorted through time, as likewise have his Jerusalem teachings and of other times. Moreover, the Unariun Moderator, when he lived the life of Akhnaton (or Amenhotep IV, the Pharaoh of Egypt), as he tried to help the people discard their beliefs in, and worship of, the many false gods; to teach them instead, true creative Principles of life, was forced to drink the poisoned cup—his life again brought to an early conclusion because of the evil and negative forces on earth—persons influenced by the underworld entities which are ever present! Yes, these destructive forces influence, control and enslave mankind through the various religions and many other means under disguise.

Due to his never-ending efforts to bring to mankind the true higher way of life has this great Intellect been, in former lives, waylaid, tortured and even murdered but never shall He renege in his continued and constant efforts! Were it not for Him and other great Advanced Intelligences, the world would be in an even far worsened condition than it is at present—if one can imagine it!

But as He has told, He feels this shall be his last visitation to planet earth. This present visit was brought about especially to project into the world the Light, the Energies so needed at this time; and secondly, to help those responsible for the Jerusalem episode that they might begin to sever their ties with their destructive pasts. Thus, they have all been gathered together, helped to relive and realize these past deeds whereby they could be discharged in consciousness and to enter upon a more positive evolutionary cycle. This is indeed, with the Moderator, turning the other cheek! As has been said, greater love hath no man!

My own personal opposition, too, added to his discomfort during the time of my personal 'Battle of Armageddon', as there were many dragons of the past which needed to be faced, overcome, and slain! For every moment of concern or distress caused him, this entity is most regretful, yet it could not have been otherwise. She is quite aware that no person could emerge from the numerous past physical earth-life accumulations without many attachments, ties, beliefs of a less positive nature, a direct opposition to such an Advanced Being; and to such a Being as the Moderator, all beliefs and ties with the earth would be in direct opposition to all He is or stands for. Thus, when effort is made to convey this tremendous achievement, the vast overcoming of the earth ties or 'victory over self', words fall short to completely relate this monumental accomplishment—an accomplishment never before achieved on earth in any one lifetime—and which, of course, could only be realized with the never-ending help of the Moderator and the Brotherhood and which are one and the same.

But He came well-prepared. He was thoroughly aware of the constant and never-ending opposition with which He would be constantly confronted on all sides where e'er He walked in this earth-world hell! One basic principle He brings is that the only way any person can begin to sever these countless ties of the past is through the inception of wisdom; to gain the knowledge, the science and principles of Infinite Creation that will set man free from his self-created karmic wheel from his past.

And so it was with myself; and change I did! As has been aforementioned, now in 1969, nearly fifteen years later, little resemblance to that former entity remains, and I'm so glad! Glad, not only for myself personally, but that it is now possible to be more compatible with Him, the Brotherhood, and with the Infinite, whereby greater help can be extended thusly to mankind. How aware I have been made of the truth of Jesus' teaching when asked for one concept by which to live and He said, 'The Kingdom of Heaven is Within'—or, as one of the ancient philosophers put it—'Man, know thyself', which is one and the same principle, for when we know the self, we know all men, and until we conceive this Infinite Science, begin to oscillate with the Infinite, we are, as an old cliché often used, only running around the outside of the house instead of coming inside. This was the state to which Jesus referred in his mentioning of being "in the world but not of it". When we know ourselves, we are no longer an oscillating entity with the past but do become 'out of this world' in consciousness. Thus it is, our Emissary has prepared for each of us the know-how; the way whereby you, too, can begin this climb from out the past and onto the golden stairway into the Infinite. To each one so striving does added help come to you; the Light, Power and Energies of the Infinite Minds are directed and projected unto you as you thus 'tune in' through your attunement with the printed 'Word'. You, too, can begin your fight to free the self of the past and the earth world. And with each victory is another step up into higher and higher states and dimensions—and to which there is no end.

Old Herod Got Through—for a Few Moments

To show how very powerful can be the lower astral forces, mention will be made of a time, in 1961 I believe it was, when I had felt they had really gotten to the Moderator. Although we do have great and constant help and protection from these influences, yet at this instance, a very strong negative force came into his aura as he slept during a 'step-out'. He awakened feeling very strange and within a short time, experienced a severe stomach pain. Although he took the usual home remedy medication, nothing helped, and within the hour, He seemed to have a serious heart palpitation and irregularity. Although we have no family doctor as our needs for one have been so rare, just whom to call in this instance, I was unaware. Looking through the yellow pages of the phone book for a doctor nearby, I found within a few blocks away, one M.D. named Jesus. I called telling him to come quickly!

During such time of great distress, time seems expanded and during our wait for the doctor, Ernest was suffering intensely, his heart jumping, pounding and acting very erratic. I was a little frightened, but when he said, "I cannot think," then I was truly scared, for with him, it is all Mind! If He cannot think, something very serious is wrong, and I have never seen this take place before. Ordinarily, if it was a person's time to change worlds, that the cycle had been concluded, it would have been different. I am sure neither of us would have fought to extend his time on earth but there was still much to be brought, in the way of teaching.

As the moments dragged on, each seemed an hour to Him in this great and intense pain with the inability, as He said 'to think', I felt an extreme crisis existed. As the doctor literally 'flew' through the door, opening his bag and preparing some sort of injection, (for I had related the problem), he administered the usual tests very quickly, then gave the injection and said to me on the side, "We've got to get him to a hospital quickly; I don't know if there is enough time to get him there or not," and he ran into the room to phone the hospital to make ready for him.

This doctor was shaken; he seemed nervous and frightened. This, of course, did not make me feel very good but I sensed no fear that He was dying, as did the doctor. Although Ernest was, by then, beginning to relax, for that was what the shot was for, the ambulance drove up and things happened so quickly, almost like magic; but before Ernest was carried into the ambulance, he said, "I don't need to go; I will be all right. I know what it is," for he had evidently made the inner attunement to locate the trouble and got hold of consciousness. He knew it was caused by the astral force of old Herod I, the one who endeavored to include Him, (then Jose), in the mass infant slaying when He lived the life of the babe Jesus. Herod is now, as you no doubt have read, incarnated as a woman living in Santa Monica, California, and it was just a few days previously that a letter was received from her; evidently the destructive astral force, (his entity), came along and interjected into the aura of Ernest as he slept.

Even though Ernest told the doctor he was going to be all right now, it did not deter him in his effort to get Ernest to the hospital and we acquiesced just as a safety measure. As I looked at him as they were carrying him into the waiting ambulance, I could see that He was coming out of it and I knew inwardly He would be all right. We felt, too, that an examination would do no harm. Thus it was, he underwent many tests for the heart which showed nothing whatsoever

130

wrong although it was performing in such a manner just a short time previously that the doctor doubted if he could get him to the hospital before he died! No further pain or trouble was experienced and, after the doctor left the room for a moment at the hospital, I spoke to Ernest and He said, "I have gotten hold of it; it was that devil Herod that came into my force field!" Of course, with this recognition he, (Herod), was ejected—and at the same time—helped! (The second day found Ernest striding down the hall to the car, heading for home.)

This realization and ejection took but a second and no further disturbances were sensed. The doctors were indeed confounded to find him in perfect condition, as they again made their tests. He could have told the doctors what happened, but would they have believed him? Indeed not! Their reaction would likely have been that Ernest was a bit 'strange', but they shall have their day of awakening, perhaps not for hundreds of years or lifetimes, but one day it is certain to come—the time of their acceptance!

No Time Needed!

It was just a short time after our move to San Diego, one of the first ladies to request help from the Moderator had a serious backache; pain she said she endured throughout her entire life. In relating her problem to Him, she said, "I don't know what it is like to be without this dreadful pain; it has persisted always!" As she sat upon our couch, she said, "It feels as though there is a heating pad behind me, it is so warm there now!" The woman had been in the house no more than four or five minutes when she exclaimed, "It's gone, my pain, it's all gone. I've been healed!" She was so overcome and so very appreciative, she broke down and cried like a baby. We saw her on the street a few times afterwards, and each time she would 'break up'. Tears would flow in her gratitude, as she would repeat, "It's just fine, the pain has never returned!" Surely, demonstrations of the Powers of a truly-developed Mind, no prayers, no affirmations— just Consciousness and Power, healing Energies!

My Fine Feathered Friends

As our Emissary has often said, however, mine has been a definite example of what man can achieve in one short lifetime. "It would be most difficult to estimate how far into the future you have been projected!"

Be not overly anxious or impatient, for these are but negative states. Be patient, persistent and positive. When you make your study periods the most important, the predominant thing in your life, you will see yourself changing. You will change from the animal-like homosapien to a spiritual Being who shall not need to return again to these earth worlds but can, through the changed frequencies within you, be attracted to planets and places where we count not time by the rotation of the earth around the sun but is realized only in achievements; in fact, where time is nonexistent!

Doubt not my words of overcoming, of the many wondrous experiences sensed; it is but one small part of the entire story and picture. Yet, I wish not to be repetitious or sound as a braggart, for when we begin to function less from the past (subconscious) and more from the mental consciousness, the ego has begun to be overcome and dealt with. It has been recognized for what it is, faced, and overcome. There is no place or need for the ego-self on the higher worlds; in fact, it could not exist there—the differences in frequencies being too great. Let your overcoming, your personal development become with you the great and vital importance in your life; then it can be possible you can lessen the day-by-day karma normally incurred and instead, begin to build; to add to the Higher Self which is created only from the good, the positive, the creative thoughts, acts and deeds. Yes, man can become a god.

In the historically famous vision of Moses, where he was supposed to have seen, as he believed, the bush on fire, yet not consumed, and countless other biblical portrayals, these are but child's play to the numerous personal experiences this one has encountered, and which you, too, as you walk with the Light, can also visualize and experience. What Moses saw was not the bush afire; but one of the Beings of the inner who 'appear' as luminous or brilliant fire. He was not likely, at that time, of such consciousness that he would be in rapport with the most high Spiritual Beings, the Unariun Brothers, who do come to you, the student, but was no doubt of a lesser degree of advancement due to the unscientific preachments he expressed.

Many of you readers may very likely wonder, "Was the overcoming easy?" And to this the answer is": overcoming self is never easy for it actually means the dying of the self, dispensing with all one has formerly believed or been and, in place, attain the wisdom that will set one free of this former past; beliefs, ties, living, etc., an ego deflation of which there must be many —not pleasant, but painful—however, necessary.

One of the most difficult ties or attachments (of which my psychic anatomy had been partially formed) was a time in Atlantis in which this entity served as a priestess in the great temple there. Buildings, termed temples, were often huge edifices which covered several city blocks and would hold many thousands of people. No buildings of the present could begin to compare with these vast and enormous structures—more like cities—in which were held various gatherings, symbolic celebrations, etc., and which almost the entire population would attend. May it be pointed out, however, that Atlantis endured for a great length of time; it was not only for a certain group of people who incarnated the one time, but many of the inhabitants returned again and again to that great island or body of land. And so it was with this person; I returned there several times.

As the Higher Ones were inspiring our Moderator one time, I believe about the year 1957, they described one lifetime in which I incarnated there, and their description is printed in the Pulse of Creation books, Volume 5, "Muse", page 1127, of the Peacock Princess —the Bird of Heaven. The spiritual one told how, at a certain yearly celebration of the Festival of the Peacock, this entity, as head priestess, dressed in garments made from the eye of the feathers of this colorful bird, in a beautiful ceremonial dance, along with other priestesses who were similarly gowned, paraded about, as does the bird itself, in symbolic remembrance to the great god, Amen Ra, the colorful feathers being reminiscent of the Radiant Energies used by this and other great Beings, called by the Atlanteans, Amen Ra.

This priestess, as goes this true story, was so in love with the Amen Ra, and grieved so at his departure that she swooned, and He left, in his place, a most beautiful pure-white peacock as his gift to her in memory. It is said that it was He who added the lovely color to these so-called 'Heavenly Birds', by placing his finger upon the feathers; thus, they retained the colors of the energies of the cosmos—the radiant spiritual colorings. I would be amiss if mention was not made of my very odd previous contact and working out with these rare, white 'Birds of Heaven'.

Many years ago, I had taken my little granddaughter, who was about ten at the time, to a flower show in Inglewood. These displays were truly a most remarkable experience to behold, as anyone who has seen them will agree. Many thousands of dollars were spent creating the arrangements. During our stroll among the displays, there stood a most unusual ar-

135

rangement of three gorgeous pure-white peacocks standing in a low tree—most graceful. As I caught sight of the trio, I froze in my tracks; I seemed transfixed and awestruck. I had never before seen the elegant white birds but, of course, it was more than just the birds. Here again, time stood still, or perhaps more correctly, the past many thousands of years bridged the present.

Little Peggy yanked at my dress saying, "Come on, Grammy, you have been staring there more than an hour." I couldn't tear myself away—not yet. She became quite annoyed before I could jar myself loose from these wonderful past memories! Oh, how I loved them, but they were, of course, only symbolic of my true love.

Yes, it has been, many of my past lives were lived on a grand scale, lush and with great wealth; as wonderful as they have been, in a physical sense, they all had to be severed, changed in their relationship with me, in the present. The attachments have, of course, been a great part of my struggle—to free myself from them—during these many past years. It has been some time, years now, since the past oscillation has been the predominating influence with me. Now, forward is the only way. The science, the Unariun endeavors, consciousness, etc., occupy my time and mind so that now the Higher Beings and Powers can and do also oscillate through this channel. What could ever be a greater joy—to know we can learn to function more infinitely and be a help to mankind!

At the time this Atlantean discourse was being voiced, tears poured during the entire chapter. It was a complete reliving with me and took repeat reading of that manuscript and hearing it on the tape which the Moderator voiced, quite a few times before it could be done with no remaining reaction or emotion. Of course, I just loved it all, the same as I loved that beautiful ceremony long ago in Atlantea; yet, when it

136

was given, it was just as if it were yesterday.

Oh, the longing to return was so great; it was a very sad-glad time and I just did not wish to let go these fond and glorious memories, yet go they must; all to be viewed completely objectively and which was eventually done. After the severance, no remaining thread or tie existed and it was then, simply a pretty story. For many years before this discharge, however, peacocks held a strong 'thing' with me. When a child, we lived near old 'Lucky' Baldwin's estates in Pasadena where they had several hundred of them. As the motorists drove past these spacious grounds which held his many race horses and stables, the beautiful birds all over the place, the drivers would often have to stop their cars while the many birds wandered across the street—and how I loved to watch them! I used to beg my dad to park there so I could watch and it was always with a feeling of sadness when we would finally have to leave them.

Then after Ernest and I had been brought together and the mission started, we were living at the time in San Diego where there was a large zoo. Now it seems comical perhaps, but when we visited the zoo and I saw the many 'Heavenly Birds' there, I just drooled and—the most frustrating part—there were two children going about collecting these tail feathers. They had a large handful of them and I wanted one so much, I said to them, "Could I have just one of those feathers? I'll give you a dollar for it!" No doubt I would have given five (or more) if they had bargained but, instead, they walked quickly away saying, "No!" I was quite sad for a time until I got hold of myself and it was not until the discourse was given by our former Brother in Atlantis, Sharamute, that I became conscious of why I had this strong attachment for the beautiful birds, that even one feather from its tail which held the iridescent colors was so reminiscent of the Radiant Energies on the Inner. Yes, this love and tie was one of the most difficult of all from which to free myself.

Laughingly enough, on an occasion a year or so later (after the strong tie had been worked out), a young couple came from San Diego for a consultation with the Moderator and, of all things, to bring a huge bunch of the colorful peacock tail feathers! There must have been a couple of hundred. But they meant nothing at this stage—all hookup with them had, by then, been severed—but the irony of fate! A few years previously, they would have been a priceless possession—now, nothing—and into the trash they went.

And so, spiritual progress is not easy, but anything truly worthwhile comes hard. The things that come to us so easily and with no effort on our part, result in little real and lasting value, and especially so with spiritual values. We must sever bonds with the past and gain the knowledge that will carry us forward to replace these oscillations in our psychic of that past. But surely, nothing on earth or in heaven is so thoroughly worth the effort—no thing! These are the values we take with us eternally!

The Negative Phase of the Cycle

The wonderful guidance was experienced so continuously, but on the other hand, to show how, in our growing up and working out, we retain ties and blocks in the subconscious that can and do serve to recreate the situation time and time again, of former experiences that were at one time of a pleasant nature, yet in the present, after a certain degree of ascension into the future, these past recurrences are often expressed in the negative phase and take on negative appearances—for they are all negative in nature to the present and tomorrow will be more positive in relationship with today. I am speaking again of the beautiful peacock, which served to bring about a most frustrating, distracting cycle, taking up much valuable time and energies from our most vital cause. So strong was the tie and love for the heavenly birds from that ancient past and due to these oscillations within, they were out-pictured to the point of drawing us to a city up the coast, Santa Cruz, there to locate property of several acres. At the time we found this seemingly bit of paradise, which was sort of a basin; natural beauty, surrounded with hills, tall pines, abundant with flowers, and a lovely stream winding through fruit orchards, so peaceful did the area seem on our two casual inspections that we had no hesitancy and were so carried away with the beauty and quiet of the place that we decided on it quickly. If you remember, during the first ten years as was mentioned, we were always having to run or move for one reason or another, due to annoyance or distractions.

It was just a couple of weeks after selling our former property in Eagle Rock and purchasing the home in Santa Cruz that suddenly, in the middle of the night, we were abruptly awakened with shrieks and screams which sounded like a woman in pain! After regaining our senses from deep sleep, we realized it was the cry of a peacock which they make during mating season. Oh, no! We hadn't . . ! Our hopes for the quiet quickly vanished, but even at that point, we had no idea that it would keep up as it did. Night after night, right after we were soundly asleep, these screams and cries would break the silence, filling our bedrooms and making sleep impossible. Well, I thought there would be some way to overcome this great interference, and I tried; first, to buy the birds from the owner, offering her five times what they were worth; then, after her refusal, I offered to give her a large sum if she would have them devoiced—which can be done—but she wouldn't hear of it! Ernest made a tape recording of the horrid noises but could get nowhere with the law. They said it was the owner's privilege, and, after all, they had lived there many years. Subconsciously, she was a channel for our opposing forces, for she was hostile rather than co-operative, unwilling to accept my 'deal'. She was not aware of our efforts in humanitarian work, as we never became acquainted with neighbors nor did we relate our affairs to others, knowing the normal reaction would be anything but a positive one.

Now this may sound strange, but it is true; so completely advanced is the Moderator in his great knowledge to the earthmen that their natural reaction is to rebel, to get on the defensive. It has been proven countless times. Man fears, hates and tries to destroy that which he does not understand! Thus, the woman refused our offer to buy the birds, even though it was many times their worth. (Of course, my offer included her signing an agreement that she would not purchase others.) Her only reply was that she had kept peacocks for many years and did not intend to stop now; no apology for the noise which made our sleep impossible.

Consequently, the property value was nil so far as we personally, were concerned. Other noises, too, soon came into the picture; a church bell which tolled every hour of the day and night; a neighbor with a loud-speaker system outdoors blasted out jazz and bebop records at full volume. Thus was our quiet disrupted and, after a few weeks, we were again on the move in search of another retreat—forced again to run. We learned that the acreage in Santa Cruz had been on the market for more than three years before we bought it; yet when we had to take leave, there was our buyer, waiting on the property!—a neighbor who had wanted it before but could not afford it previously. The point I am making is how ties of the past constantly assert and reassert themselves into the present. Though my conscious memory with these birds was one of delight and fondness, yet that tie with them served to attract me to the (probably) only place within many, many miles that kept the screaming birds—a sound that penetrates right through one and which caused Ernest inconceivable distress.

Yes, our help was there to free us of that obligation and from which we were again most grateful to get away. Oh, yes, there have been many 'rabbits pulled out of the hat', so to say; we were always doing the seeming impossible! The guiding hand of the Brotherhood was ever-apparent. We felt that it was a close shave; the negative forces nearly had us cornered that time! It has been one constant battle to keep one step ahead of them!

It is very likely that the reader will be unable to believe that in another city, Santa Barbara, the next place we chose for the annex, was again close enough to peacocks to be heard! When Ernest heard them again screaming in this town, he said, "We'll never get free of those pesky birds until you get rid of them from your subconsciousness!" Well, that made me do

141

some serious thinking. Fortunately, He did not stay at the annex; it was just a place to store the book stock and for an office, etc., but I did feel terrible and, at the time, did not know just how to go about changing the phase in that oscillation within me; but I learned. Now, the lower self or the subconscious cannot get through. I have locked the cellar door to it! But no one gets by without a great deal of effort, work, and discharging these countless thousands of past ties. It is a seemingly endless process, but we do have the necessary help when we, ourselves, put forth the effort!

An Interdimensional Contact

I know of no single happening or experience that factually did so much to project consciousness into the future as the following. There are again no words to adequately describe the experience, but as I typed a concept relating to interdimensional relationships, the teachings conveyed how interrelated are all things, the combined force fields, planets, planetary systems, universes, atoms, etc., I actually 'tuned in' and became part of this tremendous truth! It was as if consciousness suddenly stretched out to include this great expanse of so-called space, and I inwardly knew the full meaning of the Principles He had brought in. My work stopped, and I drifted out into the most tremendous state of awareness that has ever been my wondrous pleasure to experience. It was as if I had stepped up on the ladder unto the Infinite, which projected me out with it and I became aware of many of these abstractions He had been relating. The vast and tremendous feeling of Infinite Oneness lasted for but a few moments but left me so transcended for hours, I just wished not to speak, so all-inspiring was the awareness.

The Infinite had literally picked me up and engulfed me within Itself! Then I knew what his so-often-used words of 'frequency relationship' and 'interdimensional oscillation' really meant! Wonders of all! With this extension of consciousness existed a humility never before known. Such experiences cause one to feel very small comparatively, with the Infinite and to realize how very, very little we actually know and how infinitely much more there is to learn! For this hand reaching from out the very heavens, I was so eternally appreciative! This wondrous event surely must have been "integrating personal consciousness with the Infinite!" And I loved it! Although there is no way of measuring the time or distance that one is projected into the future during, or as a result of one such happening, surely this must have been as tremendous as any previous benefits realized. Thousands of years into the future I must have traveled—psychically speaking!

A Physical Visitation

During one of the times when some of the Higher Ones were projecting thoughts which the Moderator would voice to me, the few following notes were mentioned and which I thought you would enjoy: (Speaking to Ruth) one called Menonsob said, "Sonaba, woman, thou wert indeed the High Priestess of the Temple of Isis, and thou comest into the 'Chamber of Separation' with many fine linens and myrrh, and waxes and aloes; for thou comest with other women of thy kind to help sealeth the bodies against the time of the 'Second Coming'—the time that the Mt. Ptah will be split with lightning and the vaults shall be liberated and the wax shall be melted, and the linens torn asunder so that the flesh may riseth up, triumphant over time!"

He had said previously that there were one hundred of these men of that ancient time who had entered into a state of suspended animation and had left their bodies in this under-rock cavern or mountain. He said that Horus, son of Osiris (intercessor) wears the square of white quartz with the names of the one hundred priests whose bodies are buried in the rock of Mt. Ptah in Egypt. I asked what might be a few of their names and he said, "Cornetius, Armantius, Sharamute and his twin, Sharazar, and himself, Nemonsob (or Menonsob), etc.

This particular contact and experience with these 'preserved' men has been one of the frustrations within my consciousness much of my life, for I have dreamed of happenings so similar to this on many occasions; however, there was one time soon after his relating it that I was mentally re-attuned to that time. I viewed these men in a close-up; it was as if someone had put a huge flashlight in each of the faces, as I would see first one, then the man next to him, and all around the wall I went in this viewing. They appeared as Egyptians, dark-skinned, and were all standing in front of a dirt and rock wall, their features very clear and distinguishable. They all seemed familiar; some of the names I knew and who they were, but it all happened so quickly, and only several were seen in the very close-up way. It was as though I was actually there and, no doubt, this was the way it happened. No limitations with consciousness or attunement!

A Visitation From the Movie Stars

As a change in pace, thought you would enjoy a laugh with us at a few comments some of the 'movie (so-called) stars' gave as they passed through the consciousness of the Moderator. It was truly an eventful evening, for no less than seventy-five or eighty of the 'old-timers' came marching (psychically) through the room. He would name them, and there were some who we were not even conscious had died. But one, Will Rogers, said as he passed through, "Some of us were over with you at the 'smoker' last night; sure had the sheep mixed up with the goats there!" This delighted us for Ernest had just given a talk the night before, and some of those present were smoking! Of course, tobacco smoke to him is most obnoxious and I'll never know how He maintained consciousness with the smoke and noise from the 'unready' ones! This was what Will was alluding to.

Another of the 'helpers', an Indian called White Feather said, "We came alongside and took many scalps!" (Meaning, they removed many lower astral obsessions from these people). This little session of chit-chat with them took place during the first few months of the mission; the Moderator had not yet become quite as perfected a Channel as He now expresses, and here White Feather said, "Soon Ernest talk like clear bubbling water over the falls!" How right he was—so much so that the Moderator voiced the entire "Cosmic Continuum" book in one afternoon without hesitancy, other than a five-minute break! This book was printed exactly as He gave it—all in the fine sentence structure and of the advanced science that it is! Proof of the pudding! A feat I am sure that has never been duplicated!

147

White Feather, I might add, was at one time an American Indian, now a spiritual entity, who has worked with Ernest all his life; even as a small boy he would see this great, strong, fine Indian by his side, wise in the ways of spirit and science! He continued, saying, "Ernest can do many things, but being away from Spirit is not one of them!" He has long since left this (earth) dimension, and for such an Intelligence to again attempt to return and to live in it is a drastic measure for him, his frequency has been so changed. Such a Being is very foreign to the earth plane and its lower vibrations, and the fact that He can remain here is a daily, hourly miracle!"

One Ishmael of the great Unariun Brotherhood says, "Sharamute, the one who we call the Moderator, could have returned to his planet Lemuria, but foresook it to work with the earth people, and could well be the only one on earth who was originally from the planet Lemuria! Sharazar still comes and projects from that far-away planet their powerful Energies." Sharazar was, in that long-ago time (over 150,000 years) when the twelve Supermen came to earth and started what has since become known as Lemuria (on earth), the twin of Sharamute (Unarius' present Moderator). They were at that time, two giant men, over seven feet tall—giants not only in physical stature but mental giants as well—the far greater importance. They were, as were the other ten interplanetary travelers, highly-advanced Spiritual Beings. So advanced had those who inhabit their planet progressed themselves that they controlled their planet by mental and spiritual means—psychokinesis; they could direct it to any place in the countless universes which they so desired! But many would not be able to so conceive this type of development, however, there is a higher goal for mankind when he evolves from the present existing animal-like homosapien existence. Little semblance will remain! The differences in appearances and abilities are even far more so than is the lowly earthworm caterpillar compared to his later state as a butterfly, or of the many other complete changes in all nature ever about us.

Will Rogers again popped in to say, "You know, I haven't lassoed any four-legged critters since I came over here, but there are a lot of two-legged ones that need lassoing!" The brogue in which he said it was indeed Will's! It sounded just like him! He said, "I was hanging around the United Nations delegation the other day, and when the Russians came out, I was too close and got my sleeve torn!" (He still retains his unique sense of humor!)

Yes, the prediction by our dear friend, White Feather, of the Moderator speaking as the bubbling brook, has indeed come to pass. Whenever the need exists, from within our Moderator's Consciousness flows what seems like an infinite and never-ending fount of inexhaustible knowledge, of wisdom unknown to earth-men, with no limitations as to subject matter! This, to me, is definite and irrefutable proof of infinite development—an attunement with the very Infinite.

The many movie personages said they were making the contact as there would be, in the future, great and important movies made regarding Unarius; they related, too, how several famous musical composers were working on musical scores for the movies—thus, of course, we can look to the future time for these developments.

Healing Attunements

Now it is, too, with myself, and it has been so for several years, when the need exists, and it very often does, as students are contacted through the mails, their conditions are 'tuned in', often in a physical way, and for a few seconds, their pain is sensed within my psychic in whatever portion of their body it exists with them. Then the Power from the inner is projected and healing experienced by the individual. Very often the heat, the power and energies come in so strongly that suddenly, I break out in a violent perspiration and become soaking wet! Thus, I am aware that the person is experiencing healing, regardless of what portion of the body it is that is impaired—ear, eye, feet, etc.,—that is where it is sensed within myself. However, this does not always occur, and it is not necessary that we here know consciously their particular problems! In other words, we take on their physical conditions in our psychic!—the Higher Self knows what to do with it. Sometimes the attunement is only slight; other times the pain can be quite severe but short-lived as it is objectified in consciousness and discharge occurs.

An interesting phenomenon—and proof of all that 'goes out' when we are in psychic contact with the students, is the great amount of water we two take in. It perhaps amounts to four or five times the usual amount one would drink, for as we oscillate outwardly to them, the psychic and physical need to be replenished, and we drink, very often, a quart in an hours time. Especially when the Moderator was dictating the Works, we both drank constantly of the spring water, otherwise, we would become dehydrated, as it is a catalyst in the creation of the writings and a necessary adjutant in all healings expressed from the Center. I often fill Ernest's two, half-gallon water jugs several times a day—when He is delivering his Message into the earth world, and otherwise, as He is constantly in attunement with—who knows, how many thousands of students, souls and entities on the inner, as well!

Many students too, who have begun to study and even though they do not thoroughly understand, find also this need for much additional water, especially when near other people. Yes, in many ways the, principle taught is being proven daily.

Well I remember in early 1956, one of the first such happenings: as a letter was being answered to a student, suddenly a sharp pain shot over my entire head; it felt exactly as if I were being scalped. I screamed with the sudden pain and told Ernest, "I've just been scalped alive!" The experience was so real I jumped high out of my chair. When He attuned to this lady, that was exactly what had happened to her in a former lifetime. She was caught and scalped by an Indian and now she is plagued with constant headaches. She, of course, realized her healing; healing not only of her headaches, but several other organs as well had been giving her great distress and they too, suddenly became well. Her eyes had caused her much pain as well as the ears and she underwent severe foot trouble—all relative to that lifetime and the death which she experienced. The fears and subconscious memories of the Indians' screams, their threats and all the countless fears such as one would retain from such an encounter were hers.

The wondrous testimonial received from this out-of-town student would serve to prove to any open minded person the great powers expressed from this channelship in her behalf. Hers was a tremendous change—a sudden relief of all her ills and from that day on her life changed completely in many ways. She said, "I began to 'live' for the first time in my entire life!" So completely did this past experience influence her that her every deed, thought and contact served in some way to re-attune her with that past so that she was oscillating in-phase with that past. As this past attunement with me was made she could, from then on, live more in the present and out of phase with that negative past—principle in action.

Remember, this sort of thing is not rare but is carried on constantly when the student studies the texts—even at times when we go about our (few) daily chores in the shops, etc., as we contact people.

However, we are less concerned with non-students, for it is most important for the individual himself to make the effort to study and understand the science. Yes, this is all a part of the science of the future—the way man learns and prepares himself for a better future and the New Age, incoming. For the most part, man is, at his present position, too satisfied with his personal, self-erected pedestals upon which he so staunchly stands, believing that he knows all, when the truth is: he is very uninformed and quite unintelligent when it comes to understanding himself! Thus, again may we point up, make the most of this rare and wonderful opportunity, dear reader; it can save you many lifetimes of reincarnating back into this cesspool earth world so filled with misery, problems and negation on all sides; and compared to some of the higher worlds, it is just that—a plague-infested cesspool. Fortunately and happily, our Moderator has placed within your hands the key to a better future—the choice is yours.

Recalls—Past Flashbacks

Many realizations and releasements too, took place quite naturally and quickly as, for instance, one day in Santa Barbara as we walked across the lawn to the lovely library there, the arched structures forming an overhead buttress of the building served to 'tune me back' to the times in more than one era where structures of this type were used; Persia, Mecca. As I approached the building, noting the arches or curved roofed passageways, I suddenly began to cry —a good hard cry. The waterworks were turned on full blast! This took place just as we were driving into the city for the first time—another lifetime or so, down the drain! Ernest felt it reminded me of the lifetime I had spent as a Persian princess that brought the reaction.

Another time in Pasadena as Ernest and I visited the Huntington Library, surrounded with beautiful park-like grounds, one huge building, a structure symbolic of one of the lovely old southern mansions, served again to re-attune me to another life—my last, just previous life, in Georgia. As we left and walked away from the earthly paradise and palace-like home and furnishings, the strange, sad 'loss' feeling overcame me. We sat in the car as I cried my very heart out! I was having to leave this glorious estate—a former home! This was a real tear jerker, a difficult one to sever, but fifteen minutes or so, after a good hard washout, 'twas all over, and we both had a good laugh, for it seems comical after it is discharged.

This flashback and discharge was a reliving of a cycle in the South in which I had a large plantation, a colonial estate near the river and often heard the river-boats come steaming down playing their music so gay. It was during the war that I had to flee for my life; that I had to leave that beautiful home and this Library grounds served well to re-attune me. Memories of this, just past life, are very vivid to me—the clothes, activities, etc. I would feel most at home amidst the huge crystal chandeliers with the highly-polished dance floors of gleaming oak—the ladies with their high coiffured hair and long lamp-shade dresses—the men tailored out so regally! Fond memories, never to be relived, for in their place will be many times and places and worlds of far greater beauty; those which die not with time, but places and worlds of the eternal Infinite, where death and termination are nonexistent!

Although mention has not been previously made in these notations, along with the others could be included the name Isis. On one occasion when we were viewing a television movie—a Herculean picture—a scene was shown regarding the Oracle of Delphi. Ernest said to me, "This should mean something to you; you're viewing yourself, then!" Yes, He was of course right, but I had, many years before, experienced a flashback and working out with that life and experience as the entity then, who prophesied and foretold for the townspeople as they came to the Temple of Isis. Isis, as you know was called, "The Mother of earth" (symbolically).

Television Can Bring About Reattunement

There were many times when some television program 'did it' for this entity too—Egypt, Persia, Greece,
Rome, India, in which several lives were spent in each
country and brought into focus for the working out.
Sometimes the strong feelings or desire to want to go
there were present, as I viewed the travelogue and
always, with the realization that the love or yearning
was only a past memory, the attachment was severed.
Yes, it has worked many times; in fact, there is nothing
man can do in the present that is not a connotation
from his past; that is, until he works them all out and,
when he does so, he will no longer be an earth man.
He will, when he leaves the earth, be attracted through
frequency relationship to planets of a higher vibration.

Some of these past ties of such historical areas
as Greece, India, Egypt, in which I had and/or, built
a temple or palace were more difficult to sever, to discharge, due to the very strong attachments; these certain ones required more working at to finally change
the oscillation; which freed me from that karmic past
tie.

Of the most difficult ties or memories in these
countries, and the need from which to be freed, was
my attachment with the Taj Mahal, one of the so-
called 'Seven Wonders of the World'. Every time that
beautiful structure was shown on the television
screen my heart would leap right out to it! I just loved
that place although I have never seen it in the present
lifetime. Often tears of sadness, of longing, would well
up within as it seemed a very part of me existed
there. Even with the mental working with and objectifying that it was an oscillation from the past, memories of architecture in Mecca (as Khadijah, wife of

155

Mohammed) and of other similar structures, I just could not resolve the block; not until one day when it was again shown, (as it has been so many times on travelogues), Ernest noted my reactions and tears that it continued to cause and said, "You know I believe that structure reminds you of the places on the Inner, the lovely Energy Centers that are built so similarly domed, our true home!" Well, that did it! Now all the ties, the love and reaction no longer exist; again I had been robbed, as we often laughingly remark. And we would not have it otherwise, for these workouts are truly invaluable to the aspirant. Now, the lovely structure is just that, no more—an artistic and graceful building. It was the beautiful celestial cities we visit at night that it reminded me of and for which I longed but, with recognition, it is now in a different relationship with the present, just as it should be, and all emotion and reaction with it has ceased to exist. I am at peace with it.

The Ray Beam—Our Psychic Sustainer

Of most vital importance to this incredible metamorphosis were the countless daily sessions of energy projections. Months on end, (in fact, they still continue), day after day, without fail, at a precise time, just as we would be finishing our evening repast, a strong ray was directed to me, so intense most of the time in its effects, that it was impossible for me to move about; I would just have to sit quietly for the duration, as my legs seemed like rubber so long as the beam was projected. It usually lasted about fifteen to twenty minutes before walking could be resumed. Occasionally, there was need for a more extensive inflow and the energy would continue to oscillate to me for thirty to forty minutes, or more.

These instances were after times when I had made more than the usual, necessary contacts with students through the mail, or in my daily shopping, etc., which took this energy that, in these receiving sessions was being replenished; and it was, of course, also beneficial to myself as well. This Infinite Power was interjected into everything we did or touched—or even gave consciousness toward! Now this Light comes in more, whenever the need exists; not necessarily only at specific or regulated times; and which was also for the personal development and preparation of this entity. But as the Moderator says, "This is the only way I have been able to live throughout my entire life: in this infinite power and energy." I am sure his own Higher Self or Superconscious as well as the Brothers on the Inner, other Higher Minds, have extended constant watch over Him and his endeavors! Yes, over the very Light of the world.

During the first few years of these lengthy sessions

of energy inception, Ernest would not necessarily sense it or become transcended with it to the extent that I would as I was serving more as the battery; but it is constantly projected unto him in his need. This energy so directed is, of course, the same Infinite Power of which Jesus spoke when the woman with the issue (hemorrhage) touched his robe and He said, "Who touched me, for I felt virtue leave me!" She, in her less positive or lower frequency, drew upon his higher vibrating psychic and took from Him in a way which could be harmful to him. It can be quite a shock to one transcended when a physical person interjects his lower vibration through personal contact. This has been experienced by us both and, to He, who has never really been 'of this world', it can be very shocking, indeed, and especially so, were he unaware of the action beforehand. All, lessons in life!

My Brother Becomes My Own Grandson

The following is related as factual evidence of an entity returning to earth rather quickly after his demise, although many come back even more rapidly than this chap. Let me reiterate the story of one of my younger brothers, Clary. It was on the Fourth of July, 1940, that Clary, then twenty-three years old, went to the mountains for the weekend with his new bride. About eleven P.M., next day, a friend brought me a message stating that my brother had been hurt—to come to mother's at once.

The full realization hit me instantly. I knew he was not only injured, but dead; I told this person, "Don't try to shield me, I know he's gone." But he continued to try to break it to me gently, for he knew Clary and I were rather close and got along very well. I did admire the dear young boy; he was such a wholesome, kind person with ne'er an enemy.

I hurried to mother's house only to find my inner promptings to be correct; he had been killed. Clary had fallen as he swung from a long rope tied to a tree limb; he lost his grip and, as he fell to the ground some twelve feet below, his knee hit a rib which broke and punctured the liver. His throat was punctured badly, just beneath the chin, from a stub growing in the ground and, within a matter of a few hours, he was dead.

Clary was very fond of my daughter, Doris, his niece, and she thought he was just great. There existed between them, a beautiful love feeling; she, much the younger. About six years later, after she married, she had three daughters; then, five years after the last child, another was on the way during which time I overheard her say several times, "Oh, I hope the baby looks like Clary!" No such thoughts had existed with the others! Although she was unaware, she was sensing, psychically, Clary's presence with her, for it was he returning—to her!

When the fourth child was born, she was most happy that it was a boy and her reception to his entrance was quite different than with all previous children. She dearly loved this child from the start while the others made her nervous, frustrated and irritable. She named this babe Paul, after his father. When Paul was only a few months old she would say, "Doesn't he look just like Clary?" He not only looked like him then, but has since grown more and more like him; not only in appearance, but in all ways, mannerisms, personality, even his hobby, baseball the same. At just fifteen, he is a little league player. When Paul was but a few months old, a very strange defect showed up on his neck right under the chin exactly the spot where he had been jabbed by the sharp tree stubble when he was killed in the fall. This peculiar wound would fester and drain for weeks on end. The doctors were at a loss to define it and operated twice with no benefit; still the same reaction took place and, within a short time, the wound was again draining. He also developed stomach trouble when he was just a few months old and was unable to keep any food on his stomach. His parents thought they would never raise him; this gave my daughter great concern as she was so close to dear Paul. These two completely identical physical problems and areas in the body were sufficient to verify the fact that this entity was Clary returned—returned, indeed, to one of whom he had been so fond but a few years previously (about twelve between incarnations), with the same physical injuries that caused his death.

The two have a very strong rapport and it grows even more so as time passes. I doubt Doris has ever spoken a cross word to the child, as she adores him so. I am unable to relate the truth to her, as she knows nothing of our wondrous work and the truth of the continuity of life even though her son is good evidence of the principle of reincarnation.

Note: It is doubtful that they would have raised little Paul had it not been for the wonderful spirit help from the Unariun Brotherhood. A very interesting phenomenon I will relate here: just a short time before one of his operations on the throat, the Moderator was lying down contemplating, before retiring, when he called to me saying, "Little Paul is here; they have him on an operating table and several spiritual doctors are standing around the table working with the energies on electronic instrumentations for his condition." The scene lasted several moments as He viewed them, then suddenly right beside us there sounded out a very loud bang! It sounded as if a large firecracker exploded, quite like a pistol shot, but there was no one about. It startled us momentarily, then we realized it was the 'left over' energy from the work they were doing, physically discharged in this third dimension. It was real physical phenomena!

Here he had his spiritual operation and would have healed without the physical work being done. Although it was after midnight, I was so happy for them, I phoned Doris, Paul's mother, (my daughter) to relate to her the wonder and phenomena but I was foolish to have done so, as she could not conceive the wonderful manifestation.

Quite phenomenal it was, and it was during this session of viewing, too, that Ernest also became aware of him being my dear younger brother Clary, who had left the earth-plane so suddenly several years before, returned, and expressing several former traits, habits, etc., which I recognize, as well as his physical hangovers. There have been other times we have heard of this physical sound effect from the inner—of power being discharged so—as some students have written of similar happenings.

I would love to talk with Paul, alone, about the accident sometime, to see if any reaction or memory remains, but so far, no opportunity has existed. Surely, the fears and reactions of such an accidental death would have left its subconscious scars and blocks. However, this too, could have been a reliving of a still more distant time and life as are all persons so oscillating and regenerating their past. This, a reason why wars, etc., are so terrible. But we, dear reader, know the better way; we are learning how to escape this treadmill-like repetitious existence and how to step out onto a more positive upward motion of life.

*   *   *   *   *

Note: In my effort here to try to help the Unariun student realize the vital importance of continued and never ending study, I might remind you of the student who just recently passed over to the other side of life when making a contact mentally with the Moderator said, "Oh, if I had only known, I would never have laid my books down one minute!" And Bessie had been a very devout student. I doubt if any person studies more than she did for never a day went by without her delving into the texts for at least two hours—yet much depends upon concept or conceiving. One can read for hours on end but if he does not try to mentally digest what he is reading, his time is wasted. Attainment of the Science is life-changing, life-saving, and the life you save will be your own! We are very conscious Bess has been projected into a much higher position in the inner world she now occupies than that to which she would have been drawn had she not studied well, the Science of Unarius.

He Sees All!

During my daily trips to the post office, it has been a common occurrence to find myself surrounded with cigar smoke. Someone always seems to come in puffing on a cigar during the several moments I remain, picking up the mail there. So, of course, during his frequent viewings of my activities away from home, Ernest saw this smoke encounter and related it to me. Then, a few days later, I pleasantly missed the cigar; no one entered with one while I was there; as I walked out of the door, I thought to myself, "How wonderful not to have to fight that smell this one day." Later in the afternoon he said, "Oh, you didn't get the cigar today, he missed you!" "Yes," I said, "what a relief." He then proceeded to include something I did not even know. He continued, "You dropped a letter out of the box on the floor just before you realized the cigar was absent." Well, I could not at the moment remember having dropped an envelope. Ernest went on, "The envelope was a long one, having heavy ink imprinted advertising some business machine; it was from Burbank, right?" Well, this was a complete blank to me for I hadn't looked at it, but here he saw it all in a flash. Although I knew, if he saw it as such it was true, I had to go see to test-prove to myself, though I have never seen him in error! A quick trip to the post office proved him right, for I had dropped it on the floor and seeing it to be some kind of an ad, didn't even open it and into the trash can I tossed it. It was there, of course, for my verification—and exactly as he saw it—a business machine ad; a duplicator, and it was from Burbank in a #10 business envelope! Exactly right on all counts; yet he could not have picked it up from my conscious mind, for I was not even conscious of these details. Incredible? Yes—until we follow it through with the science —energy, frequency relationship, attunement, etc., then, it is principle in action. Here, he saw something that I had done and was not even aware of!

It is this sort of testing and proving, and re-proving that goes on day after day, after day—and I, loving every moment!

*   *   *   *   *   *

And speaking of cigar smoke, let me relate the phenomenon of the odors which the Higher Ones projected occasionally during the first few years. On more than one occasion, we would sense cigar smoke psychically and at one time it was so strong it caused both Ernest and me to choke! This, we learned, was the calling card of the psychologist, Professor William James. He also visited many students with this identification and they always enjoy this proof (not that the Higher Beings would or could smoke, it was simply James' little joke).

Of a more enjoyable fragrance was one particular sensing which would often occur when I would least expect and was unaware. Into my consciousness would float the beautiful incense fragrance of an oriental sandalwood; this I took to be from a teacher of the Orient, one who was especially endeavoring to help in my necessary metamorphoses. Always with the scent, which was most delightful, would exist the feeling of buoyancy and gave a 'lift'.

Now, after purposes fulfilled and I have grown up spiritually, so to speak, as I project out to others from the inner, they sense a certain fragrance from this one. It is, of course, from the Inner or Higher Self and the particular scent others experience as my contact is made with them (as many have written) is quite like the gardenia—actually more of a tuberose, but it is not a common fragrance. Many connect my fragrance emitted as Lily-of-the-Valley or Gardenia. Personally, I am fond of the Lily-of-the-Valley, it is so ethereal. Thus, dear reader, while in contact with my words here, if you should happen to sense this particular scent, know that I am near to help where needed and this, my calling card.

The Psychic Viewing of an Advanced Being

Among the countless psychic experiences so realized by myself, without a doubt, the following relatings were of greatest importance due to the realizations which resulted. I have become more 'aware' of what a Higher Being is, how such an Intelligence functions far more so than before these visions; at least, as much so as conscious mind could conceive of these abstract, infinite expressions. Although the Higher Beings have appeared and reappeared to me in consciousness on numerous occasions, (in fact, they are always with us), but with phenomena of the type I will attempt to describe, something wonderful takes place. Usually their contact or vision remains in consciousness for only a few seconds, their huge light will flash in and fade out, after a short time; however, this particular visitation is by far the most unusual and outstanding ever to be witnessed by the writer of this missive. And, as our Moderator has said, "It is very doubtful that the like has ever been experienced by man previously on earth!" For a time, I could not see why this would be so, but now it is all conceivable —due to frequency relationship, compatibility, etc.

The visitation of which I speak has appeared to me on a few rare occasions, with several months between visits, usually. The first visitation took place about five years ago (1963) when a great electronic configuration projected into my consciousness. My 'Great Light', as I call it, comes to me as I lie waiting sleep. With no conscious effort, a great ball of luminosity slowly drifts right into my bedroom. It hovers overhead and remains there for a time, oscillating in a pulsating manner. The Light moves slowly into my vision. The very center of the pyrotechnic display

166

(Light Being) is a concentrated, very brilliant bluish-white area of light, so bright that I can scarcely look directly into It. The immediate surrounding area is somewhat softer in its hue, then the outermost part of the ball of luminosity seems lighter and less dense in its intensity. In other words, the Luminous Ball becomes more and more dense and brilliant toward the center, until the very centermost portion is similar to a sun in its brilliance, yet much whiter—the blue white. To determine size in such state would be most difficult, but we can say about three feet in diameter. Very possibly this Great Being could be the size of a house or a mountain if one were on the inner, or so properly attuned, for such attunements are always relative to the awareness of the viewer.

As this configuration hovers overhead, it shoots out long threadlike streamers of light from its center. At the ends of these fine trails or threads of golden light, there seems to explode tiny stars! It is all similar to a fireworks display; there it has remained these various times, hovering and oscillating, creating and shooting out golden threads of energy, each with its tiny star-spark emitted from the termination of the energy thread.

Perhaps the overall time involved as it remains in view would vary from ten seconds to about four minutes; impossible to tell time in such suspended states (as time does not actually exist in the abstract), but always, after this Great Intelligence has 'delivered its cargo', the oscillated intelligence—and that is exactly what It brings—it slowly drifts away, leaving the room filled with its fluorescence! So light does the room become after one of these 'Visitations' that it seems one could nearly read by the light. Upon the first few appearances of this Super Being, I would become so transcended it would seem to take me right out and away with It; and this, I do believe, is exactly what happened! Now, having become a little more relative to its frequency (due to my change), it does not 'knock me out' so readily. Always after one such Visitation, there would exist with me the feeling of a greater awareness, of having suddenly learned great wisdom not previously known. This, we learn, is the manner and way people are taught on Higher Worlds, through mental projections.

And speaking of the brilliance of this Higher Being, it was during one of the many times that the Brothers were speaking to me through the Moderator's vocal cords when they were endeavoring to describe the great luminosity of the Higher Self of Him—we call the Moderator—Jacobi (Einstein) was relating, saying, "His Light is so bright, we have to wear sun glasses but even that does not diminish its glare." He continued, "And even we do not see Him in a completely compatible frequency; but when we do so, He will appear far more brilliant and larger! Yet, it would be utterly impossible to convey the Intelligence of such an Advanced Being, for this, too, must become to each one, his personal realization, his growth and awareness as he conceives the science of living. The One whom you call husband is, you know, the leader or Administrator of the Great Council of Twelve—which heads these Seven Spiritual Planets; you remember Him once on earth as the man Jesus who has since ascended into far greater heights, and has now ascended into even higher planes and to which there is no end!" Jacobi was, of course, joking when he spoke of using sunglasses, for they—in their Higher state—have no physical body but it was expressed this way to try to impress the intense brilliance (Intelligence) of the Higher Self of our teacher.

And by the way, these little visits They used to make through his voice were, to me, most wonderful. They would, at times, come in for fifteen to twenty minutes and talk very informally—often about any problems that may be in the future confronting us—

and always with the contact, the concern was quickly resolved. There was also Ming-tse who usually accompanied Jacobi; Ming-tse in his adorable Chinese accent, Jacobi in his heavy German brogue—just as he spoke when on earth. I shall never forget; one time they were doing a little experiment, one would talk a few seconds, then the other and to show how the energies would become impinged with the opposite one, the Chinese was inflecting German accent and vice versa—it was quite an interesting and comical experiment. We all four were quite amused. Although it has been many years since we have experienced that sort of physical visitation, we know they are ever with us in consciousness. I have come to love them dearly, as well as the many others who gave the discussions through this means.

Along this same line of 'seeing', I experienced a very extensive series of nightly energy phenomena. These 'teaching sessions' extended over a period of about four to five months duration. The glorious and utterly impossible to adequately describe, electronic configurations have aided greatly in the necessary preparation to oscillate more compatibly with the Moderator, as I learned of the energy concepts. Less frequently now, do they manifest in consciousness and always it is a joy to see the heavenly Visitor come drifting into nearness. 'Tis a magnificent display of pyrotechnics—all infinitely Intelligent!

Of especial interest to me on one occasion I remember so well is how I was rather saddened as It started to depart and the thought crossed my mind, "Oh, must you leave me so quickly?" And wonder of wonders, the great Being reversed its direction and returned the distance it had progressed in the opposite direction, came back, and there, in my consciousness oscillated to me again for another period of time! Then I went right out with It as I sensed its final departure and which proved to me that it not only communicated Intelligence unto me, but received my conscious thought and returned to dispense still more of its treasured, creative, regenerative Intelligence!

I could never put in words what these viewing sessions did for me. I could scarcely wait 'til morn to relate that one to the Moderator. However, it was no doubt He, himself, in his true Higher state, making the psychic contact in that wonderful manner—The Light of the World and of many worlds! He has, throughout the years, yes, through eons of time, been so actively engaged in helping, lifting, shedding his Light and Wisdom unto this one and unto the entire world as well—yea, and far beyond, unto the many worlds and dimensions unknown to man—for such a Developed Being is not limited with time or space and is, of course, an interdimensional (planetary) traveler. As this Illuminating Light so regenerates and impinges Itself unto other seeking souls, so shall they, too, in time, regenerate this Infinite Intelligence unto others who are likewise reaching for the Light.

Moreover, always too, there is far more that takes place and is done from the inner than we are aware of, for the benefit of the seeker. The sincere dedicatee can receive all the higher help needed, dependent, always, upon his own personal efforts to learn, to conceive and to apply. May your efforts be constant that results be thus realized.

Yes, wonders upon wonders, my only regret is that the words cannot factually convey the complete meaning, for only through personal experience can such inner experiences be factually realized.

Phenomenal Energy Manifestations

Equally as important, possibly even more so, if one can relatively evaluate such abstractions, were the countless times I viewed inwardly the inner energy patterns, the true manner and ways in which all things are factually manifested on the inner! Night after night for several months continuously did I experience the rare phenomenon of actually looking at the inner workings of energy (again impossible to draw the word pictures). At one moment, I would be viewing, seemingly, an entire network of criss-crossing golden, very fine, thread-like energy formations in some one pattern, always in indescribably rapid motion, all seemingly going someplace or activating something. There were vortices of all sizes and descriptions. As I would try to focus consciousness upon some one spiraling configuration, it would seemingly branch out at its apex and oscillate other whirling vortices. Larger and larger they became in motion, all at an incredible speed. To say these formations would be oscillating in all directions at one time sounds incredible, yet this is the way it appeared, the patterns were constantly changing and criss-crossing in all ways at one time. As near a description as I can think of to similarize it would be: were one to drop a room-full of golden dust into a larger room and it would slowly drift down into space and each speck of dust would become a golden thread intermingling with all other threads, yet each one maintaining its identity and intelligence. Now imagine this picture stepped up to say a million miles per second in speed. This was something like what I viewed in these most unique sequences of nightly teaching-visions, each subsequent time, different patterns were conveyed.

The particular pattern which I could make out would last only as long as I could get a glimpse of it; then other patterns would take form but for the most part, large vortices, then larger ones would predominate. I am sure this helped me realize the meaning of interdimensional relationship and how energy-filled is space—that there is no space. It is all infinitely energy filled; every living object on earth is so inter-connected.

This particular energy viewing became a regular, nightly event and I found myself hurrying to bed so I could again become so attuned; the moment I would relax, there it was—the room was filled with golden streamers of light; threads all actively oscillating and pulsating. In fact, there was, during these times, no place that I could look that this energy network was not existent! Other times, configurations would appear similar to, for instance: if you would take, say, about a dozen or so of the common, fine-screened vegetable strainers, placing one on top of the other, look through the many layers of this criss-crossing, fine wire— this could give one some idea of the intensity and density of the golden energy which I viewed so many, many times, appearing always in rapid motion.

This display was not only momentary, as many other psychisms have been but it was there, seemingly, every time I would become quiet and it would remain with me just so long as I would give it attention —hours on end! All this seeing of the energy in action did indeed convince me of the truth of the principle our Moderator teaches: that all things are energy and there is no thing that is not. Now I know! This, I felt, was creation in action! Now, after these several months of continuous viewing, it is fact to me—there is no such thing as a solid! It is, indeed, the wonderful world of energy! And physical man is, but an infinitesimally small fraction of his true self that lives in these energy fields and which, too, grows as he gains the knowledge of his true nature and life.

During this phase of my development while this energy viewing was taking place, it would cause my psychic to become so alerted that sleep was sparse, nor was it necessarily desirable. I wished only to ponder upon this most wondrous of all phenomena. The sleep was not missed for, with the inception of all I was experiencing, there was a sustaining infusion as well. I am sure our dear One must have become quite tired of my frequent reiterating of the nighttime happenings with these energy fields and displays; yet I know full well, it was He who was helping to make it all possible and that it was most necessary in my development. Oh, that every student could so likewise view! When one is ready, I am sure this will be experienced. With phenomena such as was witnessed, one could never wonder about the structure of the material world—I viewed it all in action.

I do not believe these countless times of energy viewing were manifest for my particular benefit but rather, that this is exactly as it exists at all times in the inner or causal dimensions. I am sure this tremendous program and schooling I so frequently attended in these transcended states in the Higher or Inner Worlds which the Brothers had so perfectly planned, had been long in the planning and most infinitely inspired and motivated. To say that it was successful would be understating, and I am sure, mission accomplished! Yet, too, with all this tremendous attainment, achievements, etc., this entity knows full well that it, too, is but a beginning of all that shall be in the Higher Worlds to which we shall travel and in which progress shall never come to any point of conclusion. It is ever on and forward!

To reply here publicly to a mention made by a student a few days ago when she wrote, "I know that you, too, are one of the 'chosen ones'!" But the only choosing that is done, is by the individual himself;—

whether or not he chooses to follow! There are no few selected ones who receive some special benefits. All is fair and equal so far as the Infinite is concerned. Man works for what he receives—it is first, last, and always 'development' that makes the difference!

In the misstatement in the Bible where it states "Many were called but few were chosen," this, too, is erroneous in its translation. It should have read, "Many are called but few choose to follow!"

Yet, it must not be believed that this mission has all gone off—up to the present time—without the ever-present opposing forces—indeed not. We have realized their strong and negative effects more than once. Now, as in Jerusalem, from the dark powers of forces of evil has there been infiltration attempted in the guise of 'serving' and of desiring to learn the science. This one strongest surge and endeavor to 'destroy' came (as was mentioned very lightly) in the form of a group of persons supposedly seekers of Truth. Yes, the lower astral powers had them well under tow, as they did in that long ago time, and the same persons were victimized. They could have been helped had they been receptive and realized when they were warned but the ego was too strong and they had not arrived at the point where they were sufficiently sensitive to know Truth when it was so presented to them; thus they (about six persons) had to renege when they realized they were blocked to deviate or divide we two and, back into their shells they crawled. Of course, such action set them back many thousands of years or possibly lifetimes before they will again even arrive at the point where they were before the evil was attempted. No, indeed, as the saying goes, crime does not pay! It returns again and again until the person is willing to work it out.

For, as I have mentioned, there were two or three times when the negative powers—forces of evil got through to us that either one or both of us were put

174

quite out of commission for a time. But the 'turning away' of the few, after the realization that they could not divide us as a polarity was, frankly, the most devastating thing that has ever taken place with our Beloved—due to the great psychic implications involved. It is doubtful that He has ever really recovered from that tragedy—and tragedy is what it is, for those persons. However, we are victorious, the mission well on its way as so planned and we shall expect other oppositions before we leave this mortal flesh. But, as the saying goes, "We have just begun to Fight!" And fight for truth we shall, fight with Rays of Light. As our Moderator had related on more than one occasion, "Any Truth brought to the earth world will be met with great and strong opposition—and if not, then one can be sure it is of little importance, for always there will be the two factions, the negative in opposition to the positive." Thus, this overcoming, too, is all a part of one's spiritual growth.

Rescued from Death—Thrice

It was during our second year of the mission when we were living in Pasadena, we went to a publishing house in Glendale to inquire about the first booklet, "Mars". The owner of the place, as soon as she learned of the nature of the work and of the Moderator's rare abilities to psychically diagnose and of his abilities to help people and 'see' into their past lives the causes of existing conditions, told us about a close friend of hers who, she said, seemed to be near death's door and asked if He would help her.

As this friend (Elsie Smith) lived nearby, we stopped in to see her on our way home, to find the poor soul actually more dead than alive. Her face was ashen gray, she felt lifeless and just lay there and stared. She had a sister staying with her who was very fearful for her life but knew of nothing to do; as she said, they spent all the money they had saved on doctors but no help was received. She had been ill for over three years.

Immediately, the Moderator saw she was completely obsessed with a horde of evil or negative forces who were sapping her very life forces. Elsie had a little altar in her attic, she had been a 'devout' Catholic and spent much time in so-called prayer even to the point where she was practically paralyzed with these countless lower astral obsessions.

Because of the tremendous Force Field surrounding Ernest, and with his strong projection of Ray Beams of the Radiant Energy from the Infinite, after a short time she began to change appearance. He talked with her about ten minutes as we watched life forces return to the woman. Her face began to take on color and she moved from her horizontal position saying how different she was feeling. Both the women smoked cigarettes which also made a compatible frequency for the lower astral forces to enter, but her religious ties were first cause. Elsie changed so that before we left, a little later, she scarcely looked to be the same person; her face flushed and in that short time, she gained a sense of well-being and a desire to live which, as she said, she had not had for three years. The negative forces had her down and almost dead so much were they draining her energies; they were sapping her very life.

Just three days passed when a phone call to her informed us that she was back doing her clerical work, mimeographing, etc., which she did at home and which she had been unable to do for many months! She seemed most grateful, but not to the point where she would enter into the study. It does take a great deal of doing for one to sever himself from these religious ties. In appreciation, she asked if there was something she could do to help in my many duties and I gave her some duplicating in order that we could again visit her and help in the further severance of her negative ties with the past until she, herself, reached the point of wanting to study. Ernest said he removed twenty-seven negative entities from her, who were clinging like leeches to her psychic self and very likely, had He not come along, she would have been dead within a short time.

About three months later, Elsie informed us, and seemed quite proud of the fact, she had been able to throw out her altar! This, of course, was a big step for her.

There was an equally interesting happening of Elsie's which took place about a year later. As I walked up her drive, I sensed a strong odor of formaldehyde, the embalming fluid. I know of no use to which this liquid is put other than to insert it into the veins of dead persons for preservation. It was very strong and

I asked, when her sister came to the door, what it could be. She replied, "I don't know, but something has happened to Elsie; she is having a terrible time and cannot move." I quickly phoned the Moderator at home to learn what her trouble was. He saw her being buried alive in a former lifetime and here she was, reliving it. Just as quickly as it was related to Elsie, she immediately snapped out of it and within a matter of seconds was herself again!

In her realization or through objectifying that negative experience in her past, she changed the inphase oscillation to an out-of-phase relationship with the present. This was the means, principle and energies used when Lazarus was resuscitated (and which they termed resurrected—supposedly, from the dead. His was more or less but a state of coma).

Later on, still another time, found her reliving a life when she was drowned. Ernest 'saw' her psychically, after she had been put afloat by a man who had thrown her into a boat, then chopped a large hole in the bottom and jumped out, leaving her to drown. This time, however, she was rescued by the Moderator as He told her the story, and again she had her release and healing.

These two women had been trying for many years to leave that very ancient house but simply could not do so—not until He came along and gave this help! Then, after the third 'life-saving' (psychically), they were moved out with no trouble or effort on their part. They had some property in a desert town and wanted to live there. Thus, we could say quite frankly, her life had been saved three times but even more, she had been projected into the future many years. Before they left, she did start to study the science and her life was quite different than B.U. (before Unarius) —no magic, no prayers, no hocus-pocus, but the factual science of creation in action!

My Greatest Overcoming—and Lesson

In this, my present lifetime, there was very little physical karma to be worked out. Good health has been quite natural with me, however, in 1964, partly due to the entrance of some strong and negative forces (entities), I suddenly took ill. Within a few days, it was quite serious and I was losing ground fast. Dizziness was so severe, I had to take to bed; yet even there it lessened only slightly and the room spun just the same. I was greatly disturbed because I was unable to serve Ernest's needs in my usual way, prepare his meals, etc. This was about the only time in my entire life that I was seriously ill. About two weeks passed and I became progressively worse and unable to get any sleep for the pain and influence of the dark forces that filled the room so numerously often looking like soot!

I was most thankful that Ernest was busily engaged in a physical project that kept him from being too concerned with my problem. Taking pills which a doctor prescribed helped not one iota; even the sleeping pills had no effect. When I finally realized I was actually becoming incapable of thinking properly, this startled me for, without the mind, one is as nothing! My words would not come out properly and all the syllables ran together and, upon hearing the jibberings that emitted from my mouth, I panicked. I became discouraged—something quite difficult for this one to become, for discouragement has never been a part of my makeup, in fact quite the opposite has been true; I am a tenacious person and never say quit.

As I tossed and grumbled in my bed muttering something about getting disgusted and sick of this mess, when Ernest said as he passed my door, "Well, we'll have to get some help on this!" With that I realized how important it was for me to heal or help myself; that this was my personal problem to overcome and I said, "What's the matter with me doing it?" Evidently I, in my Higher Self, meant it. I realized, in my half-doped, half-crazed state that I had to overcome this horde of evil forces so influencing; 'twas my opportunity, my big challenge to overcome, and to prove myself. With that, I tossed all the pills in the wastebasket. The condition the doctor named as shingles was only a part of the problem; the nerve endings were sticking through the skin on my legs, like tiny sharp thorns which burned severely; the lack of sleep wore me out and I believe the pills added to my misery.

At the very moment I made the decision to heal myself, I felt that things began to change within my psychic self; the higher energies began to oscillate unto me and I could sense frequencies moving about in my aura. I began to get in touch with my true Self, or It with me. Soon there came into my view, a huge bluish-white ball of Light about three feet in diameter. It hovered overhead, then seemed to settle right down within my being! By the moment, I sensed change and a feeling of strength. Then, a second identical, higher Being appeared; it also hovered then settled right down within my aura, into me. Now it seemed they both were right within my psychic self and which was, no doubt, the way it was. What a feeling of peace came over me! The room became reddish-pink with the light. No artificial light was burning but this phenomenon lighted up the entire room and I knew I was going to get well, that I would be victorious over this monstrous evil.

I arose to test my dizziness that had been so intense and it was nearly gone, within the few minutes! I walked toward the door leading into the hall, and as I was passing through, the great bluish-white lights extended out in a semicircle from each side of me. I had the feeling, "I can't get through; I am too wide with these great semicircles of light extending out from my sides! Then I realized that energy in such form is not third dimensional and the door would have no effect, and had to smile to myself. Now I knew why they painted angels with wings! When two Advanced Beings would be closely oscillating as one person, these auric emanations would appear similar to wings to the sensitive person or clairvoyant artist!

Then I walked to another room and the entire walls were covered with fuchsia light. This phenomenon was one which lasted as long as I remained awake—which was quite some time. Even more strange were the ruby red crossbars that were everywhere. I am sure a host of Heavenly Ones came with their spiritual electronic instrumentation to create all this energy buildup, the color, the sudden improvement; it was as if I had suddenly been rescued from the depths of some horrible doom! I was sorry that no one was about to share this wonder, for it was a rare and thoroughly unique phenomenon. I was parading about with my 'wings' in the living room as it was so wonderful to be free of my misery, my heart so light! Of course, there also was transcendency with it all. The large luminous balls of Light which I sensed to be our two Higher Selves, surely brought about rapid improvement, coming directly into the body in that way. Soon a night of sound sleep was realized, the first sleep in about fourteen days!

Next day found me greatly improved and within another two days I was completely back to normal. Yes, the earthman would claim an incredible miracle, yet we say, "Principle in action!" This was, to me, much more than a mere personal overcoming, for it was a great step up and the way in which I personally had to use principle and to work with the Infinite. If others constantly did our growing for us, we would never become any wiser nor would we grow spiritually. These are the motivating factors which promote and bring about progress in our evolving—meeting our problems head-on and overcoming them; experience is the only real teacher. This tremendous experience just related also meant overcoming hordes of evil and destructive forces in order that I could oscillate more compatibly with the Moderator and, in the overcoming, I did become much stronger for other possible future appearances and encounters.

When we work with the Principles and the Infinite Minds, we are given help and for this opportunity I shall ever be appreciative. It was the one big and outstanding challenge to me, the great block removed, necessary to attain states of a more compatible Infinite oscillation.

One vital importance with which I am often impressed, which is ever present in these many experiences, is how increasingly aware of the energy body or psychic body I have become. In previous years, as a materialist, the body was the physical thing. Now, with these various experiences, psychisms, workouts, overcomings, visions, etc., I have come to realize, to see and to know that I, man, all persons, are factually electronic instruments similar in function to the television set. These many happenings served truly to prove this principle; and the truth of the Moderator's teachings become more and more apparent. In fact, at the present (1969) the realization is, that there is actually nothing solid; it is all a matter of energy in its countless and infinite frequencies, harmonics, and frequency relationships that makes the difference. Rather than the former way of acting and reacting emotionally, we learn to operate this computer called 'person', or self, in a completely different way. Now it is done more objectively, rather than the automatic, subconscious, reactive-reflex-oscillation. These principles, when conceived, give man a far greater respect and concern for this electronic man of which we become aware as we work with and learn the true science of living. Man, when viewed or realized as an electronic computer is indeed a most marvelous instrumentation, but becomes even far more so as he learns to develop into higher and higher states of consciousness when he shall, after eons of time, likewise become one of the Advanced Beings who will live in the higher planes and dimensions.

No, fellow reader, there has never been, nor shall there ever be, in the distant future eons of time on the earth world, such vast and vital wisdom brought to mankind; the enormous and incalculable principles of scientific living, the life-changing concepts such as the Unarius Moderator has made available for the earth people. The concepts and precepts He has given in this Unariun curriculum can be life-changing to any person sincerely endeavoring to conceive! Man can develop himself and progress himself into the future just as far as he wishes, according, of course, to his personal efforts; and always does he have the help of the Brotherhood to aid him, to project the certain necessary intelligent ray beams of energy as I, personally, have so experienced and endeavored to describe to you. They exist in an infinite variety.

The Brothers can see, and know far better and further, the need of the student—much more so than the person himself; and, as it has been so thoroughly pointed up in the texts, man does not know himself but, through the inception of this higher learning, the knowledge contained in the Unariun curriculum, man can, as has been proven through and by this entity, become the spiritual being oscillating with the Infinite whereby our guidance and help is ever-present; so much so, that the physical world seemingly moves right out and away from personal consciousness and we become, instead, more conscious of the Inner world as we live more and more in attunement with it.

This is what Jesus meant when He said, "My kingdom is not of this world but of another place," and it is as true today, as then. Although physical eye does not discern, it is a very, very real kingdom! (dimensions). Each step up into the future is but another rung of the ladder from which to step onto an even higher one, for there is no point of cessation. That is the most wonderful part—ever and ever on—no limitation. When any person believes he has attained all, he automatically retrogresses in his evolution. Man can evolve, improve himself and become through the eons of time and many lifetimes of incarnating infinitely intelligent. Comparatively speaking, no earthman is truly intelligent! (and we are conscious of the reactions this mention may bring about). Not until he has reached the point in evolution as has our Moderator —but He's not an earthman! Thus it is, He has brought to earth for the aspiring homosapien, knowledge that can and does change him for the better on all levels of expression.

Oh, there is so much more that could be said and written, but our Brother-Teacher-Moderator has said it all so well and completely in the various texts that I could add nothing, for it has been from Him I have learned what I know. Yet, vast as it seems, I speak truly when I say, it is insignificant to all there is yet to learn; with the many 'peeks' of the inner I have experienced and of which there would be no words to describe, there have come realizations, inner knowings and concepts which cause one to feel, "I have only 'peeked through the keyhole' of the Infinite;" so vast and wondrous as it all is compared to this physical world which seems but an insignificant speck of dust; yet, we shall have to await our arrival on the inner to truly discern. These 'peeks' do give one a deep and lasting sense of humility and awe, of oneness with all creation and that this Inner Kingdom is indeed infinitely Infinite; and I treasure every fleeting moment so shared.

Others Likewise Prompted

Mention should also be made how, through this same inner prompting that other students have likewise come to the aid financially, when the need existed. Many have been my personal promptings, guidance and knowing just what to do and how, but the following relating was one of the first demonstrations of this nature and which serves to convey the perfect planning long, long before all things pertaining to this mission were even physically started. This 'miracle' happened during our second year in the work. I had just finished setting the type for the second book and learned that the offset printers who were going to make the duplicate copies from my camera-ready master-copy of the manuscript did no credit work! They had told me they required half the entire cost upon starting the work and the balance when delivered, even though our credit may be okay. However, up to this point, Unarius had no need or opportunity to establish credit. This was a surprise to me and did stop me for a moment, but regardless, I quickly gathered up the book to take to the printer to go ahead with the plan, not knowing how it could actually be done, for such funds were, at the moment, nonexistent!

The shop to which I was going was in Los Angeles. Noting I would have to pass by a certain (new) student's house, an older lady, I thought I would simply make a short visit to pass a little time as the printer was closed during the noon hour. I had met this schoolteacher once before as she had just started with the lessons.

Well, the result of it all was that, after she inquired as to my plans, etc., she handed to me, a check for the full amount that was needed to get the book underway. She said that when it was completed, to let her know the amount of the balance and she would have the second check ready for me! Right out of the clear blue, as they say, a sum of several thousand dollars was thus manifest! What a wonderful guidance, planing and preparation from our Great Spiritual Organization! As was said, we actually scarcely knew this lady, a schoolteacher, but she sensed the prompting and followed through. A few years later, it was shown through our Moderator's clairvoyant vision how she had been, in Jerusalem, the actual physical father of Jesus and also the judge who helped condemn Him to death! So here, now, this Antipas (Herod)—sometimes called Annanias—had saved very skimpingly through her forty or more years of school teaching for this very purpose! (She had also, wisely, through guidance, made some good investments throughout the years to help swell her holdings—Spirit manifest.) She knew, too, that this was her mission, her purpose and goal in life to help create a more positive oscillation of that great negative expression two thousand years ago. Much too, has been her help since, to the complete exhaustion of her entire savings. Surely no greater cause could be served.

I must admit there was a complete breakdown with me as she passed her check to me. Oh, I don't believe I ever cried so hard in my life, for it was fulfillment of all that had gone before in the many lifetimes of effort. Now she was beginning to set her life in order and to start to change to a more positive oscillation, her previous negative acts and deeds. That occasion was over fourteen years ago and still she continues to send a substantial monthly check to help with the furtherance of the work—thorough dedication!

Thus it has been ever since; whenever a need has so existed for any sum, some one or more persons would be prompted to come forth and, as a rule, through the mails, with no mention of need on our part they have so manifest this need. They, too, were inwardly prompted! Later on, a student who, in Jerusalem, then a Roman soldier who helped in the crucifixion of Jesus, brought to Unarius a large sum—also a definite demonstration, as other books were being readied—at a most propitious time, but afterwards, I seemed to know it would happen, although the first was quite a surprise and Helen's great financial gift also came as a surprise, not only to us, but to herself as well, as some relative had left it to her; and she was most wise to use it for such an infinite and eternal cause. These contributions shall serve these persons long and well in a strong and positive way. Helen, too, is now setting up the type for the various books and is a most dedicated soul in her efforts to sever the ties of the past and to maintain a more progressive evolving. Her ability to operate this most difficult machine is a remarkable demonstration of inner help, preparation, etc.

Also, Sanosun, (Pilate's secretary—then a male), likewise had saved, for her great giving to the cause, her life savings—a fine sum and as she said, "I could not possibly have used it for anything else, even before I knew of Unarius, it was for that purpose only!" She, too is becoming most sincere and expressing most generously of her time and efforts in clerical endeavors, mimeographing lessons, etc., and is indeed in her rightful place. Both thoroughly dedicated to their cause.

And so it has been with each one; sometimes certain ones contribute a few dollars a month but it is their loyalty, the dedication that is important—to them. Richard, too, a sincere soul, has served most selflessly with a very sizable sum by which we published two of the large books, and he should be most happy that he has experienced his fulfillment in the serving; he now continues to add his physical help as he prepares the advertising literature to send to those not yet informed of Unarius. There are others, too numerous to mention, who have heard the call and have come to the fore! Even unto this very day, now that all the books have been published (with the exception of one that we women shall get together of the testimonials), there were many thousands of books awaiting hard covers and which would amount to a large sum; yet even before the statements were in, here comes little Alice with her great gift to place upon her altar of life—'a tidy' sum as she sold her little home and gave, but Alice knows of no better use for her finances! And so we have thus operated the work on a strictly cash basis; with each need, there was the wherewithal—even before the need existed! These dear ones are all dedicated students, not wealthy people, for it is today, as it was in Jesus' time, when He said, "It is easier for a camel to pass through the eye of a needle than for a rich man to get into Heaven." Thus, He meant they were too busy with the physical life to learn the Higher Way.

Our sincere thanks and appreciation goes out to those so helping; their real benefits will be realized in time as the good expressed shall regenerate back unto them. Yet, man does not do a good deed for his benefits received but rather, because he wishes to share his good and to take a more positive part in the mission; and most rightfully so, that one should so factually feel, for it is the mission not only of we two but is the mission of each individual student!

There is no greater joy and satisfaction than to serve; to work with the Infinite, the Brothers of Light.

The Error Of The Parents Is Carried On To The Offspring

Of His readings, one particular karmic tie from the past of interest, which should be mentioned is that of my dear little daughter, my granddaughter and myself. As was related in another place, this entity—myself—lived more than one life as a queen and/or ruler and it was during one of these reigns in Egypt from which the Moderator read of my past and saw, during the elaborate Taurabolia procession (as they called the Procession of the Bulls) in which tremendous parades and activities were held. This Queen Hatshepsut simply took for her temple services, gala affairs, etc., those of the young virgins she chose, to take part in these celebrations, and some she selected to remain to be raised in her temple. Ernest saw psychically how this mother and young daughter (my Doris and Peg) were standing on the steps of the temple and the queen spied and chose the young girl to be a flower girl, who scattered rose petals before the processions as they proceeded down the streets as she danced along. The mother refused to give up her child and when the queen's soldiers forcibly took the girl bodily, the mother screamed and panicked; as the child was pulled from her, the mother went into hysterics and nearly went insane—understandably so!

The mother reincarnated in this present life as my daughter and the child, her daughter, just as they were then related. Quite naturally, the mother hated this queen (me); also, because the child left her, great resentment was stored up toward the child, even though she never saw her again. She was, in effect, the queen's property, taken forcibly against her mother's will.

In the present life, the strong emotions and resentments still exist with the mother (my daughter) toward her child (and myself). In fact, the hatred was regenerated back and forth from infancy between the two. As an example, to show how very exacting these cycles are repeated: at one time I took Peg to a religious gathering (temple), during the time her mother was absent. Upon our return, Doris was screaming, crying and yelling to the point where I felt prompted to tell her, "If you don't cease with this carrying on we'll have to put you in the insane asylum." This quieted her somewhat and she searched the house to find Peg, who was then hiding in a closet, as she was very frightened of her mother; but my words sort of shocked her back to sanity and when she found Peg, (who had only been gone with me a couple of hours), she did something she had never done before—she hugged her! That episode was the definite reliving of my taking from the poor mother her beloved child!

So real was this 'dragon' of the past that at one time, when I was giving Peggy dancing lessons at a nearby dance studio, I learned that the child could not even practice her expression while her mother was in the house, so much did the mother resent this 'association' with the past—subconsciously, of course. The mother would 'eye' her with anything but admiration as she, in her creative talent, attempted to express herself through artistic dancing. Peggy Gene was reliving her talent and which she was—due to the mother's resentment—forced to give up, completely blocking herself off from her natural artistic expression. Of this, too, I am sure the future will find her with regrets for not having carried on with this latent talent which she had, in several former lives, expressed in a professional way.

In fact, once when the Moderator was viewing her life in connection with one of mine, he viewed her dancing in France as the head Ballerina in the famous Swan Lake Ballet. At that time I was a woman promoter of such events who financed and aided these young girls in their careers; and because she was especially talented she became a special protégé, receiving my attention and aid. I believe these persons who helped further these artistic expressions were called 'patrons of the arts'; now, they call them 'angels'.

Throughout their lives, there has never existed any compatibility or closeness but rather, always resentment, hostility and fear. Now Doris has become a grandmother and has overcome, to a great degree, the hostility existing toward her offspring and toward me, which she also felt—and I blame her not. This, however, is a definite proving of how these acts and deeds are carried over from life to life, and from parent to child. Although neither of them is interested in the science of living, the scene of that Ancient Egypt happening was related to them, and possibly it helped some, but not to the extent that it could have had they, or even one of them, been interested in learning of life, evolution, etc. They were not fertile soil. Little Peg was very close to me as a child, and I would have taken her to raise were it not for her mother's opposition (my own reliving). I always felt sorry for her and the treatment she received and she, too, felt a closeness and love toward me; however, it has by now, almost all worked out and, although she is a fine little mother and sweet girl, she relates to me now simply as do all persons—like a good friend, completely impersonal. We no longer oscillate from a past tie, and that's progress. Doris' youngest child, a boy (my former brother) is loved as much as she disliked Peg, the difference being from previous associations in former lives.

To show how precise and exacting are Ernest's readings and viewing, He saw Peg scattering the rose petals at the start of the celebration, Taurabolia, the very flamboyant, extravagant and colorful processional display of dancing girls and all the trimmings.

Then, in this, the present life, during my marriage to George (at the temple), Peg was asked by me to be the flower girl and the minister gave her the basket of rose petals but when he instructed her how she was to hold them for him to use, she became depressed because she could not scatter them! (her past memories).

Yes, we follow right through to the letter from the past until we arrive at the point in our evolution where we wish to start upon a more progressive way.

No, my daughter no longer resents me; she has worked it out with the help of the Inner Powers. Again it should be mentioned how this is proof of the truth of the Principle Jesus was teaching when He told how the sins of the parents were handed down generation after generation. Once the hostility, anger, fear, resentment or any of the destructive energy elements have been expressed and re-expressed, the one to whom it is expressed also receives the impingement. This starts the negative oscillation within that person and, in turn, she reacts and re-expresses it on to others, it becoming then a vicious cycle and it is doubtful that many persons who have had great negation expressed toward them over long periods of time, actually know why they react as they do. There is no conclusion to this ever-increasing vicious cycle that has been set in motion; not until one learns Unarius Science!

*   *   *   *   *

And speaking of that little family, I should mention the miracle of Doris' husband, Paul, who, about a year ago was suddenly taken to the hospital, his condition unidentifiable. After one weeks stay and all the tests given, his doctor told him, "There is nothing we can do for you; you just can't live more than another two months at the most!" Well, the poor man lay there for several days with this gnawing knowing, eating his heart out worrying how his three kiddies and wife would ever get along. Ernest contacted him by phone and, with our working psychically with him (and with the doctors), the doctor suddenly decided to do an exploratory operation in the chest. They were still unable to define it, but removed about a third of his lung. He was home in another three weeks "feeling fine". Another three weeks found him back at work, but Paul knew from whence came his help and healing, especially after the doctor had told him, his was a hopeless case! Paul said he sensed the energies and power coming to him.

The cause of this condition may be of interest to the reader, to further help in conceiving of the very exacting science of Unarius. In attunement with Paul regarding his serious chest condition, the Moderator viewed Paul, in a former lifetime, suffocating in smoke as his house was burning down. He was trapped in the wine cellar of his old house. He viewed Paul in his last moments as he was pinned under fallen timbers and was looking up at a large plank that had burned and split, and the sharp pointed end was slanted down toward him, which eventually fell piercing his lung. This he viewed before life ebbed from him, due partially, to the poisonous smoke fumes.

Now here, in the present life, he had a share-partnership in a nightclub which burned nearly to the ground during the night. The Moderator also saw psychically how Paul, as he later went to view the ruins, was attracted to a large plank that had splintered, and was bent down, nearly broken off. This sharp, jagged 2 x 6 caught his eye and subconsciously reminded him of his former death in the fire. From that moment on, his past negative experience and death was then oscillating in an in-phase relationship with the present and it was then that his chest condition started its negative growth.

Of course, the doctors know nothing of these former life experiences and could be of no help in discharging the originating cause. Paul was told about the experience and mulled it in consciousness, but whether or not he was actually 'aware' sufficiently to change the negative trend remains to be seen. Surely, he does have much help on it. Now, when he is in contact with smoke—and he has been a heavy smoker—this attunes him too, in a negative way, with that fire and death. Thus, each cigarette he has smoked has drawn him nearer to this former death experience. Since the operation he has, of course, ceased the unhealthy habit, but even being in a room with smoke, as he is much of the time in his work (another nightclub), serves to keep him attuned to that past happening.

Paul, like any other person similarly reliving some critical past death could, if so properly objectified and if he knew something of the science, work it all out mentally so he would not have to ever again repeat the situation; however, he does not study Unarius, has not arrived at any point of desire to, and whether or not we and the Brothers can help sufficiently to the point where he will be through with it, all remains to be seen in the future. He does, in the present time—and his near death experience has now been nearly a year ago—feel very well and works every day, a double shift, which is not good either.

But this case is a good example of a past reliving.

Even Our Pets 'Remember'

Among the many relatings from my past which Ernest brought to me during our first few months of togetherness were psychic pictures of a little pet I once had. As we were having lunch one day, He said, "Here's a little Boston Terrier, all black with a big white spot over his eye. He looks like the movie dog in 'Our Gang' comedies, in reverse. That dog was white with the black eye." He said, "She answers to Princess." "Oh," I said, "You've got my little dog I had for several years, who became frightened at the noises of the big guns when they practiced near the army camp." Then He saw in color, like a movie, how she dug under the fence and ran pell-mell to the camp where the soldiers were stationed. Interestingly, this is the place I often found her when she would get away, as the soldiers played with her and she liked them. Then, he saw her mother, who I also had for a while. He described her, telling me, "Her name, naturally enough, was Queeny!" How right He was! But Princess didn't want Queeny on the place; she would raise such a ruckus I had to give the mother away. She wanted to rule the roost. How perfect can this inner vision be!

Further Proof

If one would need further proof of spirit oneness, or the nearness of our great Brotherhood, the following should help serve the need. As sleep evades me, thoughts cross my mind and the happening of just last evening comes into consciousness. Because of the very strong force field in which we exist, such things as virus germs are very easily attracted to it, just as a moth to the flame. Thus, we need be doubly careful to stay our distance from persons with a virus and other contagious conditions. This is especially true with Ernest. Last evening, He sensed some negative influence in his throat and began to sniffle and sneeze as well. Analyzing where he could have picked it up—for these conditions are always carried by others—He thought the only physical contact made in the past few days was at a Service Station, to get gas. Knowing if He could place where it came from, He could work it out more quickly. We both were a little anxious to get him freed of it and (perhaps jokingly) we both were remarking, "We'll just ask the Brothers to 'beam' you." "Yes," He said, "Sock it to me, Brothers!" (quoting a present-day, popular, television program slogan). Well, it had been about two weeks since I had seen one of them (a Light), when He said, "Well, here's one of their great white Lights now." Then in less than thirty seconds, it seemed to me, there shone on the window drapery (but which was, in reality, in my consciousness) a huge blue, round luminosity—one of the giant Lights. It made us glad, although we know they are ever close—just as near as our thoughts. I'm sure there will be no sign of the virus in the morning, after their powerful Energy Beams were projected.

Sometimes these rays directed to Him during sleep

are so strong they burn his legs and He has to extend them out from under the covers, He says. He calls them his 'electric boots'. They apply electrodes, no doubt, which are 'hooked up' on the Inner. (Nine o'clock in the morning: yes, a perfect healing was experienced).

There have been many times in the past with me, too, when I have sensed the contact of these (to us) deadly bugs—invisible but dangerous virus—sense the scratching in the throat, the sneezing, etc., and then into consciousness will come the healing Ray-Beam, and soon I will feel the heat to the point of a good perspiring—and along with it, out goes the virus bug! Very, very real, these energy beams. We couldn't exist long without them, and especially is this true once one has made the changeover from the physical and lives more from the inner; then these conditions and diseases of the earth are all the more dangerous and one becomes—strange as it seems—all the more vulnerable to them. Yet, it is not strange when we conceive the science and what man is, and what he can and does become with understanding—quite differently than does the present homosapien exist—and which is another reason why intelligences from more highly-evolved planets do not come to earth, other than in such instances as has the Unarius Moderator, and to whom this earth world is very low on the scale of evolution, comparatively speaking, to planets and worlds from whence He has descended.

I'm My Own Grandma!

Although the dates or years of these former ancient lives (1500-1400 B.C.) were all checked out at one time, it was so long ago that today as I begin to recheck, the thoughts and feelings keep coming to me, "You're your own grandma!" And according to the dates given, it was very likely so! Less than a hundred years between Hatshepsut's life and that of the Queen Tiy, so it is very possible to become one's own offspring after death and return; and especially when certain persons would have a 'thing' going between them such as this entity did during the dynasties. So tied would the individual be, so involved, very likely they would bounce right back to come in and carry on again. The plans, however, for such expressions have been long in the making and it was not happenstance but due to much planning, foresight and calculating on the parts of the Higher Ones on the Inner to regulate and promulgate, and help carry on this rotation and particular placement of personages in these important positions, such as the dynasties of ancient times. Thus, I felt sure that I did return—to become my granddaughter!

Astral Influence Leaves Physical Proof

The following is an incident most anyone should find of interest. A certain student, Irene, had a husband, Stanley, who was not in the strict sense a student, although he experienced a wondrous miracle from the Brotherhood. Stanley had a very serious condition in his legs and another in the hands; so severe were the red blotches and rawness that he was, at times, unable to work. Within about three days after Stanley passed into spirit, the Moderator noticed that a livid red blotch had appeared on the back of his hand and he knew it was from Stanley. The blotch, about the size of a quarter, lasted—just as Ernest said it would—for about a week until Stanley could receive the necessary healing and help on the astral. Oddly enough, a few days later, the blotch was polarized with me and it appeared on my face. We knew what it was and because of Stanley's contact, he was receiving help. The mark remained only a few days. This, we felt, was a definite demonstration of how astral forces reach toward and cling to one they know can help. The next time Stanley returns to earth, surely the condition He has had for so many lifetimes will have improved. Stanley was one who was healed of leprosy in Jerusalem when the Moderator was Jesus, but because Stanley was not able to mentally work with his problem, it recurred repeatedly—a case for much consideration.

A Phenomenal Physical 'Proof'

Mention should be made of the very unique circle that appeared on the forehead of the Moderator. The first few editions of the Venus book carry a picture we used of Him then and shows this circular welt quite well. It appeared just after we two went to San Diego, just the short time after we had met. We were sitting at a small table having coffee beside a window; the sunlight was streaming in brightly when I noticed, on his forehead, a large welt in a circular form. About half of it extended down on the forehead and the upper portion of the perfect circle went around the forepart of his large, rather oval-shaped head. His hairline having receded, the scalp bare, thus the welt was very prominent. It is, I would say, about five by eight or nine inches—a sort of oval circle.

The welt appeared to inflate, become activated when He would become attuned to his Higher Self or with the Higher Minds on the Inner. I am sure this was a special mechanism formed before He entered into this earth-world dimension: a means to help in carrying on the lengthy discourses that have been brought and which form the Unarius Library. It seems to be a sort of electro-radar contact between his Mind and the world of the Inner. Possibly this great 'radiator' is what the Ancients spoke of when they talked of the 'third eye', and as it has been written, of the Eye of Mohammed, whereby He received his 'Messages', which became the books of the Koran. These works have also become so distorted, little, if any, truth He brought remains.

When I caught sight of the circle the first time, I was rather taken aback, for I had never seen the like and, no doubt never shall again; for it is very doubtful that the remarkable communication system has ever, if rarely, been duplicated on earth, with the possible exception of Mohammed. Mohammed, however, was not in any sense of the word the great Intellect, the Advanced Being that is the Unariun Moderator. As I spoke of it, Ernest looked into the mirror and was, in his conscious mind, seeing it for the first time too, for it was just then being brought into activation. When He was not in attunement, the raised welt would deflate and become less visible. It was as if there were a circular tube underneath the flesh that would inflate as He would set up the contact with the Inner Worlds and Minds. And through the years, it has been a most vital point of interest to me to note how it is activated as the energy hookup exists.

No doubt, a great Ray-Beam, similar to a laser beam, is projected down to Him, or He projects the Ray-Beam out for the most perfect contacts in consciousness so experienced and expressed so many countless times—contacts which have delivered the entire Unariun texts.

This very unique phenomenon should serve also as proof that this great soul is not an earthman. In fact, doubtful it is, that He ever was but rather, He came to this planet only upon a few occasions during certain eras to bring to mankind, the wisdom so needed at that particular time. As one of the Spiritual Brothers of the Inner was in voice-contact upon one occasion, he spoke to me, mentioning the circle, saying, "It was no accident that the circle appeared on Ernest's head just at the time you went to San Diego, as it was with Mohammed; nor was it accidental that you sold your iron camels (my milk trucks) just about the same time, for this was all the starting of the great work on earth—that which you call Unarius."

In looking back over the past nearly sixteen years, the perfect plan has all unfolded, and it is plain to see how well all directions and plans were set in motion long before, how well they were laid out and engineered. Then 'twas but a matter of we following through with the Inner guidance which was ever-present; but as has been mentioned, the earthman shall not, as a whole, be ready for this creative science; he will not appreciate the Unariun science for eons to come and then, only slowly will he grow into it. Those who have been conditioned for this, their advent, are indeed most fortunate and should work sincerely at conceiving, for it can be life-changing to the receptive student.

He Saw the Past-Thousands of Years

As has been mentioned elsewhere, during one of the earlier visions of Ernest's viewing of our ancient pasts in 1956, He "saw" this entity (myself) as Hatasu (or Hatshepsut) formulating expeditions of large boats which were sent to South Arabia for incense, shrubs, artifacts, etc. A fleet of five boats made this excursion several times to Pauni (or the island of Punt) in Samoa, the proceeds of which she used to build and decorate her famous temples at Tel-el-Amarna. As he viewed this cargo, He described the beautiful ornate boats used in detail, and the pictures he projected were so clear I could have drawn them. Yes, the love or tie with them existed indeed when He first related these times and lives of antiquity—all necessary to sever in consciousness. And, of course, after our search through the books of record it was all there, most exacting, as he has viewed it, but it was always such a joy and satisfaction to see it then in historical print! No wonder this entity has experienced inhibitions when unable to express in a 'big' way! But that's all in the past. The only 'big' desire existing with me any more is for Unarius; that we contact each one who has set it up to be contacted, and am sure with inner guidance, this too, shall be done.

No doubt, certain benefits were realized from these lives, but the only lasting effects and results of true worth, from any lifetime, regardless, are those spiritual values which are added within, as we grow in wisdom. The point which I was trying to make: even so far back in time, the polarity relationship was in existence with the one we now call Unariun Moderator, for this was most vital for His Mission in the present—that He have a compatible polarity. One can only slightly visualize the tremendous and extensive preparation and planning necessary and which was extended to bring about these various missions and the descent of such an Avatar into these earth worlds, to bring to mankind the wisdom and know-how which can enable him to more progressively further his evolution. Yes, as it has been in the past, this great plan, is now and shall be, continued on into the future.

A common reaction with students, as they hear of his looking into and relating from their pasts, has been, "How does He see this, how is it possible, and how can I learn to do it?" Well, it is not done as have many occultists claimed or believed, but it is exactly as has been taught in the teachings. Each act, thought, or deed expressed creates its particular energy wave form or pattern within the psychic anatomy of the individual; then it is a matter of the 'developed Mind' to make his attunement with these energy patterns, similar in function to the television. The picture one views on the tube does not travel through space as the picture but exists in the same manner—as energy wave forms, then the circuitry is impressed in dots which eventually appear on the tube as the picture, similar in principle to the function of the psychic anatomy. However, the science is all very thoroughly taught and described in detail in order that those ready and desirous can conceive and, in so doing, project themselves forward in their evolution. Yes, you too, dear reader, can learn through time to likewise become one such Infinite Mind, in attunement with all creation. I, personally, would not be one to try to estimate how many hundreds of thousands of years our Moderator has been working with these higher principles. No, he is not an earthean but simply has visited this planet a few times before in centuries past.

*   *   *   *   *

Speaking of similarities in personality or physical traits, if one would need further proof to verify the Moderator's identity with Akhnaton, one is in the head size. When the Moderator was born, his head was so large his mother had to keep her legs in traction for weeks until her innards went back into place, so badly was she torn due to his oversize cranium. As a small boy of seven, He tells how He stood on tiptoe, holding on to the edge of the table to help him reach up to his (adult) uncle's hat, which was size 7-3/4 lying there, to find that, after putting it on his head, he could not get it on—it was too small!

Now as I read in the Encyclopedia about Akhnaton (1300 B.C.), I learn that his head was extremely large; in fact, after they exhumed and examined his skull, history states the Akhnaton skull to be the largest human skull ever found in the world! It carries through today, too, not only as the infant, for He has always had great difficulty finding a hat sufficiently large.

An interesting memory just came to me, how one day he awoke in the morning (after a couple of days searching for a hat), with the inner knowing that a certain store in a nearby town (Los Angeles) had a hat to fit. He dashed out immediately to get it. Upon entering the shop he told the salesman, "You have my hat here!" Of course, the man was astonished when looking at his large head and questioned his remark but Ernest told him exactly where, in the back of the store to get it (as He viewed it psychically), and sure enough, the man came out with it! Ernest put it on and it was the necessary 7-3/4 oversize!

One only needs to study the Unariun Science, then read the historical recountings of his teachings as Akhnaton, as Anaxagoras, and as Jesus to be able to see the continuous similarity, the golden thread of truth running through these various missions, headed by this Infinite Mind we now refer to as the Unariun

Moderator (Ernest Norman). Even the elegant poetry which Akhnaton expressed carries this same high infinite expanse. One need not be a mystic to conceive they came from the same Intelligence, as He has portrayed in his several books of parables and poetry in this present lifetime. The one noticeable difference in the works is, that in the present, much has been added due to the scientific age that it is and which time to come will further prove.

As has been related before, that our Moderator is a most humble and unpretentious person, this too, you will find pointed up in the existing historical accounts with Akhnaton, what a very humble person he was, how he refused to abide in the great palaces and temples but instead, found and lived in an unobtrusive abode several miles distant from the throngs of worshipful eyes of the people; how he loved to walk through the streets and parks with his family of five daughters (some say six) and wife, Nefretiti, passing the time of day, holding hands as they walked as one of the towns-people. But the people did not approve; the Egyptians wanted a god to look up to and to worship. He is fighting this same opposition today and it was no different with him when he was Jesus! Because a Learned One comes with great Intelligence, they want to make of him a god or a saint to be worshipped!

Because He understood the scientific principles of life, He could help them unlock the many psychic blocks generated in former lifetimes and due, also, to the great healing powers He projected unto them, whereby many persons realized various healings, they believed him to be one to be worshipped and venerated—and which was the last thing He wanted—for so long as they gave another this power over them, they would not learn to develop their own potentials and possibilities! He taught in these former lives exactly as He writes today, how man can help himself, heal and change himself, develop his own spiritual nature and likewise, through the eons of time, become one of the Infinite Minds. Just as He taught them in Jerusalem, "Greater things than I have done shall ye do also!" And this is the Message today; He has brought the know-how for man to learn to develop this inner nature, his Higher Self.

For the greater part of the world, man is slow to want to change or to want to improve himself; he is quite satisfied with his lowly lot in life and refuses to do anything about it, but for those so ready, so desirous and willing to put forth the effort, there are no limitations. Of this I have proven in my own personal overcoming, and I still continue to prove!

Referring back again to the time and personality of Akhnaton, most interested persons are familiar with the aton of Akhnaton, now represented as the atom; of his great efforts to change the beliefs of the people from that of their many false gods, and He presented to them the true science of creation. As was mentioned, the golden thread of Truth is most strikingly visible as it is seen winding its way from these distant past lives and teachings through to the present; His teachings of the power coming from the sun and as being the source of all creation is depicted in many ways, times and places throughout the tombs, the many walls and buildings of the ancient remains throughout Egypt and other countries nearby as they have been etched in the rock caves, etc., as the sun with many arms extending out from it in symbology. Yet, these writings were done as early as 1400-1300 B.C., and the truth of the Science (of living) remains the same today, yesterday, and in the millions of years into the future.

This, dear friends, is something we will not be able to say regarding religion! Thank goodness, it is on its way out, for so long as man clings to these old superstitions, he is lost. Only when man begins to recognize his place and position in the scheme of creation as an evolutionary entity who must accept his own personal responsibilities in life rather than to blame some (imaginary) god for all good or evil that enters into his life; only when he begins to make the effort toward the progressive, regenerative evolution does he begin to get anywhere other than the constant and repetitious round and round squirrel-in-a-cage existence. It is sincerely hoped that these lines may help inspire greater effort on the reader's behalf toward a more progressive evolving.

History states of Anaxagoras, that his observations of celestial bodies led him to form new theories of universal order which disagreed with popular beliefs. He held to his belief (which was, of course, an inner knowing with his Higher Self) that all things have existed in a way from the beginning, originally infinitesimally small and inextricably combined throughout the universe; that each thing is so connected with every other, the keenest analysis can never sever them. Anaxagoras' theory of minute constituentes paved the way for atomic theory. The sincere researcher will agree that Anaxagoras was the world's first true scientist, philosopher and astronomer. One of his devoted students was Aristotle.

Anaxagoras taught then, as before, of the constant oscillating universe, expanding and contracting, which is the most vital concept the astronomers of today need presently to know. As with many truly important new concepts, it became waylaid with the passing of time but if the astronomer today could conceive this oscillation process that is constantly ever present, it would solve his many problems in space! Again, however, as the Moderator often says, "They'll just have to learn things the long, hard way." Most of their personal pedestals are too highly erected to dare to accept or to conceive knowledge or information given by anyone other than one who had read the same books they have read, gone through the same regimentation (schools) they have, not realizing there are other and better ways to attain greater wisdom! And which brings to mind an expression Ernest has related—a truth I like, "I narrowly missed regimentation; it was a close shave, I came near having to go through the same sieve they put them all!"—referring to their schools and colleges. But He has kept the channel free and clear; purposely, He avoided reading books so that whatever came through the channel of his mind would not be contaminated with anything less than the highest truth.

Of course, in any previous visitation to earth, as in Atlantis or Lemuria, such a Being would relate the truth acceptable at that particular time and era. In those truly ancient epochs, however, people were far more versed regarding life than is true today. In other words, there is sufficient proof that man is reverting as a whole! Indeed, their scientific mechanical instrumentations have exceeded by far their spiritual knowledge of life or of the true man! This is the great tragedy. He has not arrived at any measure of balance; his efforts still continue to be exerted toward the material, and which has become far overbalanced with his spiritual developments and attainments. This, in itself, would (as it has) cause such a civilization to revert and to regress in its evolution.

Let us trust that as a result of His coming to earth in this era and with the projections of the great influx of the Radiant Power, the Creative Energies of the Infinite, as He steps down these frequencies into the earth plane tolerance, and which shall remain ever as a resource from which eartheans can draw, that mankind will begin to seek regarding his true nature and start to spiritually better himself, which will help swing back the balance, at least to a more equal measure of spiritual and material values. This is His main and vital purpose in this, His return trip to earth—to channel these great Rays, the force fields and powers so necessary for man to continue on earth in a less decadent manner—that man may start upon a more forward motion of evolving, lest he be absorbed back into the abstract.

Our Formative Years

Passing in review our entire past fifteen years of the vast and unbelievable accomplishments, it does seem quite an impossible feat, indeed, an incredible work; yet, as all things were taking place, they did seem so very normal and natural at the time, it could not have been otherwise! Throughout the former years, in our efforts to reach out to those reaching, the Moderator would dictate the advertising material as it would come from the Inner, so that it, too, would carry the Infinite Power to the reader—Power which only He was capable of stepping down to be used in this dimension. I would then mimeograph this literature.

Our mimeograph machine was not the new, modern type (now being used by another Unariun who helps in this work) but was one which had to be hand-inked and hand-cranked every few sheets. The sheets were then folded by hand to fit into the envelopes— the hard way. Many things I did to economize so that whatever funds would be realized from the books could serve to print others. At the very same time, during these many months on end, in between house moves, our Moderator would give the dictations, I would copy them down from either his words or transcribe them if He used the tape recorder, reply to student letters, mail out the books, send literature to new prospective ones, keep up the house; and another very time-consuming expression, during the first few years, the Moderator was giving personal past-life readings. This entailed much time and energies and all had to be typed which, too, was all a part of the wondrous accomplishments as I learned to work from inner guidance.

The readings He gave were, in themselves, master-pieces; and in so doing, He would enter not only into one lifetime but, usually, several lives would be traced in detail, especially in regard to whatever was the par-ticular condition in question. Complete scenes were described, dates and places related; in fact, some of the readings were, in themselves, complete lessons and most comprehensive lectures. Often they would entail an entire hour or even two, as He voiced them on the tape recorder. This collection I plan to put into book form in some future time, as mankind should have these revelations. Each one carries an important message of life, not only for that certain individual but we can each gain much from their vast and inform-ative revealings.

My only regret—if I were one to regret, which I'm not—would be that I was unable to keep in touch with all these persons for whom He read. Time simply did not permit it and I am sure that we would have re-ceived many wonderful testimonials from them had I been able to invite their communications; but this was impossible with all we were endeavoring. Occa-sionally, one would write, years later, saying how his life had followed through just as the Moderator had outlined his past.

We became aware, too, how much more valuable it is to the student to work out these things for himself; now, the Brothers and we work instead, with the in-dividual from the inner. When one readies himself to begin to view his past karmic circumstances, to begin to face himself, then the scenes of his past are shown to him from within. This is the manner in which this work has been carried on, rather than in personal physical communications of the past life readings, since the first few months of the mission. Also, in this present manner now being used, the student can more readily accept what he sees far more easily than if another relates to him that he did so and so or that some certain thing happened to him, etc. Of course, the great importance of cycles enters in; one must be oscillating on certain cycles or the conjunction of important cycles whereby the proper discharge can take place and cancellation results.

Now, however, all the books have been published, the last one just received from the bindery. A few students have become dedicated to the point whereby they are relieving me of these clerical duties. Sanosun devotes her every spare moment in helping; likewise Helen Moore, in her typesetting, she has become most helpful and in her contributed time, saving Unarius great expense in the book printing. We now also have loyal men students, Azhure and Richard, who help wrapping books for mailing which is no small item; and it is Richard, too, who now cares for sending out the invitations to new prospective students—quite a chore. Thus these sincere students not only serve a good cause and purpose so helping, sharing with us these various duties, but it is one way to express their good, the positive expressions, to help overcome possible negations previously expressed. Thus, all ends are served.

In this stepping up and relieving me of these various duties, it frees us that we may express more from the Inner and work with the students in that higher way. We know all things are in order and as they should be, and as we look back, objectively observing, it does now factually seem an almost impossible, monumental achievement; yet, it did all happen and

Unarius has arrived! The Nazarene has returned and His Mission reinstated! It is fulfillment we sense, in every sense of the word. And I am sure such an achievement has never before in history been duplicated or equaled—regardless of time, distance, era or epoch! But only through conceiving the great wisdom He brought can man realize the vastness, the incredibility of it all.

And to the religionists of the world, for the most part, their long sought-after 'return of Jesus' will have taken place and they shall be completely oblivious to this, their 'long-awaited Advent'. He will have come and gone and they will continue to 'look to the skies' for Him to come flying down in the flaming chariot in which they so firmly believe, to save but 144,000 of 'their kind'—to cart them off to some imaginary heaven! And will their faces be red when they arrive on the inner and learn the Truth—how they have been duped in their false religious beliefs, their superstitions and paganisms!

Thus it will be—I predict in the years to come, when your children's grandchildren attend college they will be taught Unarius Science of living. It may not be called as such, in time, but it shall become the academic learning in the schools of the future, for without this science and understanding, life can but deteriorate and regress even further backward, much more so than it has in recent years. The wise parent will teach his offspring the concepts and principles the Moderator has prepared for him whereby he, too, can learn how, as Jesus once said, "My kingdom is not of this world but of another" and "I go to prepare a place for you, that where I am, ye may be also"—the Spiritual worlds of the Inner!

Guidance, Guidance—Every Need

It would be unfair not to include in this epistle, mention of the wonderful demonstrations of Inner help experienced in our various needs both to locate, obtain and to dispose of our various properties from time to time. In some instances real phenomena took place. For instance, due to the frequent sudden noises the neighbor boys would create with their hot-rod cars zooming up and down the hill in front of our home, it became impossible for Ernest to enter into or to maintain his so vital higher states of Consciousness necessary to bring about the work, the dissertations. Because it was impossible to take a rental due to the ever-present vibrations of former tenants, we went out one day and located a home in the Palisades we thought would work out because of the closed entrances to the area which were guarded at the gates —sort of a private settlement. It was only a few days after our moving in when a neighbor's dog decided to make the doorstep of Ernest's bedroom his particular spot to sit and carry on his morning sessions of high-pitched barking which continued for long periods of time. Because the owner of the dog was not cooperative, we realized it would be impossible to get any inner work done there due to this annoyance.

This disturbance began just a few days after our arrival and within thirty days after the trucks brought our furniture in, they were taking it out—that quickly had the house been sold! The escrow people said they never saw property turn so fast. And this was not the only time. When one works with the Infinite, we need not do things the long, hard and tedious way. Things just happen, sometimes faster than we can realize. It is a wonderful way to function, never planning or setting things up for one's self, for plans only serve to block; but rather, to let the guidance come from the inner and, in his present state the earthman is unable to function thusly.

Among the many wonderful demonstrations of locating, of buying and selling properties (when the sudden need arose), outstanding of these examples was the very factual phenomenon (as some would term it) of the house in which we now live and which will soon be seven years since its materialization. A student friend and I came from Santa Barbara where we were then living, and looked about for two days in the area surrounding Glendale. Although there were many older houses available, none were for us, and we returned home to Santa Barbara. The following day, Ernest and I drove from there, back to Glendale, planning to rent a motel for a week or two while we searched for our next home. Due to his extreme sensitivity, it is not easy for him to live (or even sleep) in a place where others have lived and our wonderful guidance prompted and quickly directed us to a brand new sparkling unit, furnished with our every need. We bought the paper and settled down expecting to remain there for a week or two at least, when that very evening, but a few hours later, we found in the newspaper, a large ad describing the house completely. I sensed it instantly; even before completing reading the ad, I knew! "This is it! We need look no further," I said; and had it not been near midnight, we would have dashed right over, but not being familiar with the area, waited 'til morn.

We phoned the owner, who was still in bed, at seven

A.M., and after learning the directions, drove rapidly up the hill. Even before we arrived at the hilltop, Ernest said, "Get your pen out," meaning, of course, "Write out the check." There was such a strong, inner knowing that we had not one moment of wondering. When the builder arrived, we met him with, "It's ours; where is the key!" As we both inspected throughout the place, everything we saw, we knew Ernest had factually directed it built. He worked with the builder mentally and it was all according to plan, even to the very identical vinyl floor covering which I had just been inspecting a few weeks before in Santa Barbara; when looking at it there, I had quite a quickening with it, but knew not why. The house offered everything to meet our needs and they were many: privacy, isolation, quiet, seclusion, near shopping, roomy, certain room arrangements. etc., but it was all here and much more —a lovely view, up and above, which we both always preferred. Yes, the house answers perfectly the description of the place He described many years ago and built it from the inner. After He talked about this mental attunement with the builder, Mr. LeRoy, he said, "I never built a house that went so well, so easily and quickly; it seemed everything just fell into place like magic!" Then the Moderator told him of one place he had just a wee bit of trouble, and he was of course right.

After we three began matching notes of our past plans and of the changes in plans at the same time, it was all made clear, how, when we thought we would come to Glendale eighteen months earlier, it was then the builder began leveling the building pad and planned to begin construction. Then, at that time we decided to go to Santa Cruz and he also decided to postpone his efforts to build on the hilltop pad! We were right together in consciousness, even though consciously we knew nothing about it all, although one day Ernest did say—maybe we are getting a house built in Glendale while we are here renting! It was four months before we came, just after selling the large estate in Santa Barbara and taking a rental there for the four months, LeRoy began his construction—just in time to finish when we would arrive.

All things were exactly to our needs and preferences, with no lawn, as we preferred and plants that require little or no care; everything just right to suit our need. Ernest had often said, "One day I'm going to build you a golden Roman bath, one just like you had in Egypt!" And would you believe it—it's all here! Buttercup golden, a room as large as many bedrooms with two long steps to descend into the wonderful health center, is exactly what it is, and I do so enjoy it —so relaxing. This was a fond memory, even to the celotex pattern on the walls which has a very familiar feeling, a favorite of mine, Fleur-de-lis in gold, with Grecian urns.

Ordinarily, such a deal takes thirty, sixty or even ninety days to complete in escrow. Within five minutes, Mr. LeRoy turned over the keys and the truck came rolling up the hill the following day with our furniture! And it seems we shall be here as long as we remain in the flesh. This is a most perfect example of inner workings; it was the very first day the advertisement had been placed in the newspaper and the neighbors told us no others had even come to see it—yet! (No contaminating vibrations to have to remove). The place has been comparatively quiet, other than a few dogs, which do give distraction now and then, having since moved in down at the bottom of the hill; yet we are, as we must be, isolated. Should the need ever arise that would force us to leave, I am afraid we would miss the place because it was built from the inner—an Infinite Creation.

Because we were, through guidance, directed to our new location so quickly, within a matter of hours after our arrival in town and that we could move directly into the new home, there was no need for the lovely rental in which we had slept only overnight. The kind landlady was most accommodating in refunding our rent as she related how, "There's a couple just wanting the unit!" This guidance was indeed as direct and rapid as anything could possibly take place, and that is always the way with Spirit—it's instantaneous!

Created In Symbology—Jesus' Tomb!

Few have been the times in which I have ever seen Ernest excited or really enthusiastic about something physical and then only at important joining of cycles; however, one to be long remembered was a time during which we were in Palm Springs. We had just purchased a home there, the landscaping of which had not been installed. Ernest thought it would be fun to have it done to his own plan. At the time, we were living in a new rental just a few blocks distant. To clarify—as I have mentioned how difficult it would be for us to take a rental due to other former tenants' vibrations, etc., here we were again directed to a lovely, brand-new, separate unit, all furnished just to our need, which we rented for the month, enabling us to locate a home to purchase—and which we found the third day after arriving there.

These perfect manifestations, viewing back now, seem almost as if someone had a ring in my nose leading me about, for I drove in that, to me, strange town, directly to the rental and which was a beautiful Grecian village and gardens; then, within the third following day, Ernest came dashing in with, "I've found the house!" I've often wondered if there was, in that entire area, another brand-new, furnished unit that had never been lived in that could be rented! It is doubtful. This enabled us to take time selecting carpeting, furnishings, etc., for the new home nearby. Yes, Spirit has always been out ahead of us, paving the way!

Ernest had ordered three good-sized trees planted

and the gardener installed one very large olive tree in the back. It was fine. The next morning, he awoke very early and sensed something wrong. He dashed over to the house before breakfast saying, "Something's wrong there!"

The men had worked long after we had left the night before; they had brought another large tree to plant in front and were nearly finished. When Ernest arrived there, he dashed back to me at the rental all excited, out of breath and terribly upset. I had just never seen him so seriously concerned. One would have thought some real crisis existed as he said, "Come, look, the tree they are just lowering in the hole is not right, it just doesn't look right; they must get it out!"

Well, for the moment I couldn't understand but I went back with him saying, "If you don't like the tree, we'll simply get him to remove it and get another, that's all." Oh, now it is all very funny but it was a real crisis. The tree was removed, then before Pete had a chance to install another—and such installation and removal required a big derrick—Ernest decided on a change. He said, "We'll use huge boulders—no tree." Okay, He went looking for boulders which he ordered, but when it came to placing them, He had to have them placed just a certain way, one leaning against the other, so exacting. As He drove past a place that manufactured cement garden statuary, his eye caught sight of a white cement life-sized soldier dressed in the ancient garb, which he ordered sent and had placed in front of the huge boulders. Then two smaller trees were added behind the boulders, a few plants and rugged flowers, etc., all in front of the block wall which separated the home, yard and pool from the street; thus, this ornamental display which he was creating was not inside of the wall but right on the street, not visible from the house—an important factor too, for thus it was so located, a public display (as was the tomb)!

Not until it was completed did He (or I) realize what he had symbolically re-created. It was the tomb of Jesus! The huge rocks, as He leaned and balanced them just so, resembled a tomb; then the soldier beside it, even the two Cypress trees behind the boulders! What a feeling we experienced when it was realized He had re-created in symbology that time (three days) spent in the tomb. This was something, but it meant even more to me after the 'Jose' book was manifest! No wonder it meant so much when they tried to use a big tree instead of his boulders (tomb)! This, of course, was all part of working out and inner guidance—possibly the one main reason for our trip and stay in Palm Springs! And just about as quickly as it was all completed, He wanted to leave there to return to our Glendale home, and which (pulling another rabbit out of the hat) had not been sold, even though we did have it listed during the time we were in Palm Springs. Spirit and/or our Higher Selves evidently would not permit the sale, knowing we would wish to return to Glendale and this home, later, which we did. All other times, our home sold within a matter of days or weeks, but here this time we were away about nine months—having it listed with brokers (as we were out of town), but because our inner or higher selves knew we would be back—no sale!

Well, thinking back, that house in Palm Springs had been built and was up for sale for nearly two years before we purchased it, which would indicate they do not sell very readily in that area; besides, there were many other better-built houses still to be had and less costly too. But just when we wanted to leave Palm Springs, here was our buyer, living only three blocks distant—one who even wanted our furnishings, the décor—everything exactly as we wished to leave it! Again we felt the great guiding hand of Spirit directing those to us who would enjoy the place. Our only regret—yet, we know it is not wise to regret —would be that some Unariun could have shared the energies with which all our things were imbued. The buyers were Jewish people, as were also so many in Jerusalem. They loved the home and all within and without, especially admiring Ernest's artistic rock formations with the guarding soldier. But little did they realize what it signified and we couldn't tell them, they would not have understood.

Speaking of guidance in selling property when the need existed, this has been real phenomena more than a few times. In fact, each time we found the need to make a change, it became a real demonstration. Yes, even my prompting to attend Real Estate school many years before, in order to learn of selling property was definite guidance. At the time, I didn't realize how often we would be buying and selling our homes, and which we always sold ourselves without aid of brokers, thus saving their costly commissions.

It should be pointed up, as well, how the Moderator himself went to purchase and sought out the very huge boulders necessary in the symbolic building of Jesus' tomb. It was a vital point and issue that they be formed and sized just so! Then, very quickly after the entire duplication of the tomb scene was completed, He found reasons why He wished to leave Palm Springs; however, it was a 'slow take' with us both before we actually recognized what He had actually built in effigy. This area too, looked very much like the

Jerusalem hills.

Perhaps even more important to relate, how very low He was physically—so much so, that He had to lie down in the back seat of the car to be driven to the Palm Springs area—something He normally would never submit to—riding in other than the driver's seat. The truth of the matter is Ernest was actually more dead than alive when we made the three-hour drive to Palm Springs. He had progressed toward that point, the conclusion or termination of Jesus' physical life to the extent that he had actually lost interest or the desire to continue to live in the physical body. Thus it was that I actually coerced or induced him, against even his conscious will and desire to make the trip (although we had planned on just a short visit). As He could scarcely stand, I (and two men students) bolstered him up and literally carried him to the car to lounge in the back seat during the trip.

It was but a few hours after our arrival in (the symbolic Jerusalem) Palm Springs that He expressed a desire to bathe in the natural springs water. After a few of these Jacuzzi sessions, He seemed to rather quickly improve, as the new cycle was then entered. However, it was not until after his re-creating the tomb that He actually started upon his upward climb to better physical health. And now two and one-half years later finds him in the best of health He has ever experienced, stronger, etc., in all ways. This, of course, is the complete overcoming of his actual final physical death in Jerusalem six months after the crucifixion.

An additional note of interest regarding the locating and securing of the Palm Springs house: at all other times we looked together and decided at the same time. Here it was different; it seemed He, alone, must find this particular one. There was nearby, another home exactly like it, all furnished, landscaped, etc., (at no greater cost), just ideal; but no, it would not have given him the opportunity to re-create the tomb! Then, just about as soon as it was all completed, He wanted to leave the place and area. All in symbology or reliving! Indeed, the most interesting life and story ever told!

In fact, I did not even feel 'desirous' when He returned with his verdict, "I've found it." However, I actually felt a strange sadness, but did not wish to oppose his thoughts and plan for I realized it was important to Him to express himself to climb from out the rather low cycle that was existent, so I went along with it all—but not from inner desire, and now that, too, is all understandable!

An added note of interest pertaining to incidents regarding the tomb come to mind—which was, unknowingly re-created in symbology in our front yard in Palm Springs in 1966—bears relating. Although it has been pointed up in the "Little Red Box" book regarding Louis' efforts to secure (for Unarius) an unusually large life insurance policy on Dr. Norman, I felt it well to mention the following here as well.

It was during our eight-month stay there (by the tomb) that Louis just had to come there. He seemed unwilling to accept 'no' for an answer, so strongly was his past (Jerusalem life, as Pilate) oscillating or reflecting into the present. You remember in the "Life of Jesus" book, there was much running back and forth from the Governor's office to the place of Jesus' imprisonment, to the temple, etc., and having a great deal to do about the (supposedly dead) body of Jesus, money in exchange, etc., which he was said to have refused. Needless to repeat the details here which are all given quite accurately in the 'Jose' book, but the point being made here is that it was actually while he (Jesus) was at the tomb (symbolically) that (Pilate) Louis became so frustrated in his effort to obtain this enormous policy. I believe it was to have been for $150,000 to benefit Unarius after the Moderator leaves the flesh. Louis even made the appointments for Ernest's examinations with the doctors here, from his home in Massachusetts.

However, all efforts pertaining to it were blocked because Ernest did not believe in such action; it was not set up from the Inner. Louis struggled and worked in all manner and ways for months on end to put it through, unsuccessfully. This all coincides, of course, with his endeavors in the past pertaining to the body of Jesus. Louis' failure to carry through with his 'great plan', and which too, was a repeat, caused him quite a deflation and frustration; he had much difficulty in getting over that; tied up as he was with that past, it all snowballed. He has now finished with it all and I am sure it is a relief to him as he worked it out within himself. Strange that he flew from Massachusetts, spending two days in the area for that particular purpose? Not when we conceive the great strength of these past ties!

And speaking of Louis, his efforts, expressions and experiences, mention should not be omitted of his vision there in Palm Springs. As Louis sat listening to the Moderator discuss the teachings, suddenly he 'saw' the Moderator in a transfiguration. About the Moderator, Louis viewed a large, glowing aura and he sensed His psychic or higher luminous Self. Of course, as Louis progresses, this sensing will be stepped up as he becomes more relative. It was immediately after his psychic viewing that he lost much of the zeal and zest to go ahead with his insurance efforts. The desire was not completely discharged, but noticeably so, as this Higher Power was contacted. We are glad Louis could have this experience. We know it meant a great deal to him.

I Bathed in the Energy Fountains on the Inner!

One of the most beloved of all the revelations experienced by myself was the actual bathing in the Energy Fountains. As I awakened one morning, I was aware of being under a huge, flowing fountain! I was examining the fine, golden, threadlike streamers of energy which seemingly flowed slowly down over and all about me. I was not conscious of the physical but completely aware of the manner in which the electrical ribbons flowed about me. It was such a peaceful consciousness and seemed a most wonderful state of being. There was a huge Light at my right, by my shoulder, which I knew psychically was the Emissary. He had just come to my door to let me know it was time to arise when I was still conscious of this unforgettable memory that had just then taken place.

As I told Him about it, he said, "You bounced back so quickly into the body, you were practically here and in the Inner (energy bath) at the same time,"— and He knew about this Light! When one sees from the Inner in this manner, he is actually aware of the experience—it becomes a part of one and is never forgotten. I'm sure, whenever there would be a need, and when I would become depleted, to make that mental attunement would serve to actually project me and, although the conscious realization may not exist, the influx and absorption of the Radiant Energies would, nonetheless, take place. The Energy Fountain bath was a beautiful and wonderful experience and I felt so charged and refreshed and didn't wish to return to physical consciousness.

Reincarnation Concept
Becoming Widespread

Now, due to another book just received in the mail titled, "Here and Hereafter", by one Ruth Montgomery, (published by Coward McCann, New York) which is similar in content to various others being published in these 'latter days', and because some students have written to us regarding such writings, they feel here are similar teachings to that which Unarius teaches. It may be helpful to point up to the sincere seeker that only a slight similarity exists in such comparisons. We are always glad to see more and more of this type of publication come to light (past life realizations), for they are all healthy signs of the times. These people are seeking; they are all more or less beginning to agree with the fact that man lives again and again, that he reincarnates into many different embodiments, that he is, in the present, the result of his past acts, deeds and thoughts, but the vital, and ever-present, and inescapable scientific principles of how and why, he does not know. These important basic concepts are missing! It is of little benefit to read these beliefs or speculations if we cannot learn why and how! We can resolve nothing within our consciousness unless it can be followed through in principle and sequence—cause and effect!

Life or evolution is very exacting and precise in principle and it is this science of the causal realms that they are all missing. In fact, Miss Montgomery starts out her book (which could become a best-seller in its field) by stating that no one could prove reincarnation, even though this is the very motive of her book; yet, too how wrong she is! You, the reader, I, or any individual sufficiently learned in the science of Unarius can prove these principles; and we here have done so very, very often. In fact, life itself is the proof. The great difference between these many so-called dispensers of Truth and the infinite and vast Science of Unarius is, they have not been taught as Unarius teaches, about the all-important psychic anatomy of every individual—and without which there could be no individual, animal or any other living entity!

Such speculations as she relates (as do many other similar writers) will cease to be mere speculations and will be imbued with true understanding when one learns the Truth—that man is, in fact, an electronic computer, that every act, thought, or deed is electronically recorded within this energy body or psychic anatomy in a very exacting wave form pattern. It is these energy patterns which are constantly reflecting outwardly through conscious mind that cause man to act and react as he does. Man is incepting and oscillating outwardly the sum and total of any one, or from many experiences and expressions of his countless past lives! Thus, as a proof beyond any shadow of doubt, when man, for instance, has some physical disorder and views what it was that set it in motion, what particular experience in that past is responsible—in this objectification, he cancels out the negative oscillation and healing can instantly result! This, dear reader, is your proof; this is the Science which all other schools of thought do not have and which is so very important. It is the very basis of life itself. However, needless to enter into any discussion with these various scientific concepts our Moderator has taught, for they are all given in detail throughout the Unarius texts, the lessons and books.

But do not be misled, as have many who have not as yet learned the Unarius Science, that here is another school or individual teaching the science of Unarius, for it will not be so. The Unariun Moderator is the only personality on earth so aware of these advanced concepts and you, as a Unariun student, are most fortunate to be in on the ground floor, so to say, in having this teaching in this, your present embodiment. Be not deluded by others with false claims. Read these observances objectively and if you are learning your Unarius lessons well, you will conceive the great differences and pick out the flaws and short-comings, and realize that the all-important creative, regenerative, interdimensional science is missing in all other schools. We would suggest the reading of the "Here and Hereafter" book. You will find it of interest and, in part, it does serve to prove the Unarius teachings, however, because this author, or any other earth-man, for that matter, is not aware of the Unariun Concept regarding the energy body, etc., the true creative regenerative principles, she has interjected some such phrases and beliefs such as 'paying penance', etc., but you, as a Unariun, will recognize these erroneous beliefs. The only reason any person encounters serious negations of any duration or size is due to the negative wave forms within his psychic anatomy which are constantly being out-pictured. When we learn the true creative science, then all the superstitions and mysticisms, the false beliefs of the past disappear. This is the main reason why the scientists cannot go along with their reincarnation beliefs; they cannot furnish the whole picture, thus, the scientists must label it pseudo! R. Montgomery, as so many others, still believes in the old saying, "An eye for an eye and a tooth for a tooth" . . . so to speak, which is not the true science of life nor is it factual.

I thought best to include this word of warning as I have suggested it as an interesting book to read—yet, do so with caution! Watch for misconceptions that they may not become a part of you!

Even more important is the wondrous radiating power the Unarius texts carry to the reader, the inner contact with the Creative Infinite Intelligence, and which is not found in any other earthly writings. The Power, the Light and Energies transduced into this physical dimension through the Infinite Consciousness of the Unariun Moderator are thoroughly unique with Unarius teachings—the transcending element which lifts the reader from his normal consciousness into higher states of being, the element which makes it possible for the mind of the reader to conceive the Word, and step by step, to climb to ever higher states of awareness—and to which there is no end!

Again, returning thoughts to the "After Life" book, to point up once more the incredible abilities of the developed Mind of our Emissary, although I have read only a few pages, I was relating to Ernest how, as the authoress relates, one man, a nonbeliever in reincarnation, during a visit to Egypt with others, was climbing up the pyramid when suddenly a strong fear and feeling of doom overtook him—so much so, he retreated to the bottom. While he sat there, he viewed psychically the slaves building the great stone structure, he, himself among the slaves! He saw the huge stones rolling over upon him as he labored to fit them in proper junctions, and watched himself as he was crushed to death. Thus, he joined the 'believers' henceforth. But my point here: as this psychism was merely mentioned to the Moderator, He instantly tuned into the happening and viewed not only what the man had seen, but added much more as He related to me exactly how huge ropes were laced through a large eye or ring to serve as a pulley by which the stones were moved about. He told how this man was seen stepping over large, round logs about the ground, used to aid in the moving of the stones; He saw how his feet were hurt several times in all this heavy construction. The Moderator saw also why or how it was he became a slave among the many; that, as a citizen, he had stolen a mirror and was thusly punished! Now, he should have a strong rapport, a feeling with (or against) mirrors.

Here is the kind of verification by which one can factually prove this principle of reincarnation to himself. It would be very natural for him to have quite a rapport with mirrors. This is the type of consciousness or attunement possible with such a developed Mind as the Moderator. Time or distance is of absolutely no concern to him in such viewing or relating the past, present or future! It might be mentioned, however, He does not recommend folks delving into their future; his reasons are that then the conscious mind will set up ways to try to help bring about the incident (if it happened to be a desirable one) and cause blocks to what would otherwise have worked out easily and naturally. He is reticent to relate the future for this reason. Then, too, it is in the experience that the lessons in life are contained.

Mind you, dear reader, this was the only contact necessary for the Moderator to reach out in his attunement with that ancient past—my mere mention to him of the person! I am sure to many, this ability is inconceivable, yet it is factual. No limitations, as He often says—and proves!

*   *   *   *   *

233

As for the future, one of many of the Moderator's predictions along that line (the future), has, in the present (1969), materialized, for if you remember, in his Mars booklet, mention is made of how they use on that planet, in the underground cities, radio or electronic waves with which they cook and that He predicted man, on earth, would be enjoying this manner of preparing foods before long. Well, it has happened; the Radar-range, as they call it, is not too popular as yet but I have purchased one and what a joy to be able to prepare foodstuffs without the (otherwise) smell, smoke and great length of time normally necessary to cook a roast or the like. Cooking time is cut down to less than one third and often far more, in this range that cooks (changes the molecular structures) by radar waves.

Of course, this new method of cooking serves, too, to prove his science! For, as he has taught repeatedly, heat is simply the energy produced by the resistive elements; this range serves to prove this too, for I cook on plastic, glass or even paper plates in this Radar-range. So again, he can say, "I told them so!" The Mars book, "The Truth About Mars" was published in 1956.

May 24, 1969—Frankly, there is not now, nor shall there ever be a proper point of conclusion for these pointings up or relatings. Again, in today's Los Angeles Times Real Estate Section is a brief article telling of the new, fine rapid manner of building homes and buildings just discovered, which consists of polyurethane foam panels—a company in Gardena, California, named Modular Concepts, Inc., the distributors. The article states that four men erected a two-bedroom home in six hours from this modern chemistry discovery. The polyurethane foam is inserted between two panels, serving as a sandwich. This quick, easy, durable process is far less costly and far more lasting, and serves well as insulation against heat and cold.

The point being made however, is that this new discovery of building process was described in the Moderator's "Mars" book, written fourteen years ago —another proof of how He works from the inner with these various scientists, as all such vital, new so-called discoveries are brought to the earth in similar manners.

Yes, walls of the Martians' homes were erected in just such manner—the two panels of a plastic substance erected, then the foam plastic blown in between which serves as strength, soundproofing, is weather resistant, resists soil and is beautiful, as they can be installed in a great variety of colors and patterns.

Again the Moderator can say, "I told them so!"

A Past Glimpse

October 18, 1968—Again, this very morning, a momentary flash, a glimpse into the past came into focus —a scene of that long-ago day in Jerusalem how, while Jesus was teaching a small group of women, He lay aside his outer garment (robe) upon a tree stump that he could better walk into the gnarled bushes to free a small, young lamb entangled there. When, just as quickly as He had so placed it there, the young maidens seized upon the opportunity to take up his garment and place it about themselves that they might partake of this 'Power' in which He walked and with which He was ever surrounded. Yes, each one in turn did sense the glow, the tingling Rays which radiated from, not only Jesus Himself, but existed with all things which came in contact with Him.

And it was here, then, as likewise in other times, that He rebuked them, upon his returning to them saying, "It is the Father Within that doeth the works," although he would have gladly given any one of them his garment were they in need of it. But he did not wish them to place the greater value upon the material or physical but rather, this was the vital and basic part of his teachings: that all things stem from the Inner and, the physical is but an outward effect.

Thus, it is no different as of today, as the various ones receive the letter, a word, or card sent out from the Radiating Center of Light (Unarius headquarters), they, too, do sense and feel this creative energy from the Infinite. Yes, this same Infinite Power, the Light and Energy is once again brought unto the earth world! It is projected to and impinged within the psychic of each individual so reaching out, and which again serves to prove the Unariun Moderator is the returned Nazarene—the Unariun mission the re-establishment of the mission of Jesus on earth.

Of course, the energies which would be existent on any garment or artifact such as his robe or any article among our belongings are not the same energies or frequencies as those which are needed and directed to the student for his healings. Any existing energies such as remain on a garment, etc., are but secondary oscillations, not necessarily the creative, regenerative frequencies or the potent healing charge usually projected for that healing purpose. Any card, letter or word, for instance, sent from the Center here to any student would and does always carry certain specific oscillating vortexes, frequencies created on the Inner, especially for that individual, for whatever may be his particular need. All such energy projections are, of course, created and directed from the Inner or Higher Selves and dimensions, Minds creative in nature, of the Unariun Brotherhood.

So be not misled by believing that certain healing qualities exist in some mere object or artifact, for this is not the case; but you, dear student, do have the ways and means to 'hook yourself up' or make your contact with this great Fountainhead of Creative Infinite Intelligence! Your attunement in the Unarius texts is your lifeline, as they were all created of the Infinite and are, themselves, creative in nature. They can and do serve to lift, to transcend you in consciousness, out of the physical dimensions into higher states whereby you can better conceive the Word. Moreover, this attunement is also a means whereby the Infinite Minds can come to you to help; to work with you in your efforts to understand. This is the one great and vital difference between Unarius and all other schools of thought or metaphysics—the ever-present, infinite energies and power to aid the seeker.

And as He likewise taught then, just as now, perhaps in another vernacular but exacting in principle, "I am the Way, the Truth and the Light," but the people did not understand that his wording "I am", was Principle. Principle, concept, understanding is, and was then the way to attainment, to realization, and the way whereby man can find the Kingdom of Heaven, which is within! This, dear friend, is what the writer of this word has done; I have found that Kingdom Within! These words are meant to convey and to impress with you how great is the importance of this contact with the 'Word' which He and the Brothers have brought and this is His way and means to generate unto the sincere seeker, this Infinite Creative Power—to help prepare you for those Kingdoms Within!

Although it will be thoroughly conveyed in the book of student testimonials which will be a future publication how it is a vital part of the students' development that they make themselves receptive to the frequent projections of this aforementioned Power (unique only to Unariuns), how it is they sense a transcendency, in many cases so potent that it will cause the reader to slip out, as in sleep. This trance-like state in which he 'ascends' at such times, however, is quite different than the nightly sleep state. He will awaken refreshed as though he had just experienced a full night's sleep, and often the time away from the body will have been of just a few moments duration! So much can be done for one on the Inner during such transcended states; he can accomplish for himself what he would ordinarily attain in conscious wake-state perhaps ten or a hundred, or even a thousand times the benefits or progress, spiritually speaking. Thus, we cannot over-emphasize the great and vital importance of this Ray-Beam, as we term it, and which is exactly what it is—the Energy Rays mentioned as being experienced by myself so many countless times. Thus, your time of study is the way and means whereby you, the student, place yourself in a receptive frequency to receive this Energy Projection. You, yourself, then, are the determining factor as to how much or how little Inner help is extended. In other words, your study is, in effect, lifting the receiver off the hook—into the Infinite!

Most persons on earth could not endure in the strong Force Field in which we live and with which our entire home (and grounds) is surrounded; and it must be so. On occasions in the past, certain sensitive students have visited our home—and I am thinking of two especially rather sensitive ladies in Santa Barbara, Bess and Velma, who were living in the Annex— they both saw, just before our descent down the hilly drive, what they thought was a brilliant sun coming over the mountain nearby (yet, it was a very dark, dreary day), the rays of which, they related, transcended them both to the point of wanting to go to sleep, although it was only two hours after they awoke in the morning!

Speaking of Bess brings to mind another time, relating her vision, a note she wrote us when we lived on a Santa Barbara hilltop, she at the bottom of the hill, our house visible to her. Her note read, "What on earth was that great flame I saw by your porch as I looked your way? It was taller than you, Dr. Norman, gold-orange in color. It was dancing and remained there for a few seconds so bright, but when I called

Velma to see, it was gone. My, but that was something! I got rubber legs when I saw it. Was that you, Dr. Norman? I felt it was your Super Self!"

Interesting, too, is how the insects, animals and plants are quickened by this constant energy influx. Certain philodendrons and shrubs planted about the house have grown quite naturally, yet those whereon the Moderator looks as he relaxes in his easy chair, have grown more than four times the size of all others, yet have received no different care—same water, sunshine, etc. Insects somehow find their way inside, even though we find no way they enter, spiders galore, but the most interesting was the centipede which quickly maneuvered its way across the white carpet, to climb up Ernest's leg! This happened not once but twice; it too sensed the energies or light and wanted to get into it! Yes, in many ways is this wondrous transforming Power sensed and expressed.

But time is later than you think. The dedicated and sincere Unariun has become aware; he knows our great Leader, Teacher, Moderator and Emissary did live long ago as Jesus and, as He then promised, has returned now in this era as our Moderator; yet, for the most part of the world, He will have come and gone and they will not know; no more so than did all who lived in the Holy Land believe. So be ye not as the maidens with their 'lamps empty', but enter into the study with open mind and the never-ending desire for Truth. As has been said, there will never be a greater opportunity! His years among us are numbered—and the numbers are running low!

It might be well to mention, as someone has said in regard to my endeavors, jotting these notations, recalls and experiences down, "How can you remember all these psychic experiences even of this present

lifetime? It is most difficult for me to remember incidents which took place last month, or even last week!"
To this question let it be said that tuning back, as it
were, to these various and countless experiences of
my past-present lifetime, of the psychic happenings,
etc., are all far more vivid and real than is any physical or materialistic experience. The reason is, the former have to do with the total involvement of the entire psychic anatomy! All, or any one, such experience,
changes the sum and total of the individual's complete
oscillating frequency! The spiritual or psychic experiences do not diminish in consciousness with time as
do the earth or physical happenings. In fact, it is much
easier and one can be far more exacting in relating
such happenings than one would be in making an
effort to recall some physical happening which took
place in this third dimension, for all psychic experiences take place on the inner or fourth or fifth—whatever one wishes to term the higher planes of existence. They are not actually numbered anyway, only in
man's mind, for it is all frequency relationship that
counts or makes the difference.

Moreover, these transcendencies, visions, Ray Beam
projections, visitations of the Higher Ones, or whatever may be the particular personal experience, are,
each one, a step-up in his progression! Many are what
man would term an initiation and there are countless
plateaus toward which man may aspire and attain;
but each such happening will leave its frequency or
perveance (energy) in the consciousness of the individual and, he can, after certain attainments have been
realized, tune back unto that psychism, for it was another important point in his more progressive evolution. This tuning back, however, is a different function
unlike the former conscious-subconscious oscillation

which relates only from the physical past. Man's so-called mind is not as he thinks it is—a thinking mechanism. It is exactly as our Moderator has taught: a switchboard or a television computer, incepting and out-picturing messages; an electronic computer!

However, your lesson courses, and especially the second or advanced six lessons, describe this mental function most exactingly and understandably and it is doubtful that there is any one concept more vital to any earthman than to learn this vitally important principle—mind function!

Three Thousand-Year-Old Fears Remain

The little lady, Velma, was the third who had realizations of being buried alive with me when this one died back there in Egypt in antiquity. My psychic memory tells me there were twenty-six in all. The others have not as yet made appearance in the present life, but possibly shall in some future time. This would, of course, be most helpful to them—each to again make this contact in this positive way whereby the higher Energies from our Inner selves could aid them in unlocking and overcoming the great psychic impingement with them, and which any such occurrence would naturally create. What a terrible practice to carry on!

One of the other girls—which they were at the time of the burial with their queen which was so ridiculously believed to have been an honor for them, is a most dedicated student, Lillian, who was, in that time a lovely Ethiopian Princess, and now in the body of a colored girl. Lillian was, for months on end, unable to go into the basement where she worked as housekeeper. She would become terrified going into the dark place and was simply unable to do so, so completely did it attune her to going into that tomb from which she never emerged. She would freeze in her tracks; but after relating it to us here through her letters, she was told why it was and her next mail told of her releasement; now there was no reaction or repercussion whatsoever. The basement was, to her, no different to go into than any other room.

As an added note of interest, when Lillian came to California on her vacation from Illinois, she made contact with us for certain reasons and, just as she was leaving, I gave her an artifact I had had for many years. It was a tiara which is worn in the hair with evening dress, this one looking quite like a crown with a high design of rhinestones in front. I did not know at the time of her having lived the life of the Ethiopian Princess but, just as she was leaving, I suddenly had the urge to go get her my 'crown' which I did without a moment's hesitation, placing it on top of her head! Well, she took me by such surprise when she grabbed and hugged me so tightly, for the moment I was startled. Lillian is a very strong girl and it was more like a bear hug! She did have a strong reaction to 'receiving the crown' which, of course, to her was a flashback or reliving. I noticed as she walked away, tears were spilling and I asked the lady who drove her away of Lillian's further reactions on the way and she said, "She was very silent; deep in thought, quiescent, contemplating."

Her progress since has proven that much of the past was re-contacted and discharged. Lillian has been, for quite a few years now, a most devout and dedicated student, her past fast falling from her; and, for her, we are glad.

Lillian's recent letter states how the power, the heat comes in so strong where she works, the employer believes the furnace is out of order and calls the man to fix it, saying it is too hot in some rooms! Of course, this is protection for Lillian and healing for the lady employer. These signs of progress we love to hear, for it means she is now serving in a way as a polarity in the healing with us. What could be more wonderful! Principle in action!

Backtracking here a little: when Lillian first made our contact through the mail, she wrote how she felt so unrelative to both the Negroes and the white people. She said, "I just don't feel compatible with either race, why does this strange frustration exist?" It was viewed by the Moderator how, during a lifetime several cycles past as a white girl, she was attacked and

244

raped by a large colored man, resulting in an illegitimate child, which set in motion this resentment, tie, and oscillation. Thus, through the principle of harmonic attunement, she was, in one or two previous cycles, as well as the present, drawn to a Negro family parents, whereby she could work out this association, tie, resentment, the foreign feeling with the Negroes— and of which she really is not one, for Lillian is simply 'trapped', as it were, in that female colored body to work it all out.

Just as soon as she read the words of the Moderator's psychic viewing, all things changed with her, she objectified the entire situation in consciousness, and her outlook, well-being, etc., did all immediately change, as she wrote and was so happy about it all, to learn she was really one of us. Quite an adjustment did she make; so much so that very likely her next trip to earth will be in the body of the white (race) person. She will be—and always via this frequency relationship—attracted or drawn to seek out the parents of a white family, and in which she so rightfully belongs.

An added note of interest regarding Lillian's youth: she states, "My mother used to yell at me so often saying, 'You're always trying to act like them white people, you don't act like we do'." Lillian related, "I just didn't feel I was a part of the family!" No doubt, this was her first contact with most of them, other than the one Negro man responsible for setting the terrible tie and psychic block or shock in motion, but sufficient negation existed to create the strong tie with the Negro race.

Lillian has adjusted well and is now a fine and sincere dedicatee, most devoted to her study and progress, and is aiding Unarius in her own selfless way. It is doubtful there exists a more grateful or appreciative soul than dear Lillian for our help in her great severance and for her complete change on all levels of expressing and living.

I felt the reader could conceive many principles in action by this relating, thus the details were not spared that you may conceive these all-important, ever-existent, never-failing concepts and regenerative principles which motivate and influence our daily living. Had Lillian not come into this realization (Unarius), very likely her resentment, etc., could have built up, the ties made stronger with the black race, and she would have regressed in her evolution, heaven only knows how far back! But she had so set it up on the inner before incarnating in the present whereby she would work it out, and that she has, now the severance and discharge is complete. She is indeed progressing upon the regenerative cycle into a better future, more positively biased, and with the help of the Unarius Brotherhood, we have great confidence in Lillian becoming a polarizing agent with the Light as she maintains the consciousness and effort to conceive the great Wisdom of Unarius.

Richard, too, then a female, was, I feel, another of those likewise entombed with this one. It is doubtful if I retained any guilts there from for I had already died at the time. Others 'chose' and brought the girls into the tomb and I have heard that often the girls themselves would volunteer to be taken believing it to be a great honor to die with the queen and that they, too, would travel in spirit with her. Well, maybe we do not practice that particular belief any longer, but there are many others far more devastating and far-reaching presently practiced—beliefs that cause far more damage than any physical death; yes, I refer to the death of the spirit one enters into when he becomes a devout religionist!

Heaven Descended!

Although the reader may feel that too much already has been said of the Luminosities, the Personalities of Worlds of Light, yet the comparatively few mentions have been only one small fraction of all that has really taken place. And again, last night was to me another wonderful and memorable occasion. As accustomed as I have become to these Luminaries as They make contact in this way into this earth world and into our consciousness, and due to the newer and higher state to which this person has been climbing— a more compatible state of consciousness with them— the trance state has been but slight, a scarcely noticeable difference occurs anymore when their Presence is sensed.

It was a different story last night! A certain television program portraying the 'Sea World' was shown and a large portion of the film was devoted to the 'Dancing Waters' there. I have seen other such displays, one they exhibit at the Music Center in Los Angeles, and other times at the large Ice Shows, such watery displays have been quite pretty to watch, but the collection of fountains shown in this film was truly unique. These glorious fountains of dancing waters were so numerous, the configurations which the water took were seemingly infinite in variety but the color was the outstanding element. Colors from within the fountain patterns, then others with great color beams projected onto them from all angles, and the entire display served to tune me into the wonderful Energy Fountains on the Inner! Oh, I was glad it lasted more than a few seconds for they were most generous with the time spent photographing them and it was the most glorious sight I have ever seen on earth—or in the physical—glorious especially because some certain ones did look just like the golden and other colorful energy sprays and fountains on the Higher Worlds! Yes, it did 'send me'. Oh, I just didn't want it to conclude! Ernest enjoyed it too, and although we never travel physically anywhere (due mainly to the tobacco smoke, etc., everywhere) we vowed we would try to get down to San Diego to see the beautiful display.

What added so greatly to the trance state was that one by one all evening long, our Visitors from the Higher Worlds came in! Every few moments seemingly, as I would begin to slip back into physical (normal) consciousness, there would be another Light, sometimes right at my feet or in front of the divan. I lost track counting them and when I attempted to walk about, found I had no legs! The 'rubber leg' condition, previously spoken of, was again present but good! Oh, the peace that descends over one at such times is simply tremendous. I felt so outgoing and in love with all things—this, of course, their love coming into myself. At one moment, Ernest would sense one and say, "There is one right there, a golden, bright Light!" Then one would come into my consciousness and it would appear on the drapery or ceiling and I would say, "Oh, here is a bluish-white Light." Then, when an especially huge Luminosity would appear, I would really take the dive! I just didn't move from the divan all evening long, so near 'out' had I become, and loving every moment. It was a five-hour session!

As I went out to sleep in that state last night, sad I was to find this morn, normalcy had returned; but not by choice! After all, we cannot live in that state always, we have our earth life to live and many deeds to be done, but it was a wonderful night of Heaven on earth. The Dancing Waters served well to attune me to the Inner Worlds where we so often travel psychically, thus it was like a homecoming to us.

It should be mentioned, too, these Energy Fountain configurations on the Inner are the ways and means whereby the Beings keep themselves charged and from which they actually live, rather than breathing air and eating food. Thus, when we take what we call a 'step-out'—a few minutes of what may seem like sleep—yet, it is quite different from sleep for we slip out on the Ray Beam which is projected to us, and there, in the wonderful fountains of living energy, we repose and incept into our very psyches, life-giving, sustaining energy. After these few moments of freedom from the body—and the time can vary from a few seconds to thirty minutes or an hour or more but, usually about twenty minutes—we then feel refreshed, as if an entire nights sleep has been experienced; very scientific! Many times when we become depleted from having gone into a shopping area, for instance, or a market and there have been a few persons there, back home I come and 'take off' for the few moments to become recharged; similar to putting the battery on the line when it gets low! And if one needed proof, these things indeed do prove the oneness of this Higher world; of how, as has been told, this dearly beloved and great Soul, the Unariun Moderator, has brought Heaven right down to earth!

So, friend seeker, when you sense in your readings of the Unarius liturgies or even this little book, for the Power is likewise existent, the drowsiness, a lassitude, recognize it for what it is: the wondrous Infinite Power, the Light and energy which has been directed to you to lift you in consciousness, temporarily out of your mundane subconscious state into higher dimensions unto the place where you, too, may bathe in these wondrous Energy Fountains to help cleanse the psychic. Permit yourself to 'go out' with it in what you may think is sleep, for great benefits can then be experienced. Then, in time, it can become a regular cycle, a period for your personal 'pickup and recharging', to help sever some of the debris which is constantly being impinged into our psychic from this carnal earthworld. It matters not if you are not conscious of what takes place, benefit is derived nonetheless, and someday or time when you have conceived well of the science, you too shall begin to become more and more sensitive and bring back the memories of these many Higher Worlds and of their everexisting help so extended. There is nothing by which to compare such visitations on the earth, but these lovely watery fountains did it for me and, perhaps you, too, may experience the familiarity from memories you have retained. Most all persons—those who are actively studying the Unariun texts—have been on these higher planes, either in between lives and/or during the time their body sleeps; otherwise, they would not be able to comprehend the teachings, even slightly!

This is the way one is able to live on the inner after losing his body of flesh and when he no longer has to fight the gravity pull. Thus, if one is not aware of these vital Principles, he can become very lost and distressed! As I have oft' repeated, and not nearly often enough, there is nothing so vital to any person as learning this life-changing Science. As our Moderator says, "The life you save will be your own!"

I Saw Through the Building

September 25, 1968—The following few brief notations each hold a certain proving of Principle. Although this first incident may not seem an outstanding happening, yet it is definite proof of how we are led, guided and prompted by our Higher Self and the Brothers when we live or work from the Inner. Since the beginning of our 'togetherness' in this life, there has existed with me a desire (and which too, no doubt, was an inner knowing) to have an oil painting done of our Moderator, although I knew He would never sit for a portrait, for several reasons; one being, he does not place importance on these physical or material values, and secondly, He would not be able to sit with another person for any length of time due to the great outflow of energies from himself unto the individual. This is one reason why we are unable to have other persons work near or with us, even though the need has existed at times. Only one so polarized and who would oscillate in a compatible frequency would draw less heavily—and such an individual has not been found; this out-flow, of course, is due to development and attainment, Infinite Oneness.

This, too, is one reason why I have made special effort to locate and remain with one beauty operator, for instance, that she could be polarized at least to some degree, that less drain takes place; and I have been quite successful in this effort. However, one day, driving to downtown Glendale, I suddenly spied a rather shacky little house with a 'Beauty Salon' sign out front. I stopped short, went inside, to find there a fine-looking, esthetic-appearing young man who, after inquiring, agreed that he could coif my hair. Ordinarily, I would have had an appointment days before, but

251

here I was in this rather unclean little place and wondered what I was doing there—but I did not wonder for long!

As soon as he began working on my hair, I queried him regarding his hobbies and interests, other than his work there. Of course, he loved to paint! When I asked him which type, the reply was "Portraits!" Oh, for joy, for joy! I said to myself, "Well, here's where we get a painting of Ernest!" He proceeded to say, however, he had not done any work for over twelve years and didn't know whether he would ever return to it; but my spirits were too high to be dampened so easily. Now I knew why I sought out this dingy little place: to seek out this individual and I told him so but he insisted that he could not do sufficiently good work, for he did sense our spiritual nature.

Dear Bo, which was his name, was quite a timid, humble and introverted man; he simply turned red with blush as I said, "I know you can do it!" The upshot of this meeting was, that before that day had ended, Bo was taken from that lowly place and given employment in a far better shop. In fact, the man who employed him was leaning on my car when I came out; he remarked something about my hairdo which Bo had just finished and this, (my contact) started Bo's new employment arrangement, for the man went directly into the shop to talk with him.

Later, Bo notified me where he was then employed and upon my first trip to contact him, I took with me complete art paraphernalia that he might practice on his artwork, knowing he had left all his equipment in Sweden many years before. He then showed me a painting he had done of Greta Garbo and it was an excellent likeness. Again, I told him, "You are the one to paint our Moderator's portrait; you are the one!" I couldn't take no for an answer as it evidently was all set up from the Inner. Bo never did agree to do it but, regardless, he did so.

After two weeks or so, he asked a student with whom he had become acquainted for a small picture of the Moderator as he wished to make an attempt. Of course, he came up with a lovely, very lifelike portrait, a fine, large size and, best of all, he actually caught the very esthetic and ethereal nature of Ernest. We had it framed in an elegant five-inch frame and I'd not take the world for it, for I know how, in future time, it will mean much to many people and can serve many to help make inner attunement with this great Source of Light. Then Bo asked for a photo of myself from which he made a similar portrait, but that is immaterial. My positive inner knowing with the first contact did prove itself and worked out exactly as I just knew it would.

We furnished Bo with a tape recorder, books, lessons, etc., so that he would have material to help him along the upward pathway as well. Always there are the two-way benefits derived in our contacts. After only a short time, an even better position and location was offered Bo and he was on his way. He was lifted right out of that low financial rut in which I found him. No limitations with spirit!

Before the last time we saw Bo, he told of a trip he planned to take. Imagine, just the year before, he was practically penniless, now with this far better shop and clientele, he had saved enough for a months trip abroad! Spirit works in many ways to help. During his brief visit in Palm Springs with us, the Moderator told him that he could expect trouble in Sweden, to use extra caution. He said, "Your trip over will be most enjoyable, but something will take place which will spoil the return trip for you if you're not very careful!" And so it happened: very foolishly, even after all the warning, Bo left in his hotel room all his valuables, camera, tickets home, money, luggage, etc., and his room was burglarized, everything he had was stolen! How he and his pal ever managed to get back to the States was no less than miraculous—penniless in a strange country, knowing no one! But he made it, returning very saddened. This, no doubt, was a reliving with him for it shook him up more than normally. He went into sort of a depression due to it, as it caused him to 'lose faith' in mankind in general; but this is the way it is when we regenerate these negative cycles and experiences. I do believe, however, the part that hurt him most was, as he said, "And Doctor Norman told me to be careful there!"

But even our negations hold for us lessons in life. This is the way we learn and grow—by overcoming. Perhaps the little gift presented to Bo as appreciation for his artwork has helped compensate his 'let-down' feelings; however, we are sure he had inner guidance and help as he painted. The picture seems to grow in loveliness as time passes. It has been several years now since hearing from him—however, mission accomplished; the portrait was the purpose of the contact and, of course, to oscillate to him, the Infinite Radiant Energies that will help him start upon his upward climb into higher states and dimensions.

Yes, always was our guidance present; what e'er would be the need was just so manifest if we'd just cease to put forth the physical effort and instead, 'let it happen'. Quite a difference from the manner in which the 'so-called' metaphysical schools of thought believe and teach! For, after all, the conscious mind is not a creative mechanism. Yes, whether it be a piece or two of furniture, or an entire set, an office need or some artifact, it would always materialize and most often, in the least expected ways, so it was a joy to watch this frequent manifestation. For instance, just the other day, we had a good example as the need was met so seemingly 'naturally'.

A short time ago, we arrived at the point where our stockroom had become full beyond capacity. Soon there would be a need for additional storage space as several of the books were being reprinted and they take up much room as several thousand of each must be ordered at a time. Upon my first realization for this need, I thought, "I'll order the local paper and watch for someone who may advertise a large stucco garage for rent," but which is not a common thing. After the paper had been delivered, I was unable to even look at the ads, the desire no longer existed. Evidently, the Higher Self and the Brothers already had things in motion for it. I told our Unariun sister, Sanosun, who helps to care for this storing, "It has been placed in consciousness, now we'll just let it work out!" And sure enough, within the week or so, a couple from Canada bought the property on which the Annex is located (which has two houses and two double garages on the lot) and they have no need for the garage! They have no car or things to store! They were more than willing that we rent it for our stored books! Coincidence? Hardly! The beautiful part of it all is that this fine stucco garage with cement floor is just a few steps from the first storage area! How handy can they make it? Thus, with this constant inner help and guidance, we have learned never to underestimate the powers of Spirit but to rely more and more on guidance, on our inner self and the Brothers with whom we work so closely.

And still further proof along this line, and pertaining also to the Unarius book stock which has reached an all-time large supply, the following notations: although there was no water evidence noted after the most unusually heavy rainy season to be coming either through or under the wails in the store rooms, I sensed, psychically, as I stepped into the number one storage area, that some of the lower books in the bottom boxes of the piles were showing effects of the weather, mildew, etc., for it had been a very rough, several weeks rain-storm. I mentioned it to the lady-student in charge of the Annex and something to the effect that we would have to get someone to move them out and examine them and then to build shelves for them, getting them up from the cement floor.

No word was spoken to anyone about it; however, on the second day later, the owner of the property came to Sanosun saying, "If you folks will get the lumber, I will build some shelves for the books in both storage areas." This man, by the way, has no interest in our endeavors; and which serves to prove also, that we can work mentally or inwardly with any persons, even other than students for I had barely seen this man a few times to nod a 'good day'. No we were not surprised; glad, appreciative—yes. But that is the way it is when we work as do the Moderator and myself, from the Inner or Higher Self. No effort made with conscious mind whatsoever During the time the man slept, Ernest—or myself very possibly, or one of the other Brothers, simply contacted him in the astral and arranged for him to do the work, then it was a matter of following through in the physical. Despite the fact that much time will be entailed, he offered to do it gratis although he has no particular or personal interest in Unarius other than our renting his unit. Now, but another day later, the work is started and soon will be completed.

Oh, yes! When they moved out the tall columns of stacked books and unpacked the lower boxes, they found, just as I had seen, the lower layers had begun to mildew! No secrets when we see inwardly or with our mental attunement. Yes, man is a living radio; a sending and receiving station. The objective: to learn to 'tune in', as it were, to the higher dimensions.

*   *   *   *   *

The following notation is a factual demonstrating that we can learn to function from inner sense or consciousness with far more perfection and exactness than the mere five senses. I just loved this little demonstration. Sometimes these lesser importances give us great joy!

When we moved into our first home in Eagle Rock (Los Angeles), there was a huge front circular window, nearly the size of the entire front wall, that needed a certain heavy drapery, the pull-to type. My cycle in this house must have been reminiscent of my cycle in France, for I found myself going about collecting French lamps, hangings, etc. There existed in my mind (and which too, no doubt, was the inner knowing) a certain scenic French Provincial drapery pattern, a specific soft green in color, in a heavy, textured material that I felt would be right; I felt it was the only thing to properly serve. After looking in three drapery shops I found no sign of anything similar or that would do. Then the sight of another store seemed to cause a strong stimulation within and, after relating to the sales girl, she said, "No, we have nothing like that at all!"

There was, at the back, far side of the wall, a huge counter-like affair and I walked around it to find there was a huge hole cut in the back and odd bolts of yardage had been stored there. As it was dark inside, I couldn't see what might be within, but I reached down in and got hold of a large bolt of something. I was so quickened, I told the lady, "I've found it, here it is. But I had not even had a glimpse of it! She came and, after some difficulty extracting the long bolt, it was exactly my need! She agreed it was just what I had described to her but she said, "This will not be nearly enough for the size you need." "Oh, yes it will; it is just right! You'll see," I said. She insisted that I would be about one-third short of material, however, after measuring, found she could perhaps make it. Then, after they made the draperies and when I called for them, she brought along the piece that was left over—one inch of material!

She would hardly believe it even after seeing! She kept shaking her head, saying, "Never saw the like!" This Higher guidance or inner knowing is not uncommon but is a continuous way of life with us. Only when we separate ourselves from the Inner or Higher do we go wrong, and we do slip sometimes; quite difficult to live completely from the Inner in this carnal world but that is the way we live when we arrive on the Inner, we do all things mentally (psychokinesis).

An Urge for Isolation

Because of memories of lifetimes past of thorough preparation for the mission before coming—and since, as well, from the very first day of our meeting, I have been particularly cautious and secretive regarding our whereabouts. Never before in this life had I experienced such feelings, but immediately upon being brought together, suddenly was the feeling present —the need for complete isolation and secrecy pertaining to our whereabouts. This, no doubt, was a definite memory of Jerusalem and a few other times! Our efforts have, as they say, 'paid off' and in this way, our Emissary is less apt to become an idol to be worshipped—and which is the very last thing he would want. He does so strongly wish for the devotee to place importance, not upon him as a person but, upon the Principle He brings.

The certain persons who have met him personally, however, know him to be very humble and unpretentious. He wants no applause or acclaim but simply to be recognized as having developed a very high attainment of Infinite Wisdom. As an interplanetary traveler, He has lived or visited many planets and states that this Earth world is one of the very lowest in its evolutionary processes, but there must always be such a place for those recently evolving from the animal-like stages; however, for those who are ready to make their start to prepare themselves for this ascension into higher stages, He has come to bring the Word, the knowledge and the help whereby this start can be realized.

To those students who have been prepared and conditioned for their personal 'advent', the point in their evolution where they too begin to sever the bonds of the earth to gain the wisdom that will relate them to planes of higher expression, the Unarius texts point the way. Many have come to realize the teachings are their very future as they become aware of the importance of the principles taught!

Yes, the lives of these individuals have been and are being changed so they too shall never be the same and, in some future time, will thus be able to move on to a more highly-evolved planet. What else on this karmic Earth world could be so worthwhile!

The Moderator's Viewing—Psychically

During the first years of our togetherness, Ernest would bring to me countless relatings, pointings up that have happened in my youth, sometimes things I could scarcely remember myself until greater detail would be added, and always with most exact viewing. Sometimes they would be rather comical, as in this incident of the old bathroom.

We were a large family and, as a child, I lived in an old, rather rundown house. Ernest said, "When you and Esther were kiddies, did you have a wooden toilet seat that had a crack and when you sat on it, it pinched your little bottoms?" That it did! How we hated that old cracked seat! He continued, "The crack was not one that went straight across but was an angle, a slanted split so when you put your weight on it, no matter how you would sit, it could not help but give a good pinch; it got you!" He was so right. "Also in that old bathroom," He said, "the square box overhead that held the water would splash out and down on you sometimes, as there was no top on it. Furthermore, the chain used to flush the toilet was an old rusty one that had knots tied in it to shorten it, and even when you stood tiptoe, you could hardly reach it!" Right, on all counts! These tests from over sixty years past were vivid memories with me. Many things he related I had forgotten until He brought them into consciousness. This went on month after month, year after year; I doubt there were many incidents in my entire past He has not seen, viewed or related at some one time or another, for he has practically relived my life for me. Of course, this served a dual purpose: one, to teach me the infinite and incalculable reaches of a developed mind, and secondly, as these pointings out were related, they lost in his 'Consciousness' any negative portent they might have contained. Such a developed Mind could not be conscious of any negation without its being changed in its frequency!

One other incident which Ernest related to me, and very detailed, was a huge oil painting of hunting dogs my grandfather had made for dad before I was born. Ernest described this in minute detail, telling how one dog was pointing his tail to the rear and how the split rail fence was falling down, the exact coloring of the two, one brown and white, the other black and white spotted. He said, "I connect this picture with you at a very early age," and it so happened "doggie" was the first word I spoke as a babe, as dad had kept after me to say it. Ernest's relating that did please my granddad in spirit. Incidentally, Ernest very often brought to me, mentally, the many things this talented man (granddad) had done, such as cabinet work, etc. He described to me all the things he had made as he lived with us for a time. Granddad loved to play the fiddle with me at the piano, and Ernest would relate all the numbers he especially liked or that we did well together! Yes, it was all most interesting and great fun. Never a dull moment!

Mental Projection

There is a young lady who lives a mile or so distant to whom I have taken a hairpiece to be styled. I have been there once or twice before but a few days ago I put the thing in my car planning to stop at her house and leave it off but failed to drive that street on my morning tour, so when I returned home, there it was, still in the car. I became a bit disgusted at my forgetfulness and then thought, "Oh, well, I'll take it tomorrow." As she met me at her door the next morning, she grabbed my hand excitedly saying, "Oh, you know I have looked all over the house for your curl-lock and I could find it nowhere; I just could not imagine where I had put it, how come you brought it yesterday but now here you have it!" She was quite emotional with her frustration until I told her, "You did not see me here in the flesh, you simply saw me astrally; you sensed my thoughts as I 'tuned in' to you when I found I had forgotten to stop." She relaxed in her anxiety but she was still quite confounded. She would never have understood astral projection!

This is what some term astral flight but we call it mental projection. It was so real to her she was sure she had actually seen me there with the object. However, it simply proves a point; but even more, certain benefit was received by her, for no one can contact this power or Consciousness without the Radiating Light being impinged within them. She will never be quite the same.

A similar happening took place this very morning as I went to do my weekly shopping. I had stopped at the meat department and although it was a store with ready-packaged meats, I rang the buzzer for the clerk and it took a few minutes to describe to him the exact cut I wished him to prepare for me. He went to work on my order and I waited. After a few minutes he returned. There was no other person about, I was there alone waiting. He held the package in his hand looking strangely about in one direction, then the other saying, "Well, where did my customer go?" I said, as I was standing right in front of him, "Here I am." The butcher replied, "No, you're not the one I carved this roast for. She had on a red dress, was a younger and different looking woman." (The dress I was wearing was pale green.) I wanted to laugh but didn't dare; he still was not convinced, walking up and down behind his counter, "looking for the younger lady with light hair and a red dress," he said. (My hair is dark auburn.) He finally satisfied himself that I was the one who wanted the meat by concluding with, "Oh, I guess she had you pick it up for her." Even when I said, "Mister, I, me, myself asked you for the meat—took time to describe the cut," he only grinned foolishly, as if I were 'putting him on'! I simply could not convince him!

So what happened there? The clerk was transcended right out of his physical consciousness as he contacted my force field; he was viewing my psychic and saw so much red in my aura—healing frequencies—that it impressed his mind as a red dress; likewise, other areas and he could never be convinced that the person who ordered the cut was the one who picked it up! This is the sort of experience we encounter so often. But again, something wonderful happened with him during those few seconds of his inner attunement. The force fields in which we walk transcended him or we could say the Higher Self here engulfed him, oscillated for an instant with him—no conscious effort extended on my part!

* * * * *

Another interesting phenomenon, but which involved my own personal development was during the stay in Palm Springs. I experienced my first awareness of being in several, or many, places at once. I was standing at the electric stove cooking dinner when I was thinking of several different persons; students, persons with whom we then had contact, etc., when suddenly I was there—with each one in his particular location, hearing and replying to his words. I could see in color each separate home or shop at the one time! Then, within a matter of seconds, I was flipped right back into conscious mind and it seemed very strange; I had to stop to figure out just what I was doing there in that kitchen, so real did the trip to the many at once, seem. As I related the incident to Ernest, He said, "I'm glad you are getting it—so-called astral travel or attunement." There were a couple of men students present and they noted that I had a different—'vacant' look about me—during the few seconds I had 'left'.

One day, not long before this night, I had been wondering if I would be able to 'see' and to 'read' as does the Moderator when, that very night, came my answer. I viewed pictures that were evidently projected into my mind: the scene a lovely garden, flowers, trees, even vegetables, all as a movie, moving and in color. There was my answer. I would be able to do whatever was the need. During this moment of viewing, I opened my eyes to see if the scene would be visible with the physical eye and it was! It was as if one were projecting on a screen, so plain was the viewing—just like real.

To Reminisce—Brought the Contact

As I was thinking back over what I had jotted in the way of recalls for this little book, wondering if the descriptions of the Higher Ones could possibly be conceived and I had felt that the highlights had been sufficiently pointed up to give the reader a general idea of how marvelously does the Infinite work through consciousness when one has prepared himself and endeavors to attain. I was lying in bed before dropping off to sleep thinking thusly when there appeared in Consciousness—just as if the Higher Ones were prompting—and I viewed a glorious sight I had so very often seen. The entire ceiling seemed as a great soft white cloud or canopy of subdued light and, interspersed at frequent intervals, were sparks, tiny lights of an infinite number; some were larger but, for the most, they looked for all the world like stars, yet I knew they were hosts of spiritual beings. Always was there movement; they would flash in and out and looked very much like the heavens on a clear summer night—only much more thickly populated. With such visitation, there was present the transcended state, the feeling of buoyancy, of lightness. I could not help but feel our dear Brothers were saying in effect, "You forgot to mention us," but of course this was not the case. This was their way of adding their Light and Power into these lines, to help this needful world.

And if these pages seem lengthy and voluminous, they are, frankly, just a brief thumbnail sketch of all that has taken place. As was mentioned, an entire set of volumes would be necessary to contain even a small part of all the wonders which this entity has experienced, seen, and taken part in, and of which no words exist to adequately describe; moreover, it would sound repetitious. But I do trust my recallings can serve in some small way to aid you, the reader, in your personal pursuance of wisdom in your efforts to attain Infinite Consciousness and which efforts, extended in this present life, can be the beginning of personal development and attainment.

To say that I have walked with the Angels, been aided and helped by the Masters of many ages past and have oscillated in consciousness with the Infinite is all true; and it has made me very humble. When we learn Infinite Principle, as we learn to step from this treadmill-like existence, the reactionary way of life, we could do no wrong to our brother. When we arrive at the point in our evolution where we start to seek the higher way, we are given infinite help. We are never alone. We become more and more receptive to the Infinite Principle or function and, in this ever-growing awareness, we learn to oscillate and integrate personal consciousness with the Infinite—man's purpose and goal as he slowly leaves the earth-world ties to so attain infinite realization. Thus do we also become an interplanetary traveler, reaching out the hand to help the struggling earthean so bound by his past.

And, as you struggle in this pit of clay to loosen the feet so tightly mired, know too, dear friend, and truly so, that our hands are ever outstretched to those reaching out!

Psychic Depletion and Damage

There have indeed been many more persons helped and healed unknowingly than even those who have
become aware of this spiritual help, for wherever the
Moderator goes, or those of whom He is conscious
there oscillates to them the healing Powers, the Light
and Energy. This principle is also now functioning
with this entity as well, and it is, of course, the "Father
Within that doeth the works".

No, we are not desirous of having any limelight
focused upon us for if it were so, then we would be
unable to continue. We can carry on to help and work
with the many only so long as we are able to maintain
our isolation. Crowds would draw so heavily it would
soon bring about conclusion to our expressions.
There was a time during the first few months of the
work in which the Moderator did give a series of lectures and personal audiences but now He has, in fact
we both have, been stepped up so much, and progressed so far into the future that it would not be possible. In fact, so great is the draw or pull when in conscious contact with any person, that He immediately
suffers psychically because he has factually over-ex-
pended his time on earth. His cycle has passed when
he was to have left the physical but he wants to aid all
possible, any additional souls who may be reaching;
but he has actually extended his stay among us.

Immediately after one lecture He gave in Santa
Barbara, several years ago, He experienced a severe
psychic breakdown for far too much energy had been
projected. He went on and on in his teaching and instead of the planned forty minutes, He gave steadily,
of his Self for over three and one-half hours as the
students continued to present questions. He was com-

pletely unconcerned about himself, of his personal well-being and it did cause great psychic damage. Six or seven months passed before He regained any semblance of normalcy (for Him); yet that far-too-great out-flow can never really be compensated for. This is the sensitivity with which a Higher Being such as He must live, must cope with and endure. But it is the same today as then (years ago); He would give of his very life for any who would need his help and energies, so completely selfless is he.

More than once we both suffered greatly for several days after some student came for counseling. I recall three or four times, both of us could scarcely get up from the bed so psychically depleted had we become. But the visitor never knew all that had gone out from us unto him, or that his contact practically grounded us for several days and such psychic illness is the worst possible kind of distress; one just wishes he could die! What it amounts to is that we used too much of our own supporting, psychic powers; thus, anymore, as tremendously delicate and sensitive as the Moderator has become, we try for complete isolation that He may remain on earth a little more time to give from his Inner and Higher Self without the physical contact, to avoid becoming depleted. A very fine line He walks, impossible to describe. No, there has never lived on earth a more selfless Being. His concern is always for the many students with whom He is connected in a psychic way and which number many thousands, both in the physical and on the inner for, with such an Advanced Being, whether one is in the flesh or out of it makes little or no difference or importance.

In my mention that his cycle had reached the conclusion point, this occurred right after the 'Jesus' book manifested and when He found or repossessed (symbolically) his long-lost Red Box (chest), for this was what we were striving toward through the years

—to arrive at that point and time which formed the bridge of time from Jerusalem two thousand years ago into the present! Thus it is presently, we both sensed the fulfillment of completion of all He came to express. We look not for other works to be brought in the future but if any may be added they will be due to his sheer determination, his creative ability and complete compassion for all mankind and creation, to push on and on. Yet, well it is that we know so factually there is sufficient science, teachings and wisdom in the Unarius library to change, completely, the life of any earthean so desirous. This I can verify and which is, in essence, the very purpose of this book— to help the reader realize here is one who has met and faced her past, one who has conquered and overcome the many blocks and obstacles of the past, has learned sufficiently of the Science that it has changed her and it can also take place with others likewise ready and dedicated.

Thus it is, we remind you, never feel you have learned completely the science contained in the lessons and books of the Unariun curriculum. Let them serve as a way of attunement, for they can be your means of a better future. When you sense the drowsiness or heat, the lassitude often felt as one studies, it is the infinite, creative, radiating, regenerative Power and Energies projected unto you as you make this inner contact. Those who have sensed the quickening and desire for the Unarius teachings have striven long to arrive even at this point of conception and readiness! Let nothing deter your forward motion into your higher future. The key to this more progressive future has been placed within your hands in the Unarius texts. Use it wisely and often; moreover, learn to be conscious of principle in action where e'er you may be. Let the Unarius Science become the dominating interest and concern in your life and you shall indeed become the victor. You, too, shall begin to become victorious over your past that has bound you, lo these many thousands of years and lifetimes. Now is the time to start severing these fetters!

Another book (or two) that should serve to be both interesting and enlightening shall be published in the future, a book of student testimonials; excerpts from student letters telling of their progress, changes, healings, overcomings and which we promise will be a great accumulation of proof; proof not only of the great wisdom of our Moderator but also testimonials which prove factually the science He brings—his Word made manifest! (Man cannot live by bread alone.)

Thus, dear reader, if you are one of the sincere dedicatees and are experiencing from day to day your own personal phenomena of various sorts, let us hear about it so your account may be included with the many other grateful students' recountings.

An Astral Entity Pushed

An interesting psychic experience I recall and one which we've enjoyed reviewing: during the time the Moderator was dictating the "Hermes" book in 1958, a dear soul named Karl was directed to us; Karl wished to help in the work in some way. It so 'happened' he was artistically inclined and did the few drawings in that book. He had spoken of an electric air brush he wished he could have the use of, thought he could get some unusual effects, etc. Although at that particular time they were quite costly, we bought him one such tool and mailed it to him as we lived in another town. After a few drawings and, in the following months and years, we heard no more from Karl. He had been a devout student but eventually dropped out of communication.

Suddenly one summer day in 1963, after moving from Santa Barbara to Glendale, a strong urge overtook me to go to Karl's home. We had been past it only one time years before as we drove him home, so I wasn't even sure if I could find it but the pull was so strong to go there. When his wife came to the door, she said, "Oh, I'm so glad you came; I want so much to get your air brushes back to you that you bought for Karl's use." She continued, "You know he died Sunday, don't you?" (This day was Tuesday.) Well, I was rather startled, but here he had been prompting both she and I on the inner so he could be free of that guilt! The interesting thing to me was how very emotional she was in her anxiety to get rid of it and how relieved she became when she placed it in my hands! There's just nothing quite like working with spirit! We had never even heard he was ill, nor were we even conscious of him, as he had not been in touch for the intervening five years, but here Karl came through to both his wife and me loud and clear!

Our Greatest Miracle

The Jose Book—The Capstone

As it has been said, every day holds its demonstrations, its psychisms and experiences but it would require one to follow us about constantly with pad and pen to tally all that takes place in the realm of 'so-called' phenomena, but which to we who work with, and live from spirit, is quite the normal way of life. It would be strange to us were it otherwise! We are really never surprised at anything that comes about, for inwardly we know. It is similar to watching a movie being run that you've helped make; you know what's coming!

Yet, there have been a few instances that took me by surprise. As one of the Higher Ones said one time, "We like to keep the element of surprise, to hold your interest." They knew how disinteresting this old physical world has become to us—in fact, it has always been so to the Moderator for, after one has discharged all his former karmic ties with the past, the physical world becomes quite a bore and very monotonous. The time to which I refer as really receiving a complete surprise was in regard to the "Life of Jesus" book, the climax of all others, brought into our consciousness here in 1968. I would never be able to find words to define my feelings, realizations, etc., but the week of its reading was truly the climax to all other experiences as I delved into that book. It was such a tremendous thing, and most astounding to actually find verification of much that the Moderator had been teaching written from the pen of another nearly seventy years ago!

Of course, there exists also much science in the

Unarius texts that Jesus did not teach, due to the times; people were not ready for this New Age Science He now brings; however, to say I loved every moment of the reading of the Jose book is putting it mildly. It held me suspended; I walked about in a semi-trance attempting to do my usual endeavors, but only half here. A most memorable and unforgettable week it was, a week of unexplainable joy. I felt very often I simply could not contain myself; the excitement was tremendous and here was someone saying, "Unarius Moderator, you are right; you're right and here is the proof!"

When the entire impact hit me and I knew what it all brought about, I said to two lady students, "if I can't reprint and get this book to the public, I'll just die!—and felt that way! Spirit had worked it out so precisely, that it was possible for us to reprint it; the original copyrights had run out and the publishing house was no longer in existence. It was ours to do with as we saw fit! Spirit was pushing, for all things connected with it went well and smoothly in the re-production and distribution. I was in a daze, how-ever, for most of the month and was so alerted that very little sleep did I realize during that time. The 'Jose' book served, you see, to prove much our Mod-erator had taught and written through these fifteen years! Yes, the Mission of Jesus has now been re-established in Unarius—the Nazarene returned!

As I pursued the book, chapter after chapter made clear the great hoax of the Bible, of all religions and, as I read in those past teachings of Jesus, they were quite often the exact words of our Moderator! Yes, even the very language and beautiful flow He uses— it's all there, including the most vital of all elements— the power to transcend the reader!

It took me not long to recognize that it was He, Himself (Jesus and/or the Moderator's Higher Self, and which is one and the same) who, before incarnating in the present, aided and abetted the two, Saul and Judas, in their efforts to inspire the earthman Smyth in his revelations! Yes, this book does indeed supply any missing parts! The Power, too, was all there as I read and then I knew for sure, for nowhere else in the writings of any earthman—other than that which is expressed from Unarius—does this infinite, creative Power exist. None other on earth expresses this great height of 'awareness', this true Infinite Consciousness —which makes the great difference!

The little booklet, "The Story of the Little Red Box", will explain much regarding the "Life of Jesus" book and which, of course, was brought about by the Moderator because of the materialization of the 'Jesus' book. This book meant much to Him, as well; in fact, we felt that it brought about the actual conclusion of this Mission so far as physical efforts in the way of texts are concerned. Many things have changed since, and it has come to us both that it is, in the physical sense, 'finished'—that feeling has existed with the two of us—a sense of completion, of fulfillment! Now, all the books, etc., have been completed.

The past two thousand years now have, in effect, been brought up to the present. His mission two thousand years ago, brought to a conclusion so early in life before, had now been reestablished and much, much more has been added to all He taught then and even far more than He could have given then, as people were not, at that time, as ready for the more scientific phase, as some may be in the present or especially in the future. Yet, these persons so prepared will be but one small part of the many eartheans; for man evolves so very slowly. Much time will be necessary before the masses can conceive this; vast, infinite, Creative Science of Unarius.

And so, as his long-lost red chest (or box) has been found, the Unariun Moderator's identity can now be known. The world will have become, in years and in eons into the future, a far better place because of his visitation to it, because of His Word and of the Light and Energies that, through his Consciousness, have been radiated unto this earth plane. The most remarkable life ever lived by any individual upon the earth world and yet, words are so empty and futile in any effort to describe such tremendous expressions and accomplishments! Only in realization, in the sharing and experiencing of these vast powers that are interjected into the mind of the student can one realize and, even then, only a small part is conceived, for these things take place so subtly.

Would it be that man would quest of Him but one final vital point by which to live, He would again say, just as He did in that long-ago Jerusalem time, "Seek ye within," for when man knows himself, he knows all men. His life will cease to be filled with conflict, with ills, with wars and evil, with strife and want, for he will have found that "Kingdom Within", which is within each man, awaiting his personal realization.

And now, dear reader, although these various recalls, notations, etc., of our efforts to bring about this accomplishment of the Unariun Mission may sound incredible and fantastic to some, they are, nevertheless, factual and all true. There is so much, much more that could be added of the countless and infinite number of healings which have been brought about through the direction and help of the Moderator, both before and after the physical contact of we two, for many were his years devoted to that particular phase of expression, healing others, long before we met. Countless were the ways of his demonstrating the abilities of a Higher Mind as was proven in his predictions into the future many years ahead; of so-called miraculous healings of an infinite variety. A goodly example of these will be written in the student testimonial books—and which will indeed be the most monumental works ever written proving Jesus and the Unariun Moderator to be the Greatest Lives ever lived.

Yes, very possibly the last book (or books) to be published will be the student testimonial books. You will read an overwhelming accumulation of evidence; excerpts from student letters written by those who have experienced their own miracles; evidence, too, that Unarius is the continuation of the mission of Jesus and that He has returned! Moreover, that He is also teaching and making available the Wisdom whereby others ready, can likewise begin to pursue and prepare themselves that they may also attain!

No, dear friend, there are no adjectives to properly and adequately describe or define the great Mission and works of Unarius. Insufficient, too, to merely state that the great hoax and farce of religion has changed for the worse, the history of the entire world; and how, now the Unariun Moderator has brought again to mankind wisdom and truth, not only for the present but especially pertaining to that long-ago time when He walked the earth in the form of the earthman; that He is now unraveling and making known truth of the many former enigmas of the past in his texts, which can, when man conceives these great works, change or move mankind back onto a more even keel to what they were before the great religious perpetrations were so expressed and made public.

It is fact to say, "Unarius is the very pulse-beat of the future of mankind." As our great and Wise One the Unariun Moderator, has endeavored to convey how history reveals in past ages that at crucial periods of transition in man's life on earth, there has always risen some great Movement, some great Avatar who has somehow succeeded in 'Turning the Tides' of destructive, materialistic confusion into more constructive channels. Again, history is repeating itself! Inasmuch as at the present time the earth is going through a great and tremendous change, it is extremely important that certain advanced preparatory work be started among many thousands of Earth people who have, through many lifetimes, been preconditioned for this Advent.

The 'Messenger' lives and walks upon the earth today. He stands, as a living monument to the past, and a Guiding Light to the future. He has delivered His Message to mankind!

Thus, this wonderful story of truth, "The True Life of Jesus" book, stands as living witness to the true teachings of Jesus. Moreover, I who walked by his side in that long-ago Holy Land, not only as a seeker and disciple but also as his espoused, thus you may envision my feelings, the love and upliftment which I experienced as I again read His Message, His words of love and of teaching to me, there in the Garden of Gethsemane. Yes, it was, as those moments were again brought into consciousness (by way of the pen of Smyth) a truly most heartwarming and touching occasion as I read again His Message, word for word; His Words which carried then, just as they still do today, the Light, the Power, the healing Energies and transcendency that are ever existent, as any reader can experience as he 'tunes in' to His Words of Truth.

As He spoke his thoughts of love to Mary, it was as if time stood still, for I was, indeed, in that attunement, right back in that garden listening to the Master's Voice! Needless to say, how I just did not wish for the dissertation He was giving to come to a conclusion, as it was all so wonderful; needless too, no doubt, to say the truth of that story has become a great part of my new present life.

You could well imagine the touching and moving moments we both experienced as we viewed again (on television, during one of the movies of Jesus' life) the scene as it was expressed in that lifetime of Mary bathing the feet of Jesus with her costly oils and perfumes, for which she sold costly possessions to obtain for that purpose. The eyes of us both were moist with the recalling, and my heart welled with compassionate love for Him, as we relived in Truth those memorable moments.

Now we each can hear again His Voice in the recorded Messages He has prepared for us—the Voice and the Wisdom which has, from time to time, through the ages past, been brought to the earth world from the Inner Kingdoms. However, the knowledge, the accompanying powers and Light have been—for this present time and era in this, the great master plan with the present Unariun mission—all stepped up due to the great need of the earthman in this, the most perilous of all times. Thus, not only the printed word and books have been made manifest but also the very Voice (verbal teachings) of the Unariun Moderator (the Emissary from the Kingdoms within) have been tape recorded for the aspirant's benefit; the pleasure is yours.

It Couldn't Happen—But It Did!

It would be unfair were not a few words included in this little epistle of the wonderful and constant inner guidance that has been realized from the very first day of our efforts and endeavors toward the Unariun mission. This is in no way said as a boast or to brag, for there is no desire for applause or praise, or that any sense of ego needs gratification for efforts extended. But rather, it is with humility and a sense of deep and sincere oneness, or realization of Principle in action that our accomplishments have been so stupendous. Never have we wondered or not known each step to take, for always was the inner guidance present in all efforts and expressions. No words were repeated to me, but simply there existed the immediate strong, inner-knowing, and this, of course was possible, too, because we helped set up this great plan from the Inner before coming to earth; thus, it has been a sense of fulfillment.

I refer especially to such things as printing and publishing the works, for I personally have never had any such contacts or experience; never has this one been even slightly interested in such matters (nor has Ernest had personal physical experience in such, in the present). In fact, quite the opposite has been true with myself; I've disliked any exacting work; anything needful of precision, etc., I have never cared for. Thus, to me it has all been a doubly remarkable demonstration! In fact, it would have been quite difficult to 'go wrong'—and if so, we would soon know it, so strong and positive were we 'locked in' with that guidance. If ever we would go against it, our entire being would be off key and would vibrate negatively; and in such state, one becomes psychically ill, for the inflow or oscillation has been interrupted.

For instance, just as soon as the Moderator voiced, in part, the "Venus" book, although I knew nothing about typing, I felt upon awakening one morning that I could type; felt the letters on my fingertips! So I purchased an old typewriter and covered the keys with caps so I could not see the letters, as I wanted my typing to be, not from visual, but completely via 'touch' method. As I had felt it would, the writing went right off—like automatic, staccato, rapid-pace! Sleep teaching! Thus it was with every procedure and process necessary; all things went right along as if we had done them all our lives!

I quickly learned of the great difficulty and pitfalls of getting a large publishing house to publish the books and realized the better way was to do them ourselves. In my sleep, I had sensed there was some sort of machine whereby type could be set up, then lo and behold, within a couple of days there appeared a man at our house with one of these particular machines! Imagine a person soliciting a residence for such a business machine; yet this was the way it came about and how I learned of the very wonderful Vari-Typer which has since served to make the master copies whereby we have published the many books ourselves. I very quickly learned the very intricate function of it and thereby, with much inner help, brought about the books that have since become the Unarius Library. However, since that time, another student has taken over that work and Helen is doing a masterly job setting up the original master copies on a greatly-improved machine, since that long-ago 1955. Her efforts, too, have been wonderful proof of spirit having prepared her for this most important work.

Then, after the perfect master copy was produced, to the offset printer to be photographed and thousands of copies duplicated from this original; then to the binder. Then the big problem of how to get them to those ready and desirous! Without a moments wonderment, this too was shown; in fact, there came to me in the mails notices regarding the brokers in New York who rent out such needed names, all categorized according to particular interests. Quite a costly way to advertise, but it is the one way to reach those interested in self-improvement; and it has been ever since, that one source which has supplied that need. It has been the way and means whereby many, many thousands have been contacted; we have reached out to those reaching to the Light and those whose lives have been changed are without number.

Our files fill an entire wall of one room which contains testimonials of those who have realized healings of all types and natures—healings from the slightest physical condition to the most serious and critical. Completely obsessed persons have reached out and they have been healed; mental cases of all imaginable types have changed from incoherent persons to individuals capable of taking their proper position in life; family relations which have been intolerable even to the point of suicide, have been resolved and the partners become compatible, happy persons again; many in financial distress have had their needs met. Very often, after these countless and infinite number of conditions and needs have been resolved, the individual experiences such a seemingly natural solution to it all that he even fails to bother to drop the word to tell us so! But we know, regardless.

I'm thinking of one such particular case, and of which, many likewise exist: the poor woman had a very painful neck condition. The misery must have been unbearable for she wrote frequently—sometimes every week or two—and always were her letters filled with her misery, how she would just give anything to be freed of the distracting neck pain. This went on for some three years, I believe, even after it had been placed with her something of a hanging, and the knot in her neck was due to the knot in the rope which she either attached to another or she was on the other end of the rope. But she had not reached the point of acceptance where she would work it out and free herself. Instead, she would continue to 'expect another' to remove her condition. As you know, as the science teaches, it is only in our personal overcomings that we gain wisdom and, through the experience, do we grow spiritually.

Of a sudden, her letters ceased to be filled with her complaints of the neck problem and instead, they then took up other conditions. It was easy to see the poor soul was having a very rough time to exist in her misery. It slipped into my consciousness, as do these inner promptings, "Sue has experienced her neck healing," and although she had said nothing, after my questing her, she did admit, "Oh, it is fine now!" And this is the way it is with so many. The healing takes place so subtly, they even forget they ever had a condition! So they fail to do the important thing of letting us know; however, in spite of all this, there are thousands who have written and who constantly speak of their great change with hearts full of gratitude.

So it is that we know each and every one who has been contacted through the mail, or even from our advertising, has, in some way, been helped, been touched with the Radiant Energy, that Light of Infinity which will one day lead them up to the point in their pathway where they, too, shall start to seek; and in their seeking, shall they find the key to a better future.

Thus it is that in the accomplishments of these two persons (the Moderator and myself), that we feel sure there has never been an equal on earth; especially so when we realize the vast and incalculable value and benefits of His Message . . . scientific principles given that could change the world greatly for the better when man arrives at the point of receptivity; knowledge and information given throughout the texts that would cause prisons and hospitals to be nonessential, nonexistent, when man conceives and learns to live by the concepts this Infinite Mind presents to the earthman!

Yes, would it be that mankind learned these Truths, all so-called child or teenage delinquency would be nonexistent. When the great Truths included in His curriculum could be realized by men of the nations, they would never be at war! There would exist no need for strife or racial hatreds so prevalent. And if the various races, namely the colored, knew the Science of Unarius, such resentment as he feels would not be and he would be able to take his more proper place in society as he realized the truth of evolution and all its encompassing precepts; however, we know, too, that these people have not arrived at any point in their evolution where they could be receptive to this intelligence! So the World must suffer. But which way is man, in general, progressing? We wonder!

Yes, man changes very slowly; only those who have prepared themselves for this advent on the Inner, before coming to earth, shall be able to enter into the study and remain ever steadfast in their efforts to understand.

Referring again to the mention made in the Bible, "Jesus wept": let it be known that He wept, not from his pain and misery—although to such a 'sensitive' Person, the pain would be intensified at least 100,000 times—but He wept because of the great karma which He knew these perpetrators were so inflicting upon themselves, the Infinite and mankind. He knew full well how their evil deeds would follow them through the ages for many thousands of years and lifetimes into the future and that mankind, as a whole, would suffer and would be deprived of the great Wisdom and Truth He was then endeavoring to bring. He was quite aware, just as He is now, how the negative factions, the forces of evil would change, distort and destroy His Message of Light and Truth, and the Mission.

Thus, these persons—in their efforts to stop Him and to destroy his physical body—were, in effect, changing the history of the world for the worse for thousands of years into the future! Looking back, had the dark minions not so used his body to release their pent up hostilities, had the worst crime in history not have been executed, the world would indeed have progressed far more than it is presently expressing, for the false religions which resulted would have been nonexistent and man could have at least had the chance to gain the true Wisdom He was then attempting to deliver to the earth.

In other words, his (so-called) followers, namely, Saul and others did, indeed, factually lead mankind decidedly backwards in evolution. The religionists thus became enslaved by the dark forces and powers of evil and regressed to its present depraved and deplorable state, all in the name of the Spiritual, which is anything but a true representation of Jesus' teachings.

Yet He (and the Infinite) does not stop there with the blocking of the Light and His Truth, for today in the near Twenty-first Century, again He comes to the earth in the body of an earthean—to appear as an earthean—to continue to carry the Torch, the Light of Truth for those who will heed. And even those who will not heed do also receive, to a degree, of this infinite, creative, cosmic, regenerative Light and Power which He radiates and wields, that they, too, in time to come, will start to reach out toward the Light.

The Unarius Moderator came especially at this time to earth, to reach out to those who had created for themselves the heavy negative karma in Jerusalem two thousand years ago and to again make available to them, understanding and teachings that point the way to a better and more progressive way of life. Thus, it is up to each one to make the wisdom his personal knowledge; and, in so doing, he will, step by step, evolve himself out of these jungle-like worlds and enter upon a more progressive pattern of life— one which will eventually lead him unto the Inner Worlds of Light—the Heavenly Mansions of which Jesus spoke so long ago. Heed ye now His call to prepare!

And so, as an example, who can say how many hundreds or thousands of years or lifetimes this entity has been projected into the future compared to what little might have been accomplished without the Unariun knowledge and help of the Brotherhood!

The very purpose and goal of man's very existence, his objective on earth is, of course, to gain the knowledge he can to move himself forward in this ever-present evolving. The lessons gained in his various day-by-day experiences in life are the motivating elements which either project him forward or, conversely, the opposite is true; where he does not apply himself constructively he thus reverts.

So how many thousands of years or lives have most persons been repeating these squirrel-cage existences and how many more into the future will they be continued? You, as a Unariun student, can do something about your position and direction! Through the constant effort to assimilate the Science our Emissary has prepared for us, with consciousness and concern upon the principles as you go about your daily endeavors you can step up this otherwise 'slower than a snail's pace' motion (if any) to a more steady and positive forward motion. One step forward and three backward availeth one naught. Thus, constant vigilance over self is necessary to attain and retain the upward regenerative motion for any individual and, to which there is no end.

If in the various recalls recorded in this booklet

regarding the writer's experiences, it may appear that she is attempting to convey the belief that she has attained 'all', this is indeed a great misinterpretation. So vast and almost incomprehensible have been her projections into the future—much more so than has ever been accomplished on earth before by any individual in any one lifetime (so states our Moderator) yet, compared to all there is yet to learn, to experience, and to evolve into in the eons of future, all this which has gone before in the present is but as one very small step; as I have said, like looking through the keyhole into the cosmos, for the Infinite is infinitely Infinite and which can be realized only step by step, as we grow with it. These 'so-called' peeks do give one a glimpse and slight realization of the tremendous vastness of Infinity; also to conceive the abilities of a Mind such as the Unarius Moderator, does prove how mortal man can become godlike through eons of constructive, progressive evolving!

And so we, each aspirant should begin to realize that every overcoming in our daily problems, the workings out of negative appearances, of resolving unpleasant relationships, the making into a positive solution any existing negation, and that each singular concept of the Unariun principle so conceived, are all ways and means whereby we can and do step upon a more positive, progressive movement; that every act, deed, expression and thought we express is impinged within our very being—the psychic anatomy, there to oscillate always. By the same principle, the hostile or resentful, fearful feelings we project outwardly are, at that moment, impressed or created in its never-ending, regenerating oscillation within the self. Thus, when these vitally important concepts are realized, when we become truly aware that we are, factually, day by day, moment to moment, creating our future, then man begins to become more selective in his expressions; and as he thus becomes more aware and less reactionary, does he truly begin to prepare himself for the kingdom of heaven which is within. As man is today but the result of his many past yesterdays, so the present becomes his future.

Proof of Attunement
Called Astral Flight

There are, of course, countless wondrous testimonials from students and which, as has been mentioned, shall be put into books one day and I had not intended inserting any in this particular collection of notations; however, a letter received from one student today, does serve to prove so factually how we two can, and do, come to students, oscillate with them in consciousness, even to the point where they become aware of this Presence and I felt it would be of interest to the reader.

We had run short of the lesson sets and I mentioned, to another student who has been doing this clerical work, that I felt sure Irene would be glad to help with the collating. She was, of course, and today came her letter describing her experiences while she thus endeavored. Irene is a very heavy woman, thus it was doubly difficult for her to so work. It reads:

Dear Ones: Thank you for letting me help with the lessons; I enjoyed doing it. I know I was overshadowed by Ioshanna! I had the feeling we were one, getting the lessons together to fill orders. I started one day and continued on until all were done and I was completely one with Ioshanna! My physical body ached all over, I was stiff but I told myself (the lower) the books had to get finished whether my body ached or not. Thirst! I drink and drink water but my thirst does not quench; I'm still very thirsty.

(Note: This is due to the necessary catalyst that must go into the healing energy which the water supplies.)

My head ached from temple to temple; it felt swelled up but was not really. (This, the effect of the inflow of the power to her.) Every bone and muscle felt very hot but it was not a fever. Every night I was wringing wet and had to take showers. I also did a lot of purging. My eyeballs would not focus but that was soon corrected. The top of my head seemed to have a great pressure, in fact, this pressure still remains! I'm not the same person and will never be again!

One evening while working on the lessons, I could feel and see a piece of flesh in the right side of my stomach—possibly the gallbladder; it appeared full of little holes which tore off and disappeared! (This, of course, she saw psychically.) I have perspired like Niagara Falls every two hours since I started with them. Also I felt a pop in my throat and felt and saw a large piece of flesh come up and out!

Last Thursday, I awakened at 9:15, came right out and started on the work again, putting them together. I was here and yet, very much not here, doing these things! It was seemingly automation! The eyelids would not stay awake; I had to lie down for an hour, then I thought I heard the phone ring, but no one was there. (It was exactly at 10:30 that I had 'thought' of phoning Irene—to sort of, as we jokingly term it, 'build a fire under her', but decided not to bother her; to just let her do it best she could. But here my thoughts of ringing the phone did just that!) I guess you sent it psychically to get me up and going. I felt like a punch-drunk fighter, no control of myself. I left the lower (old) self down and rose very high, overcame myself so I could complete the work; I completely let myself go so I could be one with Ioshanna and it was wonderful, like a team.

When I do things for Unarius and my little dog wants attention, I tell her just as Jesus said, "I'm about my Father's business and cannot bother now and she goes to sleep 'till I get to her. She listens so attentively to the Moderator's Voice on the tape. (Animals love this vibration.) When I tried to eat, the food tasted so flat; even today, it is still tasteless.

291

(She was projected so far into the future that food became foreign!) When I study before going to sleep, I awaken later and the room is filled with seemingly thousands of tiny blue and gold lights. It is so wonderful, they appear to follow me in other rooms. The light shines so bright, I don't need to put on the electric light to see my way around!

I'm still (three days later) not back to normal but I suppose I never shall be on that level again. (And we know this is quite true. Irene had some very wonderful experiences and healing for various parts of her anatomy.)

During my visit to the doctor he said he could not understand why, even though I have every symptom of diabetes that my blood and water showed no sugar. He just shook his head! But he does not know of Unarius. Thank you with all my heart.

Irene.

(Indeed, great, wonderful and marvelous were the experiences and healing which was projected to Irene a huge step into the future for her! We are so happy for her.)

Richard told me on the phone the other day as we were speaking of Irene and her wonderful experiences, "Yes," he said, "I saw Irene and my, but she looks different! Her entire personality has changed and she feels so much lighter; in fact, her whole house feels different".

Richard's observations go to prove what can happen when the Power comes in.

Our Need Ever Fulfilled

There was a time when I had been doing an unusual amount of advertising, sending personal notices of the Unarius Library to prospective students that a sum of some two thousand dollars was the immediate need for this work. The demonstration manifested, just as has always been experienced but the manner was, to us, quite unusual. As I picked up the daily mail from the post office, among it was a large package, the wrapping torn, the paper old and the address almost indiscernible. I don't know how it ever found us; it looked like something ready for the trash can. After opening it, there was another old newspaper wrapping inside, which, too, had been all wrinkled; and it was with hesitancy that we did open it. Yes, you've guessed it—a large stack of currency, also old, in tens and twenties! The amount was exactly the sum of this statement just received for the advertising—two thousand dollars! This was Edwina's life savings; she evidently was prompted, and it was for Unarius she had saved it!

The point which is being made is to show the constant and never-ending guidance which is ever-present. What a wonderful plan! Those contributing could not help but progress with this positive expressing! The one who sent this valuable package, an elderly lady, was the one in Jerusalem who had to do with the robe—the one who sent the dark sweater which the several students made such good use of in their relivings and flashbacks, as it was symbolic of Jesus' robe. Interestingly enough, this lady insisted that the sweater she sent was hand-knitted, but it was factually a factory-made sweater. She could have very likely woven the cloth for Jesus' robe, as it was a one-piece garment; thus, her memory was likely from that past. This sweater seemed to mean so much to her and she insisted on sending it, even after I had suggested that she not do so, as I knew the Moderator would not wear it. Thus, all purposes were served.

Each student who had taken some part in the Jerusalem episode has been contacted and has had placed, within his hand, the key which will unlock this past—the key, the knowledge, and the inner help. As you will read in "The Little Red Box" booklet how these persons have all been brought in touch with the Center and have met and worked out these various karmic debts. What wonderful inner guidance to bring this all about!

Now, in January 1969, again a most wonderful demonstration of student prompting when there existed a need for a very sizable output of funds, and when, upon opening a normal letter from one gentleman student who had, in the past, simply sent a small tithe monthly, there his check for several thousand dollars—I had to take a second look to make sure I was seeing correctly—this time, it was rather a shocker. I had not had an inkling and both the Moderator and I were overwhelmed. But as we often say—there's just nothing like Inner guidance or functioning from the Inner, and thus, the Unarius lessons will help one to learn when one conceives the science and has severed his past earth ties. It is the only way we live on the Inner so it is important that one begins to understand these concepts and begins to work with them here on earth.

We Were Invaded

On another occasion a few years ago the negative forces really got to us. Our television failed and, although Ernest is quite capable of repairing or even building these circuitries, proper tools were not available at the time. A certain man, John, who was at the time, helping about the place, phoned for a rental television while they took ours to repair.

It was brought just after dark; there on the porch, carrying the television in were two large, unclean and very black Negroes. They set it down and left but not before they had left, also, a great horde of very low astral forces (warriors)! In effect, they got us off guard coming into our home, something we just are most careful about. Within a few moments, our beloved One was literally knocked off his feet, became deathly ill, was choking, gagging, his stomach doing flip-flops seemingly needing to regurgitate and was so nearly completely overcome, He couldn't sit or stand. Their negative force fields interrupted ours and it was real havoc for a time. After a few moments, they got to me. I, too, was choked, strangled and nauseated, my strength sapped and I was psychically, very ill.

We phoned John, who ordered the instrument, to come quickly and remove it from the house, for it was a polarity for the astral forces to attach themselves in our home. Soon after they had moved the television outside to the far end of the lot, one of the Spiritual Brothers came in and, through Ernest's voice, was telling me not to be negative or fearful as it would only make matters worse, that there was a horde of powerful, negative warrior forces, astral obsessions from the men making the delivery. The Brothers told us they were having a big 'pow-wow', as our American

Indian Spirit friend, White Feather called it, when they went on scalping parties (as he termed it) to do rescue work as they were doing in our situation.

Such happenings are not an easy undertaking, for the negative forces fight hard and are often very powerful in a negative way. Thus, the many Higher Ones rushing to our rescue, worked fast and hard to clean out our home (and selves) of these drastic, hellish interferences. Within an hour or so things were changing for the better but during that time we both were nearly knocked out. However, another hour more found us back to normalcy.

But if anyone doubts the strength, the negative powers of these dark forces, they should have seen what we went through that night before they could all be dealt with, dislodged and removed. They would dive for our solar plexus and attach themselves, which is a most miserable sensation.

I do not know how we could ever manage in this world without the close aid and protection of our Spiritual Brothers. We just couldn't! They heard the alarm and dashed to the rescue, their minds never far from ours. As they related later, a terrible war was waged—many scalps taken. By that, they meant their Light had penetrated into the darkened regions of the invaders and soon they became docile enough whereby they could be taken to where they belonged, as they were lost and fear-ridden. Because they are so much closer to the earth, it is easy for them to interject their mind energies, their fear and emotions and their hostile states unto the unsuspecting earthean; but, in this case, it was a direct attempt to 'stop us' in our spiritual efforts. Of course, in such a contact these negative astral forces were helped greatly, being so touched with the Light.

It was indeed a night I shall never forget, nor do I believe John, who removed the television so astrally loaded, will either as he watched, wide-eyed and fearful, as we suffered and fought through that lengthy attack—one I never again would care to encounter. But this experience did indeed teach another vitally important lesson. I doubt if I would have been able to believe such great effects could be expressed had I not, myself, so experienced it.

Had we, ourselves, made the phone call in the first place, in the ordering we would doubtless have, through the principle of frequency relationship, selected a store other than the one that was called. It is very unlikely, too, that another place in the entire valley would have been so obsessed or involved with such powerful and devastating entities for, as our Brothers of Light related, they were warriors of the Orient, such as the Genghis Khan, his relatives and warriors with but one strong drive and obsession—to kill! No doubt, they were, themselves, killed in a war many years ago and thus they live on with those same warring efforts and hypnotic ties.

Now, I'm sure, a natural reaction or thought by the reader to all this would be, "How can this be, with all your psychic and spiritual powers, to be so influenced?" And to this, let me reply: It is very true, we do (and must) walk in an energy shield of protection and, as we leave our home, a great tent of Light surrounds us with a certain amount of protection from these evil and destructive forces so prevalent everywhere in the astral (and influencing man). In the experience related, they came, as it were, into our environment. Our guard was down as we feel a certain sense of security in our own home, relaxed or unaware. As we leave here with our guard up, protection is in effect in a far greater measure against whatever we may be so confronted. The Moderator was not aware John was replacing his television with the rental and, when the black men suddenly appeared at our door with it, this was similar to punching a boxer before he has removed his jacket and he is unprepared to ward off his opponent.

Since that day, few persons, indeed, have there been to enter this sanctuary! I never again wish to see our beloved Emissary suffer so or, to be put through such an ordeal. Of course, we, in our Higher Selves, aided in the ensuing battle and, only after bathing in the Energy Fountains on the inner, were we able to oscillate more normally.

It is times such as these (although they have been but few and never before such a drastic experience), which cause me to truly appreciate the great wisdom, the Powers and Light which our Moderator so channels for, without his 'know-how' and our angelic Brothers of the Light, we would have been stopped and downed long, long ago.

Ours has had to be a constant vigilance against the forces of evil and only through his great awareness and the inner contact, has He been able to endure throughout the many years of his life in a constant and never-ending rising above and overcoming the astral and this earth-world influence which, to such a Being is, indeed, a hell of the worst kind. In fact, I must, even as I relate this experience, be aware of the erected wall of energy shield and be completely conscious, in an impersonal and strong, positive way, so that I do not re-attune unto them! Thus, how important it is to learn our energy-frequency principles!

I could relate too, of a most interesting experience (of 1950) right along this line which I witnessed as I attended a small circle of 'sitters' in a seance, who were observing a certain young medium (Dr. Richard Minnough), who, during the evening sessions, permitted certain astral forces to enter into his body and speak through his voice. This he did in an effort to help these 'lost souls' and to teach the group of sitters important concepts in which he, as a teacher, believed.

As this one particular entity entered, he was very violent; he was actually gunning in war! His hand was clenched as if he held a pistol and he cursed, the likes of which I had never heard before, including threats of murder and all sorts of bodily harm, all expressed with the most extreme hatred, fear and resentment. It was plain to see he was thoroughly hypnotized for, as one of the guides who brought him in for help related, he had been killed in World War I, and has continued through these many years, due to the shock incurred at the time, to fight that war in which he died. He was so thoroughly 'locked in' with that shock of death.

What a revelation to myself; it did indeed so scar my psychic that it is unforgettable. We, in the circle, were all too, a bit squeamish with his terror, so realistically was he reliving his warring experience but, after a time, one of the members began talking to him, telling him that the war was over and that he was what is termed 'dead', that he need not kill or fight any longer. He was very reticent to believe at first; he refused to listen but, after a time, he began to relax and give in, listening to our words.

Before long, the poor soul broke down and I have never realized a man could cry so hard, loud and long! It was most pitiful, yet a wonderful thing. There he had had his healing. Before he and the guide left our room, the boy was most appreciative, humble and a little confused but he did realize he had died and that death was not, as he had believed, the end, that it was but a change—another dimension. To think of these poor souls reliving year after year those warring experiences is quite overwhelming, to say the least.

It was a real joy to see him, within the few moments, change so completely; evidently, those who were endeavoring to aid him felt he needed to make contact with some eartheans that could help him. When Dr. Minnough came out of his dead trance state and questioned what had happened, (for a medium is completely unconscious of what takes place when so entranced), he looked down at his (previously very freshly pressed) suit, to find the coat had been wrung as a dishrag by his 'visitor', in his anguish and, as he believed it to be a gun, he twisted it up in a tight knot, pointing it as a gun. No doubt he, and others as well, were aided.

However, the séance room is not the healthiest place to gain knowledge. As our Moderator has often related, one can subconsciously project anything to take place he wishes and most often does so, for most often these voices one hears, of those who enter through the medium's vocal chords are, as He states, actually self-created illusions, thus we would not sanction persons to so visit such spiritualistic séances. But I was, at that time, very busily engaged in doing this type research and am presently glad that I did investigate the various schools of thought—now I know; do realize surely and factually that no others know of or teach this interdimensional Science, the creative, evolutionary science Unarius has brought to earth.

I have often thought, since that revealing witnessing, of the many thousands of similar cases there must be; those boys killed in action who were 'stopped', as it were, in consciousness with the psychic shock in such drastic conclusions. No wonder we hear of the many cases of murders which have taken place, as they often state, when the murderer was, during the time 'blacked out', when the crime was committed as the evil obsession or astral force inflicts and projects his warlike attitudes into the unsuspecting earthean. Man is indeed in need of the truth of these so vital principles Unarius brings whereby he can learn to protect himself from these countless lower astral forces which fill the astral realms. Food for thought, indeed!

We Brag Not

No, we brag not. There is nothing we could state or no claim could there be made for or about this great Mind—the Unarius Moderator—that He would be unable to do; no questions could be posed to him that he would be unable to answer in a frank, practical, logical, scientific reply, regardless of what field or interest may be the topic! Could we say more? And for such a Being, this world is not a desirable place to live; as He often says, "No wonder the spacemen do not land here!" But for any man to conceive the tremendous breadth, width and vast scope of this great Intellect, there is but one way—through understanding, through the complete conceiving of the science which He has brought to the earth and which, in itself, is a major undertaking but man can make the start; he can place himself—in his effort to understand upon a more positive footing than he has expressed in his past lifetimes.

Thus, never lose sight of the fact, dear friend, that as you study, it is a means of attunement unto the vast Infinite Brotherhood and we who can and do help, stand ready at all times to project their Ray Beams of Intelligence, of Power and Light unto the mind of the aspirant! This inner help shall not terminate as He steps from this temporal form he has so created for this purpose but shall be carried on and on. We have been the post-hole diggers for this great Advent, 'The New Age', which shall be carried on throughout the eons of time. This, the present, is but the means of delivering the Message to the Eartheans and to help prepare those so conditioned and ready, to step upon the higher pathway. I, for one, shall be most thankful for him when He releases himself into the worlds of Light, for I have learned what it means for such a Being to be trapped in the body of an earthman and again incur the wraths, the hatreds of the earthmen; and I am sure his Brothers of Light shall likewise welcome that day of his return to them, when He resumes their leadership among them. Those who He heads and teaches are, themselves, far beyond what the earthman calls a Master. This I can state, for I have viewed many times His great Light, often too brilliant to observe as He has come to me to project his great Radiance, the very Intelligence of the Infinite; and to you, dear student, likewise do these Higher Ones come and extend their Powers, each according to the individual need, to his position upon the path, and his ability to understand, and always commensurate to the personal effort which the student, himself, puts forth to conceive from day to day.

May your efforts to learn, from this day forth, be quickened and never-ending for, as you so find Truth, you thus add to your storehouse of the Infinite Self which does live forever. And, as He once taught long ago, there are many, many mansions into which we can ascend as we grow in wisdom. This world and all within it is but fleeting; the knowledge Unarius brings is eternal and shall endure forever. This is the one thing man can take with him always—Infinite Wisdom!

A Psychic Vision

There has existed throughout the ages of time, frequent controversy and question as to exactly who was the model for the famed sculptured bust so often copied and professed to be the young king, Tutankhamen. Some believed it might have been Queen Hatshepsut for, with the headgear then worn, the male and female heads would appear similar. Also, considering the fact that he was her grandson, a physical similarity could have existed.

Interestingly enough, one sensitive lady student, —Velma Wasdell—paid a visit to the Los Angeles County Museum one day in 1963, when this world-traveled and famous bust of the peculiar, ancient pink-marbled quartz of King Tut was to be on display; it was valued at many thousands of dollars. There were, of course, other valuable Egyptian antiques exhibited. Velma must have been especially prompted to go there for she told us after returning, "I spent the entire afternoon among old Egyptian relics, then I spied the statue, the elegant bust of Tut, erected upon a tall pedestal, surrounded by and sitting on a black velvet cloth, right in the middle of the large room; oh, it was so beautiful. The certain spotlights which played upon this most costly piece did it justice, for it looked so real and lifelike, the texture seemed almost soft." "Then," said Velma," as I continued to view it, and lost as I was in the observing, the head slowly turned (or changed) into you, Ioshanna, your living image! You were as Queen Hatshepsut, but I knew it to be you! I became transcended. The spiritual aura with which it was surrounded surpassed by far, any previous manifestation I have experienced." "Oh," she carried on, "It was so lovely, the lights shone not only about it, but from within! Here was all the proof I needed! I was so shaken, I froze in my tracks but knew the long-hidden historical secret had been revealed to me!" "Oh" she said, "It was so elegant, I just wanted it to remain so but, before long, found it had changed back to be just as I had first viewed it—a solid quartz—and I realized, whoever made the bust, sculptured it from Queen Hatshepsut; but, as no writings existed, all things were tallied in pictures, hieroglyphics, etc., thus, many people simply thought the famous bust to have been King Tut." Velma had quite a psychic experience for she was still all aglow when she returned; she had, in her psychic way, learned the truth of the long-hidden historical secret, a mystery which confounded many through the ages. Her eyes sparkled and beamed as she related her realization to us.

Velma had quite a psychic rapport with it, too, because she was with me in that lifetime as one of my pageboys. And speaking of pageboys, here's a cutie on Velma (and she'd not mind my mentioning it, for she has worked it all out) but just to show how factually we relive the past, in minute detail: at one time, she helped us in a personal clerical way and she came with me on an occasion to house-hunt in another city from where we were living. We stayed overnight in a hotel and, as I would look through the ads in the paper I would step to her door to discuss them. On one occasion it was quite late and she answered the door in, of all things, sleepwear that looked exactly like pageboy bloomers, short, blousy and gathered! I said, "Velma, what have you on?" "My nighty," she said, "Why?" I told her they were pageboy garments; she broke up right then and there! She had a good washout, a transcendency, then came peace and a good laugh. She said she had always loved to see pageboys in the movies and was glad to hear that she had served in that capacity with me way back when, but it was good to be freed of that block with the past. I noted the following day, she shopped for new sleep-wear!

I recall at one time, during a cycle being expressed in which I wanted to sew and make garments representing the various countries which I enjoyed at the time for Ernest to photograph, when Velma had need to make a visit and I was just trying on a very extreme and sweeping gown, a representation of something they once wore in India. It has a long, trailing sari that could be draped about one, or simply flung far out behind as a train, brilliant green with much gold braid trim. As she was a very fine seamstress, I knew she would appreciate my handiwork and left it on when she came in. Well, it served to 'tune her back' to a life when she was either, or to both, a handmaiden; or another time when the pageboy for when she glimpsed my costume, she became so weak and limp, she slipped right down onto the floor and there she sat 'til equilibrium could be resumed. A little stream of tears trickled; soon, to the present she returned. Of course, she loved the garment for it reminded her of interesting and exciting times and lives but it did serve to turn back time with her.

Another lifetime Velma, who was one of the handmaidens, was buried alive with her queen. In the present life, little Velma would always look to me as some overseer or the like, not as we had wished she could, as a spiritual teacher desirous of helping her over the rough road of life. But like us all, she was reliving that ever-present past. It was revealed to this entity quite a long time ago that Velma had been with and near me in more than one lifetime and, especially in her 'pageboy' lives, she foolishly, practically worshipped her queen. She admired and adored yet, feared her, as is so often customary with people close to such personages. Thus it was in the present life although there was strong resentment and envy within her; on the other side of the balance, she would have

305

done anything for me, so devoted was she until the negative forces influenced her, so to speak, and she succumbed to their evil obsessions. She was not sufficiently strong to walk the path of Light and it is with compassion we think of her and those who renege—who do not follow along in the plan they have set up for themselves. Long and severe will be the reaping of such karma! Great will be their repercussions and regret in their after-earth life.

The Incredible Master-Plan

Doubtless it is that mankind, or even the most dedicated Truth seeker could possibly envision the complete incredibility of the vast plan—a plan by the Infinite Master Minds of seeking out (through many hundreds of years time) those responsible for bringing about the termination of Jesus' physical life, these persons who prevented mankind from receiving his great Wisdom which He tried to teach and, of gathering together these persons, so-to-speak, preparing them life after life for this present opportunity whereby they may begin to free themselves of this great stigma—a stigma of the worst crime ever perpetrated upon humanity! Only the great and infinitely intelligent Master-Minds could conceive, direct and cause to be motivated, these infinitely vast, time-consuming plans and cycles now being expressed through Unarius; knowledge which will enable these perpetrators to step up on a more positive path of evolution! Yes, great and vast has been the infinitely wise preparation for these individuals!

Heading, of course, this vast Spiritual Organization so responsible for this help and releasement being brought, is the Leader-Master-Mind Himself, called during these earthly visits by different names, Anaxagoras, Akhenaton, Zarathustra, Spinoza, The Nazarene and/or the Moderator of Unarius (now 1969 incarnate).

Thus it is with we two who are so endeavoring to help, to lift, and to reach out to those reaching toward the Light, do we experience a sense of fulfillment. Yet, with all these countless accomplishments, healings, workings out, etc., with those 'who were there', it is but one step in the right direction. Far easier it is for man to 'pick up' or add to his existing load of karma than it is for him to discharge these past negative oscillations. Thus, it requires constant vigilance, awareness, study and, of being 'conscious' of the direction toward which one is progressing! The change-about in direction (oscillation) is so subtle, most often one is completely unaware, until perhaps after another lengthy decline or time spent reverting, he again becomes trapped in the mire of his own making, and once more, he calls out for help to assist him to climb up from the depths into which he so easily and subtly regressed.

And so, dear friend, as attempt is made to climb this never-ending evolutionary pathway into higher and higher states and dimensions, abide ye ever closely to the middle of the road, for the temptations, the thorns, the ties and bonds of the past are ever present to deter, to hinder and to bind man unto the earthworld; worlds far removed from the Heavenly Mansions of which Jesus spoke. It is these Heavenly Mansions the Unariun Moderator refers to as Inner Dimensions or the Infinite Creative Intelligence.

As ye so walk and seek, shall ye ever find in the seeking, the outstretched hand—the mind energies of those who have walked before; that as ye so overcome and attain, ye become more and more infinitely polarized; so shall it be that you, too, shall learn to as Jesus so aptly put it, "Greater things than I have done shall ye also do"—as we learn to integrate personal consciousness with the Infinite.

And so it has been, and has come about in this time and in this age, that the very One upon whom all the hatreds, the vengeance and the evils were directed (in Jerusalem) has now, after two thousand years planning and effort, returned; returned to aid, to help and to teach those responsible for helping bring about his destruction and termination!

The beginning of this effort to help release these

persons from their past evil deeds and karma was first set in motion as He hung on the cross in his death agonies, as He, in his Higher Self, projected the Infinite Light and Powers unto them! These Energies were the instigating element that made it possible for these persons to make this contact with Unarius in the present, whereby they could thusly become receptive to his teachings and start to free themselves of the great stigma of that long-ago time and start upon a more positive evolution in the future. It was He, of course, who caused them to be 'brought back' in the present whereby He could aid them in their efforts—efforts without which these persons would indeed have destroyed themselves for eternity and, no doubt, would have been drawn back into the abstract for dissolution; for there are limitations to the depths into which one can recede before the abstract absorbs such energies. This is indeed 'turning the other cheek' —"For an expressed evil or negation, I'll express to you the positive!" Greater love hath no man!

Thus it is, if one could realize, how pleased we both are with the "Story of the Little Red Box", which contains the testimonials of these persons who have sent us their personally written testimonials which relate their turning about-face; how they have started upon the more positive way after viewing their past errors and evils. What a better world it would be were man to practice the principle of 'turning the other cheek' rather than regenerating the negation in reaction as is so commonly expressed. And could it be that this one simple principle alone were put into effect, in time there would be no need for war and the world in general would become a far better place in which to live. But man constantly regenerates the negative, he adds to the hatreds, resentments from his subconscious oscillation, which is ever from the past!

Thus, look ye not unto the churches, the temples or synagogues to seek ye thy peace, for they are but tombs operated by the minions of the underworlds who would enslave man and entomb him eternally; but look ye instead unto thy secret closet and unto thy 'Great Book of Knowledge' (The Unariun Library) for, within its passages lies the secret key whereby man shall learn to 'Know Thyself'.

We shall look to Unarius as the great Shining Light which will, through the Cosmic Infinite Energies which have been brought through the Emissary's Consciousness, continue to regenerate on earth and which will serve as a lifeline to those so reaching. Let your reach toward it be constant and your grasp firm—for Unarius is the only true way to lead you out of this earth-hell and into a higher world of the future.

Doubt Not

Doubtless, my pointings up and relatings about the great book, "The True Life of Jesus",—of its effects and repercussions with we two, fall short of what they should be and are quite insufficient in description relative to the factual and entire effects which we both experienced and realized. There actually exist no words, however, to so thoroughly convey the complete truth in this most vital conclusion—a conclusion to the Unarius library which this book formed. As was stated, the information in this book brought about a tremendous and earth-shaking addition to all the Unarius works.

The effects of this book could be relative to the feeling one would experience had he somehow been striving throughout his entire lifetime, struggling to climb a tall and steep mountain inch, by inch when, at the conclusion of his life-long climb, he finally arrived at the peak wherefrom he could look out over the top to find his sunlit and peaceful valley, his 'paradise lost'. This one single life's endeavor, however, has been but one small fraction of the eons of time and great effort that has gone into bringing the Unarius Mission up to this point; and even with our sense of fulfillment, knowing our mission to be 'fulfilled', yet there are only certain, comparatively few, persons who have been properly conditioned and prepared for this advent, for their own personal 'second coming'—which the inception of the science does bring about. Yes, it can become the true spiritual awakening for anyone so dedicated to learn the Higher Way—the true Science of living.

For the most part, the peoples of the earthworld are too preoccupied with their material lives to be concerned with their future and spiritual principles; and as our Moderator often says, "It will be many thousands of years before the earthman will be ready to seek such knowledge; for the most part, the world will remain pretty much as it is for there is need for this lower type world for persons just evolving from their lower states.

For those individuals who have prepared themselves to accept, to be receptive to the Unarius texts, there are no limitations to their evolvement and progress. This entity has indeed proven that point!

Now, there are those who shall make some manner or gesture to study the science, to understand this higher way of life, and even those who 'were there' at the tragic historical event in Jerusalem and have, themselves, had realizations of their personal experience in connection with His crucifixion, have factually known momentarily that Jesus has returned as the Unarius Moderator and other truths pertaining to that and other times, who shall at different times, after returning to normal consciousness, find themselves doubting—doubting what they saw, felt, and learned in that fleeting moment of true awareness. Yet this is understandable—and the very purpose of this little inclusion—when we realize that, in those momentary flashes or realizations (illumination) of some past experience, that the past information is oscillating from another source or consciousness other than that which is normally used or expressed. In a flashback or an attunement with some past life experience, the individual is thus receiving the flow-through (oscillation) from the mental or the true self of the person and which oscillation takes place very rarely and he is incompatible with this particular phase relationship but, during the time it is present, he knows factually and definitely it is truth—yet, when he returns to a more normal reactive or subconscious state, may doubt his very self—that of which he previously became so aware. Thus, with this analyzing, you may be helped in your possible times of doubting. With true understanding, all seeming riddles are solvable.

And so, dear friend, if, after you have had a realization, a flashback from some one particular experience then, later on you find yourself doubting what you 'saw', just recall and remember this vital principle of mind function and your doubts will disappear. The reality of the situation may not remain with you for it is now in an out-of-phase relationship with the present. I trust this discussion may help clear up any possible wonderment existing within some students pertaining to these incidents.

The road upward to Truth is never easy but the results and benefits are most rewarding!

That He Grew to Adulthood—Miraculous

Someone asked of me today, "Of all the wonders and wisdom of Unarius, what would you say to be the most important or outstanding, or which will benefit mankind the most?" Well, of course, with such a great, vast and so infinite a message being expressed into the earth especially during the past fifteen years, I would say the fact that it has been distributed into such vast and far-reaching areas and distances, and which now cannot be lost to man as has been done in past eons of times of like expressing, would be a most vital accomplishment. In all previous times, this great Being has left, for the time, his high position as director on the Higher Worlds, to don the body of an earthman to descend into these negative pits called earthworld, as has been in the past, after bringing his Message of Truth and Light to the earthworld, these teachings have been, most often, so distorted and changed, that little resemblance to the Message He brought remains today.

A thorough reading of "The True Life of Jesus" book will give one a good example of how greatly these spiritual teachings have been changed and subjugated as is so related in biblical portrayals; however, Saul and Judas were not the only ones so engaged and guilty. In other previous times, this same changing to suit others wills has been likewise carried on. When these so-called dispensers (pseudo teachers) would come upon concepts inconceivable to them, they would simply change them to something with which they were familiar and build themselves a pedestal, a temple of distorted facts and lies to make their religion attractive to others!

So this entity would think the fact that we have

been successful in having the Message in print, the writings reaching the far corners of the world for posterity, is a most vital fact of no small importance. As the science is all in print, it will be less easy for others to distort and remodel the Infinite Truths. Yet, the fact that our Moderator has endured the great negations, the countless blocks and oppositions constantly directed toward him from the astral negative opponents, that he met and overcame these ever-present efforts against Truth, is indeed the greatest of all miracles. Only a Past Master could have so survived, endured and won his many battles!

No less, really, in greatness is that He brings not only the know-how, the Science and teachings that the earthean may learn how to free himself from his past —the seemingly endless wheel of karma—but also, the truly singular uniqueness of Unarius—ever present with the Word—the Radiant Energy, the Ray Beams, the Light and Power of the very Infinite, the Higher Minds, to help man in his struggle—a struggle which every human must eventually undergo in his evolutionary ascent as he begins his climb from the animal-like homosapien into that of a Spiritual Being —a being which, when his separation process has been achieved (as 'yours truly' has so accomplished), shall not again need to be attracted or pulled back again and again to this your earth world. And comparatively speaking, it is indeed very low on the scale of evolution.

Thus, the accompanying Power or radiating Energy factor would indeed be the most important of all factors and thoroughly unique with Unariuns. Remember, friend reader, this incoming energy is impinged with all writings, with every word expressed from the Center, for the reader, that he may become attuned unto these Higher Minds, who can and do aid the earthman in many ways. This great influencing power for good is ever existent as the student tunes in through the teachings—minus any meditative efforts!

Although this notation is not necessarily relative to the above, yet comes to mind the many persons who quest, "Exactly what does one do to meditate?" and or, "What other preparatory efforts can one express to hasten enlightenment?" May it be said here and now, although the Moderator has voiced it more than once, there is no physical effort or endeavor one can do which serves to aid in this development! Although mention has been made in his earlier writings of meditation, yet He was referring not to the common concept of the word. The best possible effort anyone can put forth is simply to remove one's thoughts from the existing material and physical; in other words, stop the existing oscillation between the subconscious and conscious mind, which constantly takes place. Any conscious effort stops there. Perhaps with some, quiet and restful music may help to bring about relaxation; however, I will state most frankly and factually, this person has never entered into any such efforts!

I have been concerned purely with the teachings as we worked with them—typing, etc., but never have I indulged in any so-called meditative efforts. In fact, truly stating, the many wondrous psychic happenings which I have experienced come completely unaware! For any person to indulge himself in trying to project himself, etc., he is asking for trouble. This is a fine way for lost and lurking entities to latch on—but not so easy for the victim to free himself. Thus, to you who are sincere in your development, spend whatever time you will in effort to study, to learn the Science. Psychic experiences come to us the other way about— from the Inner out—not by conscious effort or direction.

The Time Element Nonexistent With Spirit

Looking back over our experiences of the past fifteen years, I'm deeply impressed with the great planning, the extensive preparation in the past, the much forethought that was evidently extended from the Inner to bring about all that has taken place. I am thinking especially at the moment how, so long before the 'Jose' book (twenty-two years), Glaphira's (symbolic) bracelet was made manifest to me.

First, let it be said, if you have not already read "The True Life of Jesus" and "The Story of the Little Red Box" books, by all means do so, for they carry the most important historical revelations regarding Jesus —his true birth, life, teachings, of his death and return —that have ever been revealed to any man.

It was more than seven years before Ernest and I met, living as I was then in Los Angeles, that I had heard of a certain mystic or sensitive (I'll call her Rose), a spiritual teacher in San Diego who was lecturing weekly in her little temple there. A strong impulse within was sensed to go there and it was on my second visit to her school that her secretary handed me, for no apparent reason that I knew then, a wrapped package with the remark, "I'm prompted to give this to you; it is important and has great significance." Mind you, I had scarcely met the lady. Bear in mind, this teacher (Rose) was, in Jerusalem, Glaphira, the physical mother of Jesus, who gave the babe Jesus to the foster mother, Mary.

At the same time, she also gave Mary the red lacquered chest containing the true identification of Jesus, his birthright papers and one of her two unique bracelets—further identification of Jesus' heritage.

317

Upon opening the package, noting the very wide arm band, I thought, "Well, I'll never wear that," and thought it rather weird; but oddly enough, I never did dispose of it even though I did not care for it. It has two fish with entwined tails embossed.

It was only after the Jesus book was manifest twenty-two years later, that I learned the 'why' of the bracelet. Now, in 1968, is the first time I have even thought about it since that day I received it. Then one evening I was led to relocate it. I was looking for curlers (which I don't use), and I unconsciously pulled out from an unused dark corner in a closet, the box with the long-hidden bracelet. Instantly, the entire picture fell into place. I knew! It all came clear and the feeling sensed was like suddenly a huge jigsaw puzzle all fell into place on its own. This arm-band was, in symbology the bracelet of Glaphira—and this one came from her very place, twenty years before! I showed it to Ernest who had also just learned of the Jesus book. Well, needless to say, for him now too, the pieces were rapidly falling into place like the links in the chain of two thousand years distant.

We had learned many years ago, in fact, during the first year after the mission had been started, that this (sensitive) woman (Rose), although she knows she was a member of Jesus' family, is not aware she had been Jesus' true mother. It was during the time the Unarius Moderator was dictating the last part of the "Venus" book (in 1955) that John, the Revelator, inspired Him and told us it was this woman, Rose who had given birth to the babe Jesus in Jerusalem. He continued, that she was not, in the present lifetime, ready to learn these higher scientific concepts Unarius teaches; thus, we were unable to tell her who she had been. Also, John mentally said she had been in a former lifetime, Nefretiti, the wife of the Pharaoh, Akhnaton (1358 B.C.) and which, as has been related elsewhere, was a life lived by our Moderator. Thus, through this previously formed frequency relationship, He could come to her in Jerusalem as her son, Jesus.

It is in such recallings that bring to mind the long and far-reaching plans and efforts which the Higher Ones expressed in this great work; how, long ago, someone so representing this individual (Rose) was prompted to place with me, this symbolic treasure which would, in the future years, serve (as it has come about) to help form the conclusion of certain important cycles, to furnish for us the final missing and connecting links in this great historical episode; an episode which has extended through eons of time; yes, the epochs through which these endeavors have been carried on could be traced back to Atlantis and even into Lemuria in order to arrive at the beginnings of this great work of Truth on earth.

Then immediately, with the stunned realization of what the bracelet actually symbolized, came also the memory of the 'other' bracelet—one which Ernest had purchased for me during our first years together. This lovely arm band is embossed with, of all things, the bust of Nefretiti!—a personality I have often felt closeness with; and no wonder, for she was, in Egypt, a close relative of Tiyi.*

Yes, on and on do we make these personal contacts, frequencies which attract, bind or repel. Although the Moderator has written, in his own words, in "The Little Red Box" regarding the psychic crisis he experienced in the present life as a mere infant, as He relived the mental and physical torture on the cross on Golgotha, it would seem, too, the great anxiety which was added due to his knowledge of the red box and its contents, the papers and bracelets, etc., yet, his inability to get it was, no doubt, equally as shock-producing and, to such a sensitive as He was then (and still is today—even more so), the anguish surely was multiplied ten thousand times. Thus, it was no wonder it all came out in the screams and cries of the infant Ernest, as he went into near convulsions, in his great anxiety to repossess these vital birth records contained in the Red Box—records that could have changed the very history of the Earth. Now, sixty-three years later, He finds, and repossesses, in symbology, his two-thousand-year lost box and which rings down the curtain on this, our last act.

It was a most significant revelation with Ernest as he brought the box home. I was away at the time and, upon returning and parking the car, He came, as he often does, to the garage. He was very excited and elated; His eyes sparkled and he did not want to wait until I removed my packages from the car but, "Come quickly," he said. "Look what I've found!" He had placed a small table in the center of the room, draped it over with some blue velvet I had, then placed the Red Chest—the long, long lost Red Box upon the velvet. Oh, it did look beautiful to him in his conjunction of the cycles! As he first spied it in the store, time stood still for him; held him spellbound for a time.

So here was his red box, the two-thousand-year lost box which held his identification papers that would have (had they not been stolen from him) proven his true parents, his true heritage and which, too, could have saved religion from becoming the great hoax and substitute for intelligence into which it has presently regressed!

* * * * *

This finding formed the final link in the seemingly endless chain of events which were leading up to this present. Yet all this, too, is but a beginning of yet another larger and greater cycle into the future in time to come on the Inner as the work will be carried on from there. Ever must there be the way-showers to go forth for mankind.

320

*It was during the very first few months of the mission and our togetherness that Ernest attuned to his Higher Consciousness and 'read' for me from my past records, saying that I had lived in one lifetime as the wife of Amenhotep III, Queen Ti, or Tiyi, the mother of Amen IV (who later changed his name to Akhnaton or Ikhnaton). In these revelations, the facts related seemed quite familiar, as though we had always known them, yet not in conscious mind. Again, as we had done previously and at later times, we made the trip to the library as we had not yet settled down sufficiently to purchase such needs as encyclopedia sets, etc., for we knew we would not remain in San Diego for long. Sure enough, as we browsed through the historical books there, it was shown exactly as He saw it from the Inner—Queen Tiyi or Ty, wife of Amenhotep III and mother of Amen IV. We were both excited but not surprised. We had learned to rely on his findings and which we have never found to be in error! (By the way, this was my first introduction to Egyptian history.)

It was these earlier lives lived in contact with Him and, in this case, Akhnaton, that aided greatly in forming a more compatible frequency relationship for future lives as in Jerusalem when He was Jesus, I his espoused and especially in the present, the most important and significant of all lives and missions! Only time will prove the great work accomplished, the Light, the Power transduced into the earthworld, as well as the all-encompassing science He has brought and which will live on through time. In fact, it will take a great deal of time for the work to become widespread (as it shall) in future eons, just as it was true in Jesus' time; His teachings were known and accepted by a comparatively few persons. I believe He said there were only about one hundred and fifty followers during his physical life yet, already we have reached many thousands throughout the lands.

The complete library of Unarius has also been placed in various colleges, libraries, etc., in different parts of the country so that the minions of the underworlds shall not again waylay, distort and destroy the Word—His Message—a message that can change the life for the better of whosoever will conceive the Message of Truth, of Light, and Wisdom, the Higher Way into the many Mansions of which He so often spoke!

My mention of these various lives is noted simply to show how we return time after time in similar families and relationships and for specific purposes and, thus it has been with this one since Lemuria and Atlantis, in Greece, several lifetimes in Persia as a Mitannian Princess, in Japan and in Siam (Thailand) as one of the 'so-called' Royal Temple dancers; with Mohammed in Cairo, as he brought to the world the wisdom necessary at that time, in my effort to serve. Zoroaster, or Zarathustra was another of his works, vivid in my memory, but they have also been distorted until little of his great Truth remains. Yes, on down through the many ages has this one traveled, lived and died, as have you, each one. Jerusalem today seems but a few days distant as these great cycles swing.

As has been mentioned, this, the Unarius Mission, will be—and this is my prediction—the greatest movement ever brought to earth; the plan is vast and far-reaching and to which there is no end! There will be others in time who shall descend to the earth, higher Minds, but we cannot expect to ever entertain upon this earth again, such a Mind as we have had these past sixty-four years. He vows He shall not return. He says of this life, "I'd not send a boy to do a man's job," but we both feel others shall return that He may not need to do so. Yet, these inner worlds, too, are infinite and without number. Such a Being loses himself in serving. However no other Being could have so adequately served in this capacity due to his connections

322

with all who had to do with the crucifixion. He especially returned to help these many persons resolve these negative oscillations and ties.

Although we feel that sufficient of my ties with the past have been severed, there is nothing in this world that holds my interest anymore, that I have earned that Higher Way in the future yet, who can tell how one may feel after spending time there? He may look down upon the struggling eartheans and feel just as did our Beloved One, a sense of pity and compassion for them and again take the dive! And so I shall not say I will never return but, if it does happen, it will not be due to compulsion but rather, from desire—personal will and wish. When we have discarded much of the ego, self becomes quite unimportant—and serving becomes the way; however, we will not be concerned in such abstractions, only that we can serve well our cause here, now, today! As the 'Magnificent One' (a name He was given in Egypt by the people) has related, we two have much work to be done on the Inner Higher Worlds in a few years; thus, it shall be looked forward to with joy and anticipation, knowing that we shall be projecting to each one so endeavoring, our Mind Energies from the Infinite, the transforming Power—eternal.

"THE LITTLE RED BOX AND BRACELETS"

The box and bracelets psychically remanifest in the physical in an almost totally accurate facsimile of the original box and bracelets of Glaphira 2,000 years ago!

Mental Attunement

To show how unified two can become in their actions or thinking, it might be well to relate how, so very often when I think about doing some certain chore or deed, even before I have had the chance to carry out the plan, Ernest has already done it, even though it may be completely foreign to his more normal activities. For instance, just the other day after I had been thinking about a new adding machine, I stopped in a local shop to inquire regarding one of the newer models. Although the antique one I have still operates fine, it is quite noisy and I have been conscious of the sound coming through the walls into his consciousness. I had not spoken a word about it for I try not to concern him with such trivia—when he brought in a Sears magazine with the photo of a fine little instrument just like the one I had been looking at. I hesitated when observing it in the shop due to the type buttons—but here he brings the ad regarding it which was 'on sale' with the words, "I'm going to get you one of these!" He did!

The same happened with a little photo duplicator I have needed. After I had checked a few shops for one—unbeknown to him—here he brings in the advertisement where it may be obtained locally, just as I, too, had located. Very often if he happens to be adding chemicals to the pool, I will stop suddenly with my typing letters and dash out to do it—to find he is just in the process. No separation in consciousness. Any more, I just never know whether what I am attempting to do is something He has already done or whether it's of my own planning, and it's fun to watch the oneness of consciousness. The same, very often, with foodstuffs; what I cook and prepare for him he will say, I was just wishing for that.

Yes, when partners learn eventually to oscillate more from the mental consciousness, there exists a most interesting unified oneness in the physical dimension or activities, which can be most helpful. I never need call him to mealtime—he always gets the mental call the moment I've finished and am ready, regardless of what part of the house he may be in or, if he happens to be away, he will still sense my beckoning and, vice versa—I, his. Yes, mental attunement can be most useful—far, far beyond the small test-provings which the researchers know about.

*　　*　　*　　*　　*

Because some have asked regarding the extent of one's ability to conceive and progress in any one lifetime, let it be said that it is frankly very doubtful that the majority of persons would make all the headway possible in any particular earth life for, in most cases, people are too involved in their own physical material life.

In the case of this entity, as has been mentioned, due to the existing need, the briefness of time to accomplish all things and because of much preparation, she feels as though just about all has been worked out and conceived which has been set up to do. After man actually sets out upon the more progressive pathway, we plan while on the Inner just what we shall accomplish and learn while on this side; and it does seem this has been completely accomplished, other than the remaining testimonial books to be published. But there exists a sense of completeness and peace—a peace possible only through the severance or separation of self from past influences and ties.

The world and all its belongings—all things of the world have come to seem meaningless—as nothing.

They no longer hold my interest. Occasionally, I will wander into a store, an apparel shop, as ladies are wont to do, to try to find a little stimulation and if some garment may appear for the moment, a bit attractive to me, even before I can purchase it interest has already dissipated; the oscillation with these values has all been changed, and they are as naught. Some outfit that would, to the average person, cause reaction and emotion, means nothing to me. I can find nothing to quicken this one—and that's good! The only thing that 'yours truly' can get a little 'charge' with anymore is to see, when it does take place, the post-office box stuffed extra full—orders from new faces —which means others are joining hands in their upward climb and, of course, the letters of testimonial as they relate to us of their happy progress of change, healings, etc. These are the real values and which, I am sure, shall always remain of interest as they are of the spirit, the inner and higher.

Our 'Visitors' still (and shall always) continue to appear now and then but we know They are with us continuously on the Inner—and we need not have to 'see' to believe. When they do appear in consciousness, the lift or transcendency is less in its intensity with me because of the more compatible relationship which has been formed with me. The trance state is usually slight now, as I have been tremendously stepped up in frequency.

Especially if we two speak of some higher aspect, of some abstraction, as Ernest often does, then one or several Spiritual Beings make the attunement as He has attuned unto them and their beautiful, glowing Energy Bodies are viewed, and it always is wonderful to sense. The Power, the heat, Ray beams and Light have become more frequent, stronger and more intense as attunement is made with anyone in need—so much so that any more, even through the letters, the powers flow abundantly as Consciousness is thusly directed toward them.

Yes, the climb up this golden stairway into the future has been a most wonderful one. We look forward to future time on the Inner when life can be lived more fully in Consciousness and in company with the Brothers and Sisters of Light. My one regret —yet it could not really be termed regretful—is that it is utterly impossible to relate in words this tremendous flight out of the dim, distant past into the glorious light-filled Consciousness of the present. What a joy it is to view all things objectively, rather than being involved with them emotionally!

And of our Beloved One who patiently, yet longingly, awaits the time when He shall step from the prison flesh—and indeed, it has been that to such a Soul—to again take up his abode and directorship with the great Spiritual Brotherhood. I am sure it will be a welcomed homecoming! But, for the time, even though the works He had planned to bring to the earthean have all been voiced, written and found their way into print, He continues to carry on the transducing of the Energy Rays, the Powers from the Higher into the earth-plane, to aid each one in touch.

In his particular way, He keeps his finger on the pulse of creation, continues to relate with the scientists on the Inner via his 'objet d'lens', for he has always appreciated fine lenses. He was, as you know, the scientist Spinoza. Thus, his telescopes, cameras (of a large variety), microscopes, binoculars, etc., serve to furnish him a vague interest even to this day. He has a fondness for these things; even though they may not be used, He enjoys handling and the feel of these scientific objects with their intricate lenses, which have enabled man to learn many things. Just last evening, He showed me a view of the glorious Saturn. What a beautiful sight to see, the great silver disc with its rings surrounding it, so clear, sharp and distinct. Such things get one to thinking when we see these heavenly bodies seemingly floating (supposedly) in space. Surely, there can be no greater thought provoker—planets to which man can evolve!

So, as we often reminisce—who else in the entire world has so accomplished? It is not untruth or bragging to state, that with all the efforts of all peoples of all the world together, they do not begin to compare in real, true, lasting value with the works He has brought; for what it actually amounts to is the difference between life and death of the planet earth! This is quite true but, only through conceiving of principle, of personal progress, of inner growth and awareness could one conceive of that vast and incredible fact. All that man does or accomplishes in any one lifetime on earth, in a physical way, advances him very little, if any. It is the spiritual values, when added to his inner nature, that create of him the spiritual being who can and does become godlike; becomes an oscillating polarity with the Infinite Intelligence!

A First True Scientist-Philosopher

I believe it was early in 1966 that Ernest tuned into his own past incarnation, when he lived as Anaxagoras. He saw himself as the great scientist and architect—the one who helped design the Parthenon and the Acropolis. Actually, this philosopher was the father of all of these Ancients and much the wiser; for he had then, as now, the wonderful ability and development of Infinite Consciousness or attunement—which is the great difference! He viewed me as the wife of Anaxagoras, mother of his daughter, Dioneses, of whom he was most fond. The daughter was a most unusually lovely woman; in fact, he said she was so beautiful in both face and form that she became a legend. But she caused her parents much sadness; in fact, she broke her father's heart as she chose the loose way of living and became a famous 'madam', operating a very lavish house of ill repute.

After all this was viewed by the Moderator, we were both naturally anxious that she should make the contact whereby these pasts could be revealed to her and she could discharge the psychic blocks which existed with her from that lifetime and which was, as a result, greatly affecting her present physical life. The guilt retained was influential, causing psychic blockage and mental frustrations. This woman was called 'Freddie' in her present lifetime and was also a very lovely girl. Her writing of wanting to make the trip to California gave us a happy time of anticipation; a desire to again see our daughter of ages past. Freddie had been a Unariun student for a couple of years and knew that here, in this science, were the answers to all life.

Finally the day came for her air trip and arrival.

When she stepped from the car in our driveway, it was to me and, according to her emotions and reactions, to her as well, a day of homecoming although this was our first physical contact. It was such a wonderful feeling, as if she had been away but a short time rather than the twenty-five hundred years! We hugged and cried, just as close relations would do had they been apart for many years, so realistically was the past being relived! I am sure, too, that Ernest 'went back' in time as she embraced him. We three had a few very interesting days. The second day as Freddie and I looked into each others eyes, I said to her, "You know, I see me in your eyes!" She answered, "I see myself in you!" Thus, our past tie and oscillation was quickly severed. During that flash-second, with recognition, cancellation occurred.

Just before Freddie came, Ernest had glimpsed a picture of our three past lives together. Freddie had brought with her, as a gift, of all things—a beautifully packaged box which held an elegantly polished, large sea shell. This served as the key; it attuned the Moderator to that long-ago past, as he said to her, "I see you walking on the seashore as a little girl, picking up shells—a lifetime in Greece about 500 B.C. You were the daughter of the philosopher, Anaxagoras, and Ruth here was your mother, his wife." Then later on, he went on to explain other things of a less positive nature whereby she could discharge these ties with the past, and soon we all had become like strangers. This was working out karma the scientific way.

Sadly enough, however, poor Freddie was not sufficiently brave to face herself—her past. So long as things were viewed or pointed up of a positive nature, she could accept; but so strongly was she locked in with negative forces that she was unable to accept the very blocks that could have changed her life in many ways for the better. And not necessarily to be including something of a negative nature, but so the reader may get the complete picture for the help it may serve him, she again brought about a great sadness to us both. Our hearts were again broken as she was unable to accept the truths pertaining to her past that could have become her salvation, just as she caused us sorrow in Greece.

She soon left for the east and took with her a big chunk of both of us; and to such a Being as is our Emissary, it became a great crisis with him. In her refusal to accept, she turned from the great Light which He offered and the error of her ways and distant past, was only refortified and regenerated. Naturally, her error will follow her always, until she arrives at the point of recognition or acceptance and deals with it in a positive way.

But even worse—this woman committed an even far greater sin unto herself, for she induced several others to join her in her departure and rejoining with the destructive forces! For this, surely Freddie implanted within her psychic great and lasting heavy karma. Of course, this is true for the others who 'went along' upon the downward trail. This is the one great crisis in our lives together—a crisis because it meant that the negative forces were successful with them, but even this, too, can all be lessons in their future if they ever again arrive at the point of turning back, to again begin to seek for the Light—and Truth. However there is a limit to how much man can be helped and aided. The Higher Ones will help and give sufficient opportunity, but when man refuses, time after time, after time, then he has chosen the lower route into oblivion; and each man has the right to choose, he is not coerced or forced; it is ever his personal prerogative! Loud and long will be the cries of these poor souls as they arrive on the inner and realize the great evil so perpetrated.

The actions of these several students nearly cost the Unariun Messenger his life! When one such as He works with an individual in the manner and ways which He did with these certain ones over a long period of time, He has actually given a large portion of himself unto that person. He oscillates his Intelligence unto them, and which is his very Being! Thus, after this oscillation is carried on in this outgoing way for a great length of time and the person reverts, pulls away and joins forces with the dark powers, very critical damage results in a psychic way to such a developed sensitive as is the Unarius Moderator! It is a tragedy beyond words to define. It took us both many months to recuperate from this loss; in fact, it can never be thoroughly overcome—at least, until these persons, in their own time and way, again return to the path of Light and compensate for their great wrongs. To do such a thing to the Emissary surely must be, to the individual herself, unforgivable!

We have often wondered just how many lifetimes, if ever, these people will take to get themselves back up to where they were before rejoining the destructive forces. However, for one ever to get loose or freed from them, once they have locked themselves in such a manner, is indeed quite dubious. It is very possible that these souls may be headed for absorption back into oblivion but we can do no more until such time as they, themselves, would reach and put forth conscious effort toward the Light. And so here again, Freddie was repeating her Grecian negation, in another way, perhaps; but another heartbreak for Him who was once her father—the great Anaxagoras. Not only that, but she (and the others) have, in so doing, caused much of this Power from the Infinite to be made available for the negative factions to be thus channeled, for anything less than Unarius is negative, comparatively speaking.

Yes, these ladies did receive many letters of help from us describing just what was happening to them but they turned a deaf ear. The worst part was, they had all planned for years to help, to work in a physical way with the mission! One had even helped for a few years and was going quite well in her progress, yet when the time of testing came, the challenge was too great, the negative forces too strong and she too weak; she, too, turned from the Light and acquiesced to the influence of the negative astral forces.

In our reminiscing, we have often pondered just how far ahead they could have progressed themselves minus the negation; but we do not permit thoughts to linger for we must, at all times, keep positively attuned and such reminiscing can only lead to a sense of sadness for these poor lost souls! Far better it would have been had they never contacted us than to have taken so much and then reneged and reverted.

The lifetime in which Anaxagoras endeavored to bring to the earth world his great science was in effect, brought to a similar conclusion as it was when He lived the life of Jesus although perhaps less torture was involved beforehand. He was, however, forced to flee because of a trumped-up charge, to live out the rest of his physical life in a cave, and in which he first suffered great illness in his later years until the age of seventy-two, when he died. Ernest viewed this happening himself in one of the many recalls or readings; he saw me, then his wife, coming up the hill to the cave to bring food, where I had finally found him after his escape from those who were endeavoring to bring about his termination, my arrival being too late to be of help.

Perhaps too much space has been taken in this relating but it is of importance and the intent was to impress it emphatically. This crisis, as it has been called, was one we both had to work hard and long to try to eventually overcome. Our compassion for them is great, for we are aware of the eternal repercussions, and their tears of remorse when they arrive on the inner shall surely be constant; and we wonder if their cries for help shall ever be heard or noted again. This was the one reason they were incarnated and brought in touch, in the present life—to be given them this opportunity for which they had so long, begged and pleaded before returning to earth. The true pathway into Infinite Consciousness is very, very narrow and the sincere seeker must be ever aware, else he be overtaken by these negative factions which are ever present; present and awaiting the time when they can, due to laxity, slip in on the negative frequency and influence the seeker of truth. No one is immune! Constant vigilance must ever be maintained!

Of My Physical Earth Life

Although I had not intended to include any relatings regarding my physical life involvements, perhaps a brief outline of endeavors in which I became engaged may serve to help others in some way, who likewise express in what may be termed the average materialistic way of life. Perhaps revealing such personal experiences will serve to prove that, regardless, when man decides to change his ways and self, it can be done! He can, as do my revelations prove, rise from the lowlier depths to heights unheard or unknown! This is my main purpose in the following brief outline of my physical life-trail before meeting Ernest, my beloved husband, the All-Wise One.

Also in these mentions can be seen the miraculous hand of spirit guidance when true need existed, and plain it is to see now, when the Inner prompting was not present, or that I did not await the promptings, were there lessons learned from the existing problems. After all, that is what life is all about—to gain the lessons our problems contain when faced and overcome!

One very unhealthy and health-wrecking habit I did not have to overcome was cigarette-smoking. I can't say that I didn't try, for I have, but just didn't care for it and thank goodness, it was not necessary to have to remove all those negative energies from the psychic—along with those I had incepted from seeing others smoke, for great psychic damage can be impinged through being in contact with the poisonous smoke, even from the smoke of others! But I am sure, along with my personal efforts, the Brotherhood did a great deal of inner work on this old psychic in order that it be even tolerable to our Moderator—the Master Scientist—and to whom such things as tobacco smoke is the worst kind of poison.

I was the first child of nine, born in Indiana; my parents came to California in 1906, when I was age six. At the early age of twelve, I found occupations, during the summer months in the fruit canneries, the fruit dryers, or in some way to earn monies. Father was a hard worker but earned only a menial salary; so, being the eldest, I felt it my duty to help and I was ambitious. I remember well how, while working at the cannery in Pasadena, I would get up very early to get the position nearest the first outlet of fruit on the belt so I could earn more, as we were paid on piecework. So vivid is it still in mind how this very tall lady, Dora, who surely must have been five feet ten inches, for she towered over me and had huge hands which held enough fruit to fill the half-gallon cans with one swoop, always earned top wages; but tiny Ruth—for I was small for my age—strove to keep up with big Dora and, when I made it, was I the proud one! Oh, but I did tire myself out rushing to match her accomplishments but, at the end of the week, her check was no larger than mine—one of my first victories! Then there was the preserve company. I just had to operate the various machines used in this big production operation, but when I worked the jam-filling machine, the automatic suction pump stuck and the boiling berry jam scorched my legs—and I had had enough, for I was convinced I could do it!

As a child of ten years, the piano seemed a 'natural'. After a little practice, I was able to play tunes of my own composition. My granddad, a talented violinist, thought my compositions very good but I could not replay the same one—always was there a new one. But my far-too-severe dad spoiled it all by forcing me to practice, even with the switch—a fine way to treat a person with a little creative ability. He squelched it, but quickly!

337

Whether the following was simply nerve, or just plain ego, one of the incidents that took place during my first (and only) year in high school was a tennis tournament I entered. Can you imagine any person entering a tournament who had never played a game of tennis? Neither can I, but that was what the youngster Ruth, did back there when! Now it seems ridiculous, but I did that very thing. No, certainly not, I didn't win, but lasted the set out! It just looked easy to me and I thought it would be fun. I even thought, when my opponent shook my hand, I'd won! That kid! But this was the kind of courage young Ruth had.

Yes, one year of high school was all I wanted. It seemed uninteresting and monotonous, and my first chance to leave it I did—perhaps not too wisely, for schooling is important to the average person but I doubt if my life would have been any different, even with extensive schooling.

When I tried the laundry, the various ironers fascinated me but only a few weeks served and I had my fill; I was too small and it was very tiring labor; the big shirt pressers were too heavy for that little girl, but she tried! My arms ached but I couldn't give up 'til I had mastered it.

As I look back, I can see the dear devoted mother always washing, ironing or cooking, with a tot in her arms or lap and another on the way. I doubt if many other girls have actually entered into a greater variety of occupations than has this one, for I liked the new and getting into something different after finding I could accomplish it. During the many occupations I have held, I would always tell the employer when applying that I was experienced, for how else would one get a job! There were the variety stores, then the department stores—in various departments; the telephone company bought a few years of my time and, as was most often the case, I climbed right up to one of the top positions—that of supervising. I seemed to make friends wherever I worked but, as soon as I found I could do the work, my interest waned and I would seek elsewhere for a new interest (working out past cycles).

Because my dad would not permit me making friends with boys at home, I found work away from home. I was only sixteen when I was doing house-work for a doctor, his wife, their two mothers and two adult children. I kept up the three-story house, did the shopping, cooking, etc., and had to bake different kinds of bread for practically each one of them! For instance, the doctor would bring home a live goose and ask me if I knew how to prepare it. "Oh, yes, of course," I would say, never admitting I couldn't do anything—and I would always seem to manage. Then before I became eighteen, when dad learned I had been going out to dances, he phoned that he was going to bring me back home; so what to do! I was afraid of him, so told the boy whom I had seen a few times, we should marry. "Okay," said he, and that we did! What a way to enter into marriage—as an escape!

I continued to work to help with the earning, this time at a Japanese store. Within the year, I had saved enough for a down payment on a house—one I just had to build or have built and I drew the plans to the last detail. Soon I found a soda fountain that paid better wages, adding to the nest egg and, before long, I had found a nice lot covered with orange trees and had the little dream house built. It was small, but exactly to my liking and I loved it. To show how exact-ing these memories ring true, I had the outside stucco sprayed with opal ground oyster shell, the nearest thing possible to the glitter of palaces of old! On the walls of the interior, I had insisted they blow big areas of gold dust onto the wet oil paint, which they did; perhaps not too apropos for a small house but I was reliving the past, and gold dust it had to be! The second year, my one and only child came along—Doris. Although I'm not the motherly or family type, I thought her just the most wonderful thing in the world, as do most mothers with their first-born. Her dad worked on the electric rail-cars and at age eight days she was, said the workmen, the youngest passenger they knew—yes, eight days old!

Too ambitious to be a full time mother, after some months I foolishly put her into a day nursery and continued to work—not a good thing for the poor kiddies; they do need, above all else, mother's loving care, attention and presence. That was one of my great errors, for it left its scars with her. As always, when mothers give their kiddies over to others to care for, the poor children cannot reason; they believe the mother does not love or want them. Deep-seated resentment results, and she was no exception. It grew and settled within the child, even to this day although she, too, is now a grandmother! Mothers who may read these lines, above all costs, give your child that one great need—yourself, the nearness of the mother! I can plainly see these resentments which have been reflected on with the daughter's daughter and, no doubt, will not stop there! Oh, that all could have the true light of wisdom (which I did not have then).

One could scarcely expect a marriage entered into as an escape from a parent to be successful and this one was no exception. In my eagerness to help financially to buy furniture, and a car, which had not long been popular at that time (1920), and other necessities, I continued working as a part-time garment saleslady. The business world was attractive to me and I enjoyed the work, the people and most of all, this constant desire to climb to the top existed in whatever it was I chose to do. Here in this large department store in Oakland, I started out as a stock girl, one who cared for garments, etc., the beginners jobs in such a place; after but three months I was clerking in some of the best departments—lingerie, swimwear, then gowns. The store held contests with cash prizes for those who advanced the sales of their particular departments the most. You guessed it, I did win! Regardless of what department they would transfer me into, it would be the same; my sales were stepped up most and which eventually promoted me to assistant buyer and a model. Of course, I liked that phase, and the good wages! At this time, I was twenty-one.

Later, I was called back to Los Angeles as word had come that my mother was ill in the hospital, so I went there to see what I could do to help. During my few days stay, evidently husband Frank must have written while under the 'influence', for word came from him that he was ill. Back to Oakland I dashed to find that he and his brother had been on a few days spree and were simply undergoing the usual hangovers! They both chided about the girls they had been out with, but which to me was no joke when I learned they were joking on the level.

My young heart was broken but we carried on a few years regardless, until things went from bad to worse. The husband completely forgot he was a married man; that few-year cycle completed. After the separation, the Care Center which kept little Doris, then eight, did care for her nicely—much better than I could, having to be away working. The next several years found me in various positions. I did clerical work, office jobs, etc., but liked best to work with the public, for I liked people. I worked as a waitress in several restaurants in Hollywood; for a change, I would take cashier's work, then was asked to do hostess work, which I felt carried some prestige and with better pay.

But looking back now, regardless of where I was or what I did, I seemed to be, like a swimmer, always striving to arrive at the other side. In my strictly physical life during one cycle, I met and was waylaid in any progressive efforts by one who must surely have been obsessed by the underworld entities; a few years of labor and endurance not conducive to progression were spent, yet always can we learn through our experiences; now I can see that person was, no doubt, dope-influenced, as he kept me broke supplying him with funds. In order to escape this individual, who followed me everywhere, I left town, took little Doris, who by then was fourteen, and drove to the mountains near Bishop, California. There, I found a small place, a cafe, the owner of which was looking for someone to manage for a year, and which I did. Doris enjoyed the change in the mountains.

When the season was up, I was then attracted to a place in Pasadena to operate a food dispensing cafe, which was a change and fun. Foolish girl that I was perhaps, one was not enough, so another business was located and obtained in another area, then a third! It was this third location in La Crescenta I called the "Mystic Moon", I just had to spray paint the entire outside of the building, and it was huge, with silver paint!—Past life memories! This was a terrible job. The silver powder would clog up the spray nozzle when I would be at the top of the ladder near the roof! Oh, was I ever glad to get that job done! But I did it! That was the point. I accomplished what I set out to do—surely a man's job! Just the old urge or need to prove to myself I could do it; but it was fun—the people, the dancing, music, etc., and for the most part, a gay time. Then again, came time for change.

Another note of interest to show how, subconsciously, we are drawn again and again to the scene of the crime: at one precise conjunction of cycles, in 1948 I believe, came a sudden need for both a new home and business. I purchased a house in Burbank, but at the time, wondered why it must be so far from my restaurant—about ten miles.

342

Years later, I now find why. The house was within view of the cemetery called Valhalla (a name often referred to as 'Heaven' or 'Paradise'). The 'attraction', too, was a huge golden arch at the entrance, the type the India people use and, to top it off, just to the side of this beautiful gateway was their office which looked much like the gold domed buildings in Mecca! So great was the pull and oscillation when I glanced at those two structures, that my subconscious found the way to jockey me into position to purchase a house whereby they could be viewed daily. These gilded structures reminded me of 'the good old days' in most memorable Mecca and Cairo! So strongly did I oscill-ate with that past, even though it meant driving four times a day, the ten-mile trip, that I succumbed. The ringing of these oscillations, past blocks, ties, etc., will ever and on, win out for, after all, that is all man is— his past; that is, until he begins to learn and conceive the cosmic, interdimensional, creative science where-by he can create of himself a super-being that lives in worlds far removed from this physical planet; far more spiritual, where the inhabitants know these vital principles and live by them! Yes, man is constantly out-picturing his past into the present! However, more than ten years had passed before I realized this for-mer reliving and cancellation eventually took place (via a television viewing) but had I been aware of the Unarius Science, it would have been easy to cancel out the block mentally and instantly without all the physical inconvenience which was incurred in the many trips back and forth. Now, I can use the prin-ciple!

I had met at the last place of business, a kindly man, to whom I was immediately attracted. After these intervening years, I never thought the desire for mar-riage would enter, but it did, and we were. Carlos was a kind, gentle man; he thought a great deal of me and treated me well. We both worked; I, then at a soda fountain in San Pedro. Within the year, the man own-ing the place wanted to sell and we had saved enough that it was possible to purchase it, so I took the res-taurant over, doing the cooking, serving, mixing at the fountain, etc., and the place did very well.

By now, Doris had met and married a man and I was glad for her; but Carlos had a problem. He was a periodic alcoholic! The first time I saw him, he was hanging out of his parked car, 'passed out', his head near the ground, out in front of my cafe. With the aid of others, I helped him in and tried to bring him to. All he would do was laugh foolishly and topple over, so one could say I did not go into that marriage with my eyes closed; I knew what I was getting into! I couldn't depend upon any real help from him at the newly-owned Soda Fountain in San Pedro; I would send him to the store; maybe he would return, but likely not! Thus, after a year had ended there, we took a trip to the mountains at Big Bear; perhaps I felt it might lessen his desire for drink—but it takes more than that! Carlos was, however, even in his worst times, always good-natured and one couldn't get very angry at him as his deep dimples were always show-ing—smiling. (It should be interjected here, regarding this man Carlos whom I married, although I did not know it at the time, but years later, Ernest saw how Carlos, whose given name was Benjamin Arnold, (call-ed Benny) was, in a former lifetime, Benedict Arnold! And the interesting note was, he often asked and even left notes, "Please see that I get a military funeral!" (Of course, it was not possible—although he was a World War I veteran—but his long-hidden problem of the past was quite evident in his frustration that caused him to drink. He even incarnated into a family of the same name—Arnold.)

To take over the Soda Fountain cost only $2,500 at that time and after just twelve months, I sold it to, of all people, an undertaker, for $8,500! (Spirit guidance, of course.) As I related earlier, the visit to the lake put me in contact with a cycle to be expressed there and the visit ended with my signing up to buy the big camp—the twenty-cabin lodge located in eight acres of tall pines. Well, after selling the two properties previously owned, there was sufficient for the large down payment needed for the camp and to the mountains we moved, lock stock and barrel. Now, looking back, it would seem spirit was there attempting to jockey me about to help accumulate a sum for the time when the mission would begin, for we would have to leave the business world and also publish books—no small item.

The first few months at the camp, called Indian Lodge, were interesting and I enjoyed much the work. Guess I've always been a glutton for work but, as was said, these cottages were purchased without inspection. It, no doubt, would have made no difference, but I found many improvements which could be and were made. I laid linoleum on some of the floors, painted other interiors, replaced some oil stoves, also replaced some plumbing equipment, but it was all a pleasure to do, for I was improving something. The places were all kept occupied and I had learned quickly all there was to know about operating a lodge.

Carlos developed a heart condition, the reliving of being shot as Benedict Arnold, and was unable to help but in a few months I had done all the improvements needed; as it was during World War II, help was impossible to obtain. Winter came and much added work was to be done, footpaths to be kept open for guests, all thirty oil stoves to keep in operation. I remember the man Bill, who delivered the oil to me, told someone in my presence, "The first time I saw this lady, she was under the house with a blow torch thawing out the pipes—never saw such a girl!" Yes, I would tackle anything necessary to do and, at a resort such as that, there was plenty to be done! Carlos' heart condition gave much trouble, a thrombosis, and I had to keep him in bed for months on end, to the hospital, etc., then it was felt the high altitude was not conducive to improvement for him and he went down the hill.

A few weeks later as I was bustling about, I met the Real Estate lady who sold me the camp and kiddingly said, "Why don't you sell this place for me?" She took me seriously and, within a few days, had me a buyer. The price offered was some one-third more than I had paid for it, so I accepted and left Big Bear. Not at all a bad deal, for at that time property prices were a big question—with the war raging! Anything could happen and I felt fortunate to have made a good profit. Carlos had been warned by his doctors not to drink; that any alcohol would cause his heart to thrombose and that the third spell would kill him sure; but evidently when one is an alcoholic, even knowing that, they would do it anyway—and which he did. Christmas eve he was, (told one of his friends who knew), standing on the street drinking with a couple of men friends when he slipped down under a parked car and, by the time they carried him into the house, he had drawn his last breath.

It would have been well had the time been right for the work with the mission to start right then, for with my next project, I went directly against guidance! I knew at the time I didn't want to purchase the costly cafe in Glendale; but, to please a friend, I did it. I called it the "Breeze Inn" and I wished every day I could have 'breezed right out'! The equipment was all worn, I found the entire block to be rat-infested, which I had to have all cleaned out as food was served at my place, so I was responsible! Every day held its grief; cooks would fail to show up, a waitress took several sheets from my payroll checkbook, the place was broken into and robbed three times, the cash drawer robbed at other times, but worst of all, the huge ice cream cabinets all needed to be replaced. It cost nearly as much getting all things in order as was the purchase price. Then, after it was completely rejuvenated, the main part of town (of which this location was a part, near three theaters) moved in the other direction! It took quite a while to find a buyer, only to learn, after accepting mostly notes for the place, they, too, were unable to make a go of it and the notes worthless, so I let them call them off. I realized it was just a plain bad deal and I failed to heed that 'still small voice' that wasn't so small at the time. I did feel completely negative with it but simply reacted too hastily.

Soon after I removed myself from this large cafe in Glendale, I purchased a little home at the beach, and for relaxation, enjoyed planting the patio flowers and shrubs. It was there I had the urge to do some cement work. I installed the patio floor, using huge slabs of stone, pouring cement first, then laying the slabs and filling in the cracks with cement from the mixer I had rented. Then there was the barbecue and fireplace; I got specifications and built it as diagrammed, finishing off with a stone block wall! I had become too busy by this time elsewhere (in Real Estate) to finish the last wall of the cement work and ordered the one wall installed by a regular company. After a couple of good windstorms, their wall came crashing down; the one I had built held solid as the day it was built! I suppose I just had to go through all these cycles which related to past lives, lived as a male and as a female.

I shall never forget a time, when mixing and pouring the cement at this house, as I was jockeying the huge stone slabs into place, I looked up at the wooden gate I had just made and hung, and there stood three men just watching me. One I knew was an official at an oil company close by; he had brought his friends to 'show what a woman was doing'—and, they caught me pouring the cement! They just stood silently and shook their heads. The barbecue worked well and I was quite proud of the place when completed.

It was about then I went to a Real Estate school and secured my license, purchased an office and furniture, set up and opened an office in Inglewood. Spirit was pushing, for after only the third day there, a man bought a fine lot I had listed; then before the week was over, I had sold a drugstore for a party and within the month, a large costly house, so now I knew I could do it—and interest no longer existed!

During the few years I was working only single shifts, I enjoyed several different hobbies; one summer brought with it a cycle in which I became absorbed in leather tooling. As I attempted to get my daughter interested in a hobby, I found myself involved in the work with leather and made many wallets, bags, purses, etc., for friends but always would the interest fall away just as soon as I found I could do it well; with success came the sudden cessation to whatever the interest was.

The next summer I had a yen to learn to ice-skate and the indoor rink in Hollywood served to satisfy that wish; it was fun and short-lived but, with dancing, I never tired; and to this day, a good tune inspires me to want to dance, but I become out of breath quickly; with the new psychic which has been formed, too much energy is expended in any physical exertions, so I'll just go with the tide and be quiet.

For what reason then, I did not know, but I had the desire to go to an electronics school; the fee was one hundred dollars and I signed up for the course, studied and learned how to put a radio together. I bought the parts and worked on it day after day and when it was completed and turned on, to hear the music come from the set for the first time, was indeed a thrill! It was most successful, but that was that—no further contacts regarding that interest; even though the school would send us out to certain electronic shops to apply for work, I wasn't inclined that way but I had learned something of energy. Instead, I noted an ad in a local beach paper for an experienced drug clerk. Of course, I had never had such experience but found, after starting on the job, no one knew the difference: I made out quite well.

It was while working at this beach drugstore that I met, at a dance, the man George, whom I soon married. As I related earlier, I went to the desert with him to relive my 'slave' life and also to relive the selling of the iron camels, as one of the 'Brothers' called our milk trucks (in symbology of helping Mohammed get his mission started in Mecca long ago). It was this last year at Lancaster on the desert, before Ernest and I were brought together, that I experienced my first real transcendency—a new cycle; although I was not yet familiar with these experiences, I thought it quite strange; yet, it didn't frighten me. Momentarily, my physical seemed dissociated; however, it did frighten George (my husband then) quite severely, for he got a doctor and ordered heart tests, etc. Of course, no trouble was found—purely psychic. The Brothers had begun to prepare me! Then, after but a few months more in Lancaster, the sudden change and move took place and I was literally drawn to where Ernest was.

For the most part, my material life and finances were not a real concern, although I can say I do know what it is to be without. At one time, in between endeavors, funds ran completely out. A job for either Carlos or me was seemingly impossible to find. My little car stood in the street with flat tires but I had not the price of a patch or for gas. I wrote to one I felt would make me a small loan, with no results. The cupboard held only a couple of wieners when the call came from the waitress Union in San Pedro to come for work. Yes, I know how it feels to be on both sides of the fence but, during those few weeks of lack, I did not become depressed or worried. I seemed to know it would work out; however, I would just not like anyone to believe it was one big velvet path, strewn with rose petals. I have worked hard and usually, double shifts but perhaps in so doing, I have worked out that many more cycles of the past.

Oh, there have been many interests and accomplishments unmentioned. In later years, there was a cycle of sewing. I had never attempted to sew before yet, suddenly I seemed to know how and made several suits, coats, dresses—some beautifully tailored—but, after the completion of about a dozen garments, the cycle was over, and even though material remained, interest no longer existed; the cycle was concluded as suddenly as it came in. The same with art objects; as a hobby a few years past, I was inspired to make pictures whereon ground colored glass was applied and glued. I made a dozen or so for gifts; although painting by number is not really creative, I did enjoy making a few of them, a little knitting of sweaters and needle punchwork but one yearning was unrequited. I have always thought what fun it would be to drape or design clothes on people—dress designing, however, now even that desire has waned. In fact, there are no longings or wishes unfulfilled. As they say, "I've had it!" If I had a choice, to relive it all again, I am sure it would be pretty much the same—with some omissions, of course.

Lest I be misunderstood, this reference is strictly in the physical sense. Of course, I'm most desirous of further and ever-continued inner or spiritual growth and to relate, as does our Moderator, in creative writing from Infinite Consciousness, yet these anticipations exist, not as some strong ego urge or drive; I know, in time, all things shall manifest whatever be the need purposes and plan; however, with Unarius' Channel, as He maintains consciousness with us on earth, there is really no need for such expression from myself. I am sure were there a need and purpose, all things would be fulfilled.

One experience I have often wanted to try—as, have many women—that of the theater. Well, an uncle had been very active in show business and successfully discouraged me from attempting it. However, in December 1953, community plays were held in the desert at Palmdale, so I thought this would be fun and a change; as I heard they were accepting 'readings' for the various parts of a play to be started soon, so I entered my application. As it worked out, I did get the lead part (no other would have appealed), and with rehearsals two or three times a week and the study of parts, etc., it was exciting. Interestingly enough, the others were professional actors; the director (school teacher) had been in show business and the other several male and female actors all believed that I, too, had worked at it before. They kept after me to tell them where I had worked on stage but, when I would insist I hadn't, they wouldn't believe me and thought I was hiding some dark secret about who I was! Well I remember, in the dressing room, the girls would say, "Look at Ruth slap that makeup on so quickly and well and she tries to declare innocence about having done it before!" I couldn't prove differently, that it was my first effort; no matter.

The play went off very well and I did enjoy the week that it ran. That was my last week in the desert and I was on my way to meet Ernest soon—although unknowingly!

These relating's merely serve to prove how, when one has been on the path of evolution for a long time, he has learned many things. Thus, it becomes just a matter of reattuning or reflecting outwardly, repeating this knowledge of the past. I am sure each such activity has served to help discharge the past oscillations with the earthworld. There has been no one or great outstanding achievement in my humble little physical earth life but the various contacts, cycles, workings out, etc., were all necessary adjuncts in my prepara-

351

tion although, as was mentioned, the material life is of no great importance, yet it must be expressed and which contained much proof of the reliving, of the ever-present guidance urging on, all in preparation for that time and day when, through frequency and planning, we were attracted together in the church and practically, within a matter of days, we (and the work) were on the way. The rest I have written first—rather backwards perhaps, but because of the lesser importance of these physical experiences; yet, we could never claim any one day or endeavor since the 15th of February, 1954, unimportant. Each day has held its wonders, brought its great wisdom; the beauty of the Higher Inner Worlds has been entered into and experienced, step by step, and presented to mankind. As has been mentioned, only after much time has elapsed, will man begin to conceive the wonders, the great and life-changing science the Unarius Moderator has brought to mankind.

I, for one, have been the most fortunate person in the world to live so closely with the Light and yet, as the Moderator and the other Higher Ones have often said, man experiences what he has earned; what he has worked and striven for. Thus it is too, that each one can be aided in relationship to his personal efforts.

Could it be that any one word would serve to help, it would be: put foremost in your endeavors, efforts toward the true and lasting, the spiritual values; those spiritual values we do take with us when we leave this vale of tears to retain eternally. May the direction of your evolutionary pathways be ever in the forward motion, the creative, regenerative and progressive way. Again, my one wish and hope for each one who may read these lines is that you, too, may experience through dedication of purpose, the enthralling wonders of the psychic nature this entity has witnessed and become a part of; indefinable and indescribable in earth language as such realizations are experiences of the soul; revelations conveyed beyond the five physical senses and in dimensions above and beyond the third. Through continuous effort to conceive the wisdom of the Ages, the Unarius Science, the reestablishment of the mission of Jesus, the sincere dedicatee shall likewise so experience—and to those persons, our help is ever extended. Seek and, never cease your seeking.

*   *   *   *   *   *

And now, because these mentions of former lives have been rather scattered throughout these pages, perhaps a brief review of some certain past lives and eras which this entity has lived and expressed could prove helpful. A point of interest is in the endeavors and expressions of those with whom she was, in these various lives, then associated. The field which is, being referred to is, of course, Truth, philosophy, science, etc., and which 'set the stage', as it were for her present great metamorphoses, her life, work, and expressions.

For instance, in Atlantis more than 75,000 years ago, as was related to us by the Spiritual Brother, Sharazar, who told how this entity was, at that time, his (and his twin Brother Sharamute's) sister; they, of course, being some of the first purveyors of Truth, of spiritual science etc., to come to planet earth to aid the earthean. Although there were, no doubt, many other earth lives in between, she again later incarnated and became the wife of Amenhotep III, Queen Tiy, mother of Akhnaton—again in the association and contact with the Intellects from the Higher worlds. This life of 1557 B.C. was one during which Akhnaton was, of course, the harbinger, the forerunner of great wisdom and science, philosophy and poetry; thus, here again, the contact with the oscillations of

353

Energy, Light and powers from the Inner was carried on, which was the great instigating factor in her personal spiritual development and preparation.

Another contact with these Higher Minds and Forces of the Inner worlds was during the life which I lived in contact with Moses—as he was under the care of the princess who found him in the bulrushes (the very first scene which the Moderator brought forth from my past). Although Moses possibly did not teach this creative science of Unarius, his mission was one which was inspired by the Inner and especially adaptable for the people of that time and era. As it would be realized by anyone, that a following of the size which Moses led and in years later, abiding by his Mosaic laws, their leader would have had to have had the Inner help of the spiritual worlds to have made it all possible.

It is only through and with this great and constant Inner Energy and Spiritual help that any such work or movement beneficial to mankind gains such momentum and endures throughout the ages, as have the teachings of Moses. Thus, it was the Spiritual Self of Moses that also served as a polarity with this entity at that time, the Inner Energies from the Higher thus oscillating with her whereby she could again relate with these most vitally important Higher Powers. (Not that Unarius agrees with all Moses taught—not at all; but here again, an instance of how one's teachings are, through time, changed by mankind; nor was Moses the developed Being as is our present-day Emissary, the Moderator.)

As it has also been mentioned how, in the time and life of Anaxagoras (500 B.C.)—the first Master Mind to appear on earth for so long a period of time —this entity again incarnated and became his wife whose name was, at that time, Nada, the mother of their daughter Dioneses and it was Nada and Dioneses who founded the Dionesean cultures of Greece at that time through their schools of personal expression, body grace, the dance, etc. This was another close relationship and association with this great Infinite Wisdom, Power and Light. Another contact and close association with this great Infinite Wisdom and Energy, with the Intellects of the Higher Worlds incarnate on earth, was her life with Mohammed, as she lived the life of his wife Khadija, in her effort to help in his spiritual expressionary endeavors. Again, during the lifetime as the espoused of Jesus, etc., and we are all familiar with the great Infinite Powers which Jesus channeled and which would, in effect, oscillate unto her—Mary; more or further preparation for the present.

The point being made here is simply to show the great and lengthy preparation necessary to help bring this one up to such a point and position, spiritually speaking, that the great work of the present with both myself and the Unarius mission could be manifest; how, in life after life, the conditioning, learning and preparation was carried on and on, all this, too, in planning and preparation that the entity Ruth could become compatible or act as a polarity with the Moderator in the present—in this, the greatest of all missions and teachings brought to earth.

I am not conscious of how much, or how many times I may have reverted and possibly fallen back, but it would be a rare evolution for one to always move forward and to ever maintain the regenerative attitude; at least, until such person himself had so arrived at such state of Infinite Consciousness awareness and complete compatibility with the Infinite, etc.

However, in my mention of these several specific lifetimes, they were, especially, ones that needed to be polarized again in this, the present life, to be objectified and cancelled out; thus, with the countless lives and eons past, has this one viewed glimpses of these lives and expressions which has made it all possible

355

so that now the Higher Ones can enter into Consciousness here to carry on; that they, in their visits now so frequent, can appear to me as brilliant luminosities and, with transcending power, they come to help polarize and project the Radiant Energies used, in an outgoing way, to the countless students with whom we work.

That I have lived and served as queen, as pharaoh or as any political official in any other capacity is unimportant so far as real and lasting benefits or values are concerned. They all had to be worked out, severed from consciousness and cancelled out; but rather, it is the spiritual contacts with these Higher Personages that have played a most important part and the one vital involvement which has made the present progress, the rebirth and expressions all possible.

My effort here in this notation is simply to point up the eons of preparation and planning which was necessary to bring about—in my personal humble part played—the awareness, the conceiving of principle, and the efforts expressed in these most monumental Unariun works. And again we relate how it will take mankind (as a whole) many years into the future before he can become ready to incept this life-changing science.

He Speaks With the Voice of an Angel

Quite often it is that, as we sit viewing a 'silent picture' on television, possibly with the sound turned off to await opportunity to view something worthwhile, a scene may come into his view on the screen which will prompt some esthetic and heavenly verse and He will voice it. Sometimes I can catch it on paper but many times the words slip in so quickly unannounced, that the next second they are gone. Often the beauty and transcendency that is brought with them prevents me from arising to get the pen!

Just last evening as some discomfort was being mentioned—for this is a most miserable world for He who has been accustomed to living in the Energy Worlds of Light, I viewed one of our very High Spiritual Beings as He came into Consciousness—the large, blue-white Luminosity—and I mentioned it to Him as it was just beside his chair and He said, "Oh, I shall be glad when they take me out with them for this is such a negative world, undesirous of Wisdom." "But," I replied, "just think of the many persons you have aided and who, in the future eons of time, shall read your wonderful science and, even more, of the great induction of Infinite Energy that has been brought into the world through your Consciousness—Light that will regenerate throughout thousands of years into the future!" "Yes," He said, "That in itself is the one thing that makes it all worth the while," continuing—

> "I, who have braved this hell have done so
> that it may be said:
> Those who have wept at Heaven's door
> have not been unheard."

357

The Shining Presence Continues to Reappear!

November 8, 1968—Just about the time I begin to think I've seen these beauteous personalities (Lights) in all their various sizes, shapes, intensities and colors, I again find another plateau, for surely, they are infinitely varied and limitless in description.

Last night, as I was going through a new edition of one of the Pulse of Creation books now being reprinted, just before sleep, one of the Higher Ones popped into my consciousness with an intensity and depth of color I've never before viewed. The manner, too, was seemingly as if the luminosity exploded right inside my head! The brilliant Light seemed as if it was solid; it was a deep vivid gold, almost as the sun, and equally bright! The Light seemed to sort of unfold or materialize in my mind unexpectedly. With it came the beautiful feeling of love—an outpouring of oneness impossible to describe. Oh, I was enthralled. The heavenly rapture lasted some moments and each time I would think of it later, to recall, the sensation of this Infinite Oneness was again existent. To complete the picture, mention should be made of the many others of less intensity who projected their Lights after the very brilliant orange Erosean made the attunement. After the initial realization had passed, there came into view, literally hundreds, maybe thousands (I have no way to tell) of luminosities of lesser hue. They were all sizes of brilliance, similar to looking into the sky on a clear night when no bright moon is out to dim the view of the stars. In the distant background existed great sheets or clouds of soft radiance. Truly, this is heaven on earth! I just did not wish to sleep at all last night so I could carry, in consciousness, all these wonders!

As I related it to Ernest the next morning—although I did want so much to dash into his room to tell him when it happened, for it was such a rare and unusual phenomenon but I resisted, knowing how very occupied He is while his body sleeps—teaching on other worlds—He said, "Oh, you had a most Advanced Being pay you a visit, didn't you?" "Yes," He continued, "I know He was one of the old Lemurians, and I know just who!" Before I had even begun to describe this High Presence, Ernest said, as He was in contact mentally, "The Light seemed solid to you, didn't it?" Oh, yes, his ability to attune to whatever one may be thinking is incredible to most persons; but as I was recalling to him my feelings experienced at the time, consciousness of this Presence was again sensed and we both became transcended, an indefinable upliftment. Our psychic selves were right in attunement with this great, great Soul who had made the contact, and, which was in fact, as near to a physical materialization as could be.

If you, the reader, may feel I have taken too much space to relate these visitations from a Most High World, it is because I am hoping that, through my consciousness with the experience and in attunement with it, you too may experience the upliftment, the attunement, even if only partially, the joy which was my great privilege to so experience.

Again, such phenomena cannot be properly put into words but must be realized, experienced, to fully appreciate. When it was said some pages back, that the very door of Heaven had been opened unto me, that the seemingly great distance had been spanned in one brief fraction of a second, it is most factually true, as was here manifest. Man creates his own limitations; he refuses to enter into a better future simply because he is too preoccupied with his material earth life; but you, the sincere devotee can likewise experience, can also know of this infinite oneness as you travel the pathway of Truth with us—the very, very narrow road of learning into infinite vistas of the future, into that glorious rainbow-hued kaleidoscope so infinitely filled with Radiant Energies—and which some have called God. Yes, we can, and I have attuned unto the Most High Beings, the Archangels themselves as They come to us—and it is Heaven! Thank you, thank you, Beloved Brother. Do come again some time!

Further Proof

February 7, 1969,—And now, this very evening, as I was collating a few lessons for posting, my vision was attracted to a few words on one of the pages; it read: "Jesus was born in ordinary circumstances; his father was Annanias (Herod Antipas) . . ."

I had, of course, in the past few months read in the "Life of Jesus" book all about Herod's son being the true and illegitimate father of Jesus, and it was a most gratifying revelation to read it from another's writings; but I had not realized that the Moderator was aware of Annanias being Antipas—which his writing in the lesson printed several years ago does serve to prove! He voiced the fact that it was Annanias but I, personally, was not aware that He, Annanias, was also called Antipas and was Herod's son, so now, to find the Moderator had actually included it in his lessons, copyrighted years ago was, to me another shot in the arm, as the saying goes—another proof. These findings always cause me to reminisce, to realize more and more the vast and distant 'forehand-planning that has gone into this tremendous work. I know, too, how very much it can mean to others, both in the present and in the future to come—these added proofs!

Yes, I'm sure in the distant future this great book, "The True Life of Jesus", shall become the spring-board which will unlock the door of man's past, of the countless thousands who now retain their old religious ties, those bound to their pagan practices, their false gods and symbologies, their superstitions in which they become so hypnotically imbued, but will, in time, become a thing of the past as Truth becomes known; and again, Unarius vindicated for Smyth, in his book, wrote from the inspirational impulses of Saul, this tremendously important document of fact; fact, that should cause any religionist to leave his idolatrous false-god-worship and belief and start upon a more realistic and progressive evolution into the future.

It may be well to also point up, due to the great controversy of the place of Jesus' birth and which has been mentioned in the Moderator's writings, that Jesus was born in the temple in Jerusalem. The old Pope, Anasthasias II, having added the 'attractive' manger animal-stall bit as his place of birth to help build his false religion; but would it not be a most natural thing for Glaphira to have gone to the temple for this birth to take place, she, knowing of old King Herod's anger over her son's association with her? It was, in fact, the only safe place for them! Some certain maps of Jerusalem (in the Bible) even designate and show 'The Women's Quarters', a large section set apart for the hospital and a place where women who became pregnant, due to the religious rites, could go; as they believed, which the priests taught, that all unmarried women must, after each monthly cycle, so indulge in sexual relationship with the priest, all in the name of their god Jehovah, to be so-called cleansed or purified, the old priests supposedly representing their god! Very often, as the women became pregnant during these 'rites', they would, of course, have such need for hospitals and thus, the temple served as both hospital and a place to rear the babes, some whose fathers were the priests.

This was the case with the babe Jesus, or Jose, as he was called. Glaphira could feel quite safe within the walls of the temple, possibly the only place where old Herod would not run her down! And so the mysteries and false beliefs have all been borne into the true light of understanding. In fact, there was really nothing mysterious about his birth or his entire life, only that He was not understood. His philosophy of life was distorted until little, if any, of the true wisdom He taught remains.

Another point of interest along this line of Jesus' birth is pertaining to the individual who was led to obtain for us, this great Jose book. His name is Cleedos Higgins, as I have mentioned elsewhere, who was a woman in his past Jerusalem lifetime—a midwife to Glaphira, who helped care for the babe Jesus in his first months on earth. This man (a woman in that life) brings to us the word (proof) of that particular time and happenings! It was as if Cleete was silently saying, "I was there, and I know, and here's the proof; it was the temple where He was born and I cut the umbilical cord and helped nurse or care for him in his infancy." Cleedos was so impressed with the book that, for several weeks on end at the weekly group-meeting which he and a few former Jerusalemites attend, he would talk of the book and the story. He kept trying to get the others interested to read it as it meant much to him, just as it would to anyone who had lived there or who had heard the Master teach, etc., but the others paid little attention to Cleete and his book which he continued to bring; no one cared to read it, they simply put little importance on what he said.

That is, they did not, until Cleedos wrote to me about it and I was inspired to read the book, which he sent and, with our recommendations, then the others were most anxious to have it too. It must not be omitted either of the strong and continuous urge Cleedos has sensed for several years on end, in fact, most of his lifetime, he has written, "If I could only contact Jesus, my life's dream would be fulfilled." He has always sensed this urgency or inner knowing, which he felt to be the urge to make the contact and which he did, one day at a small group meeting at a park one Father's Day, when we held a surprise meeting for Ernest.

Equally as important in analyzing the entire situation regarding this facet is the fact that now that Cleedos has delivered his important document, the book, he no longer attends the group meetings which he had previously attended for seven or eight years. He tithed a very substantial sum monthly to the mission; now that his objective materialized, that too has come to a conclusion. This is being mentioned to show simply how, when cycles swing, many things change. This is the one thing he came to earth to do and it is doubtful that he even studies his texts any longer, so complete and 'finished' with his little mission does he feel; but, of course, he is a very foolish person not to continue to seek the knowledge he could otherwise gain.

For myself, I have related previously how life has been quite different since this 'proving'—the proof the Jose book carries—proof not only of the truth regarding Jesus but that much the Moderator has brought and instituted in the Unariun texts has been vindicated. The book agrees completely and thoroughly with the Science He again teaches. For me, the lid was off! That ancient, distant past from that very first day of reading, a great new cycle has taken place. All past enigmas pertaining to Jesus, his birth, life and death are now revealed in this marvelous book of fact written so long ago (seventy years) especially for this specific purpose and time. It is, of course, all a wonderful part of the great plan and mission; and now again this day, my consciousness is drawn to a mention in the text of #2 Lesson which serves to show how Ernest knew, too, that Annanias was Herod Antipas—even those several years past, long before the Jose book came to us. I am unable to put into words what these vindications do for me but I just love these proofs and do trust that they serve to help prove to the reader as well and serve to stop up a few more loopholes in this vast wonderment of the past.

If it is felt that I have spoken too much or too often about this incredible manifestation, it is because my effort is to impress with the reader, the truly great historical importance.

It is doubtful that there exists any topic upon which more books or stories have been written or interest placed than that of the various points in the life of the man Jesus. Now in this one book, "The True Life of Jesus", man can learn all the true facts, all superstitions removed and naught but fact remains (other than possibly a few slight and unimportant irregularities): Saul and Judas did portray Truth to the medium Smyth, and for which we both here shall be eternally grateful—which, of course, was an all-important part of the Unariun mission, the capstone of all that has previously been brought, to form the incredible, never-before-equaled Science—the Unarius library.

For All Problems—A Solution

February 17, 1969—A good example of how the Unariun Moderator functions from the inner, working with the earthman where possible was factually demonstrated to me again just a few days ago. He has been, as would any scientist be, quite concerned about the drastic catastrophe, the oil-well drain into the ocean water. The reader has, no doubt, read about this devastating situation and, as always, Ernest will instantly become aware of the solution. In most cases, it is not easy to get to the proper persons or channels whereby his solution would be heard, however, he was relating to me after a television viewing of the great extent of damage being done to the wildlife, seaweed, fish, etc., a proper and effective solution to their present problem.

He suggested they could obtain and lower into the water over their drilling areas a huge steel tank; this could be done in sections or rings, then in case of a leak, the oil would simply be drained into the tank the rings formed and pumped out in case of a rapid drain. Well, I knew it would work and felt relieved that here was a true and could be effective solution to not only this one critical situation but in the many that could result in the future. As I have a friend connected with oil, influential with the officials there, I thought I would call him and relate this wonderful solution of which the Moderator had become aware, when the following thoughts were: "They may not be receptive on the conscious or physical level but He can work with them on the Inner and relate it to them." I was pacified that this was the better way.

Sure enough, today's paper carried the story of a realized solution—Ernest's plan! He was, of course, delighted to read it, knowing proper contact had been made and his description put across, and that they intend to carry it through! Indeed, He has been instrumental in many ways and times for the good of the people and country, however, it is not always they heed or will be receptive. But it is wonderful to watch.

As has been mentioned, there are no unanswerable or insoluble problems with such a Mind. He could relate to the doctors, etc., many cures for their present-day incurables, but who of them would listen? Besides, if the patients of the doctors were cured, wherefrom would their incomes be derived, and just how many would stand still to have their very high and self-erected pedestals lowered? Moreover, they would be unable to understand! No, man must learn the slow and hard way his discoveries, by accident so they think, not knowing there are Higher Minds working with them when possible! So we're glad they heeded the solution to the oil-covered water, as well as many other problems of the past which the great Cosmic Brotherhood of Unarius has aided in their solutions and needs. Much, much more could be done—were they but ready to listen and to conceive.

An Anticlimax to All Previous Visions

February 22, 1969—And now this very evening's inner experiences have topped by far anything before psychically sensed by myself. As was mentioned earlier, in my meager efforts to describe some of the Visitations of the Higher Beings—that which we term, in a physical sense, 'size' of this Being was relative to one's awareness, development or ability to conceive. This night has, however, proven that fact as my great Light, the one I term the Moderator in his Higher Self, or the Christ Self, drifted into my consciousness.

Most prominent and of a diamond-like brilliance, I viewed the centermost self, the concentrated area in the middle of this great electronic configuration or mechanism so pulsating, oscillating and projecting its golden thread-like streamers, each ending in its burst of star-like sparks—the entire surrounding area of the luminosity filled my entire bedroom! I had previously made mention that, although the size of the Visitor seemed in my consciousness about two to three feet in diameter and that I felt if viewed from a higher awareness, or with greater degree of oneness or attunement, it could possibly seem in size, to completely fill a room, or even more so. Thus, it has happened just so, and fill my entire bedroom it did! The whole ceiling was illumined with the phosphorus cloud-like luminosity as the Super Being remained in contact for the greatest length of time I've ever sensed it. Beautiful to behold, transcending and awe-inspiring, it left me with a consciousness of which there are no words to describe. At this sensing, it seemed I actually became one with it all as it 'breathed' intelligence unto me.

The duration must have been at least ten minutes

that it remained in touch, and it did seem there was no separation between this and the Inner world—it was indeed torn asunder here and now. Vivid is the recall of my thoughts, "Oh, how I wish these moments could be shared with many persons!"

Then after its lessening, it slowly drifted out of range and the entire ceiling was supercharged with a fog-like cloud of phosphorus pulsating energy. Oh, how I wish it were possible to photograph such phenomena. Although in the many past viewings, the different shafts, pillars, etc., of light have appeared at some one or various places in the room behind me, in the ceiling or corners, here tonight there seemed to come from within my very being or consciousness (aura) a large ray, a beam of light which extended outward. All previous notings of this nature were sensed in other areas or direction but, now the Light came from within—outwardly projecting!

The entire pyrotechnics brought about a new and greater expanse of consciousness, a tremendous feeling of awe and a feeling, 'yesterday I knew nothing'! Yet, how very much more is there beyond and in the future to learn, to conceive and to experience as we tread this golden pathway into the stars. The beautiful Spiritual Ones did indeed give cause for me this night to become at one with them—a night to ever remember. It was truly the most remarkable and outstanding experience this entity has ever encountered or conceived.

Beloved Ones—for making these treasured moments possible, thank you, thank you, and I love you! After all, surely it is love in its purest and truest form They bring into this dimension. And I'm sure all this intelligent Energy so oscillated does not terminate here with me but becomes an oscillating facsimile, a part of this Higher Self to be projected out unto others so like-wise receptive and seeking, in time, as we go our way and walk the narrow, steep and rugged pathway. Indeed, I am on Heaven's Way!

And you, dear ones, who read these lines, as you tune into these relatings, in this consciousness, may you likewise receive of this oscillation from this reservoir of infinite Radiant Energy so directed here. I am sure some of you shall likewise become aware, possibly not to this same extent; however, a most beneficial effect can be thus oscillated, and whether or not one has been made aware, a certain benefit is derived regardless. Energy must move, must oscillate; it cannot be stagnant. May your personal intake of this Infinite Intelligence be most generous as you incept this great Concept—the Unariun Principle.

This relating just mentioned almost seems a sacrilege to attempt to bring it down into the physical word form. I wonder how many of these Ascended Ones joined in to so express! Yet Their abilities are far, far beyond our scope or ability of analysis. But, ah, this glorious experience—a once-in-a-millennium happening! May it be that I shall always prove worthy to serve the Infinite Intelligence in my own small, humble way.

*　　*　　*　　*　　*

Should, perchance, some reader of these pages not have read the beautiful book of verse by our Emissary titled, "The Anthenium", there is a most delightful experience in store. They are exquisite gems of truth and wisdom, portraying profoundly the vast and Infinite Mind of the One we call 'The Moderator'.

Of my favorites from this book, one He wrote to this entity, I will include herein, as it portrays 'recalls' of past eons, preparation for the Unarius Mission (which we have just discussed):

370

Dearest — Once again you've come to me
    from out of space into my starlit night
Borne swiftly by the magic wings of destiny
    into my waiting, longing arms.
Eons ago it was we were together
    the misty tides of time and place
Alone do hold the things of all of this, our
    love and laughter of a bygone day.
Could it be that once we walked together
    there beside the reeded Nile
And heard a nightbird softly call
To watch the stars fade into rosy dawn
But this I know that e'er the time or place
    it was, we were together
For us, love's golden alchemy has blended
    all things of life and Immortality.
And now you've come to me my love,
        a guiding star to light my darkening path
To show my heart a Shining way —
        a way to be my strongest staff
And find our Heaven far above.
Dark was the hour when hope had flown
    and in a leadened sky my sun sank down
My wounded feet had groped among the stones,
    the sight of all things good,
Was blinded by a thorny crown.
Now breaks a new resplendent day,
        a day no weal or woe to mar its Light
And in all life, our love has come to stay
        to turn all blackness to a starry night.
The shining Light 'round your head
        a halo of the stars
    Composed of all the things of earth and sky
        and by this Light my soul is led.

Time, tide, and trails—ever do they cross and criss-cross, again and again, ever to meet their source —ever and on until the time when man will look within—within himself, with recognition, with understanding and with the inner knowing, with realization of what man truly is in reality and truth; how he is brought back again and again, given the opportunity to free himself of his past, to rid himself of his error, so long in the making and in the living and reliving, of which only the stars and their dwellers would know the numbers of times of these repeat relivings!

But lo, there comes the time of each man for his awakening, the time when he, too, will come to know that he—*no longer need be the victim of his past*— whereby he, too, can step from this seemingly eternal treadmill-like existence; and with the severance of these age-old ties of the past, he will seek new avenues, new channels of experience and life; he will seek and find the knowledge that sets him free—free to travel and roam the infinite vistas of worlds beyond worlds—worlds far beyond man's most imaginative dreams! This entity, then, stands firm in the exemplification and proof of this wondrous science—the Truth and Principle so brought to mankind through the complete selflessness of our Beloved Moderator and the vast Cosmic Interdimensional Brotherhood of Unarius. It has worked for me—and it can work for you!

Mostly Feminine Workings Out

Because of the fact that one who has read through the manuscript has questioned regarding the male lives, saying that only one was mentioned and what about the lifetimes lived in the masculine gender in my personal résumé, herein, let it be said: it is exactly as our Moderator has portrayed it in the various concepts, that the individual sets up, during his stay on the Inner, exactly what he will work out when he returns, certain repeat cycles and patterns and then, upon returning to earth, this he does. It is not that man repeats every cycle he has ever lived, for evolution does not work so rapidly, but rather, inch by inch, we might say. Thus it is, or has been, that these particular cycles brought more clearly into focus were, no doubt, those which I had previously outlined and designated that needed the re-contacting or focusing into conscious mind again. No doubt, there were many thousands of former lives lived and possibly most worked out; in fact, it is very likely that this was done, otherwise, I would not have been able to take this great step 'over the bridge' into the future that has been so expressed.

It should be pointed up, too, that certain cycles can be discharged without the conscious realization, such as the several lives in which I experienced a great discharge but had no awareness of whether I was, in that particular lifetime, in the body of a male or a female, and which is factually far less relevant than most believe. It is, after all, the lessons gained from the experience that count. And in reply to this interested student, let it be said, too, that it was mentioned by Jacobi (Einstein) on one occasion that I had lived as, and he mentioned several including a governor, a priest and other positions occupied only by the men. Then, too, and most naturally so, there were countless former lives lived—hundreds of them which were simply normal earth lives and in which no particular critical blocks, shocks or workings out were primarily necessary to objectify in the present. It should also be noted that as was mentioned, for instance, as I was confronted with various different structures, buildings, as in the park, the library, the city hall, etc., which for no physical or apparent reason brought the flood of tears and these times, too, could have been lived in the body of a male—I had no way of knowing other than that the reaction was there and it was evidently unnecessary to know just what, where, or whence came the familiarity or attunement—suffice that the objectification and polarization were in the present. (I trust this may help others who may have similar wonderments.)

The average earth person will, for the most part, very likely be working on but one past life and will very often carry on into several subsequent lifetimes to try to sever and discharge the negative content of just the one life—but when one steps up on a more progressive pathway, this regenerative process can be stepped up greatly and, instead the individual can work out or cancel out several or many negative portents from various previous life cycles.

No Limitations!

The foregoing lines—in fact this entire book—has been given for the sole purpose to prove not only the Truth of the Unarius Science but, moreover, how factually and without fail man does constantly relive and repeat his past or former lives and the experiences thereof. This is the prime point that I have so endeavored to bring home to the reader. When man realizes that his every act deed and thought shall again be by himself, face to face, as experience coming to him, he shall indeed start upon a more positive way of living. And if perchance you may feel too great length has been gone into in relating our particular relivings, it was due to the vital importance of it all. There surely could be no greater significance than the truth of Jesus' return! And these various and numerous facts, our portrayals and pointings out here do prove beyond any shadow of a doubt that He has kept his word. Jesus has done exactly as He prophesied He would do—Returned (with his espoused or polarity, Mary), and with His Host of Angels.

And I, too, now personally share in the very Presence—the company of these Higher Angelic Beings. I have learned to walk with Them in spreading the Light and the Truth; Truth that will make man free—free of his age-old past, his ties, bonds and fetters that have, since man's beginning of life on earth, bound him. Incept, dear one, this great and wondrous knowledge of Unarius—wisdom that can and will, with persistence to learn, release you from the invisible prison in which all men of the earth are presently enslaved. Yes, man is indeed a slave to his past. This is the one reason our Emissary has taken this descent into this (to Him) lower hell-world. As he has often said, "Man need not fear 'going to hell' for he is living in it here and now!"

Yes, Unarius is man's salvation—the way to save man from himself, from his past, for if he does not change the course of this retrograde, the regressing inclination so presently existing, then surely he shall die. He shall pass on unto oblivion—the abstract—from whence there is no escape. But the opportunity exists for any person. The Unariun Moderator has brought to the earth the wherewithal, the know-how, that man can use this knowledge as a leverage, as a lifesaver to grasp, and that as he conceives, step by step, shall he be brought up from out these pits of the past, of negation, of fear, misery and of suffering into a new world of understanding, a world of light, where life becomes meaningful and man becomes his own master, no longer a slave to his past. He learns from this vast New Age Science how he, too, can become one of the beacons in the night shining his little light unto others as he learns to oscillate with and relate to the Infinite Intelligence rather than from his past, subconscious, now so expressed.

Moreover, no person need be without this great wisdom; it can be made available for anyone in any walk of life—regardless of his financial circumstances. The choice is yours, today, tomorrow, and always as to which direction you choose to progress; and each one is progressing in one direction or the other! —(forward or reverting). Not only is the know-how furnished to man but the Inner help, the Infinite Rays of Light shall be directed to help and to aid any seeker so endeavoring to learn this higher way of life. Your request for and your study of the teachings does so set in motion this Inner help so directed—help that can and does make Angels from devils and Saints from demons.

And there are no limitations to this progressive evolving! This I have surely proven in my own personal instance and life. And even now, as I've so recently experienced wonders impossible to describe, have had Heaven brought literally right down into my lap, and I lived in that ecstasy, that transcendent state for days again. However, tremendous as it all is—yet, I too, must relax any limitations and know that all this was but another step up, another rung on that eternal ladder unto the Infinite. For the Infinite is infinitely Infinite and no limitations exist in the Infinite Mind of God.

And now with the great added measure of Power constantly present, as is noted by the 'effects' with others, I have become aware of just what the Higher Ones meant when They told me—on more than one occasion, through the Moderator's voice—that with my personal progress, with higher and higher attainment and realizations which would enable me to more compatibly and harmonically oscillate as a polarity with Him, the inflow and Energy projections would be much greater, that it could be stepped up intensely from that which was being so dispersed at that time, in years gone by. Thus it has indeed happened. The effects of this wondrous Ray-Beam is noted to be far more prevalent and frequent and more potent or strong—just as They had promised It would.

As one proof of this, Sanosun, (as has been mentioned), who helps in the various clerical needs at her home, can scarcely stay awake anymore as she works on these notes I've written, which she retypes. Hard as she tries, down will go her head and off to the couch she must go. It was yesterday morn, I believe, she exclaimed over the phone, "Ioshanna, I just can't stay awake, hard as I try; I've gone to sleep twice this morn and am ready for another! The Power is so tremendously strong!" Thus it is. Now the world has Light, Energy and Infinite Rays of Power being projected into it that never before have been so intense, strong and prevalent. Now, this one can be a help to our

377

beloved Moderator and mankind! And, of course, there is no greater way to help than in this polarity relationship or oscillation. Yes, there is indeed a feeling of having 'arrived'. It is not a final platform—but simply another rung from which to step to an even higher awareness—on ad infinitum, unto the infinite reaches of the Infinite Cosmos.

April 13, 1969—Dear Ioshanna: As I read in the "True Life of Jesus" book about the plain of Genesareth, a much cherished spot of Jesus and noted for its beauty, I remembered your Palm Springs home and recalled that I wrote you after visiting there, "Your desert oasis jewel is a beautiful setting for You Two—and how fortunate for those on that desert!" I did have the feeling that I was 'back home' in Jerusalem when I was there.

While my tummy did a flip-flop on viewing the rocks and the soldier, the most vivid impression was watching the Moderator ride away from the Lighthouse, your Glendale home, in a horizontal position, with a feeling of never returning there; yet, within a year He returned to Glendale from Palm Springs driving his own car!

The Moderator had said many times, when He reached approximately the age of sixty-two, it would be a very critical time—a great crisis in His life; if He could live through it then, He could go on several years, but "it was very doubtful life could be continued in the physical after that period for it was a conclusion of the cycle."

While I know I cannot fully realize the scope in benefits derived in this incarnation, in the opportunity of working out the negative Jerusalem cycle, I do know in part what it has meant for Jesus and His Mary to again return to this dimension to give those of us playing a negative part in the crucifixion, a once-in-a-millennium chance to change the oscillation to a more positive bias, to lessen the impedance in our journey into the future.

As the Moderator said, my true name, Sanosun, means 'Rising Sun', I know, if I remain steadfast in my efforts to overcome the past, and with continuous study of the Unarius principles and their usage, the arms of the Infinite will surely surround me tightly.

Sanosun (Dorothy Ellerman)

P.S.—Most important, was the realization when I awakened this afternoon from a long nap. "He has arisen" was in my consciousness. Then I remembered I wrote you that my most vivid impression regarding your move to Palm Springs, was watching the Moderator leave your Glendale home in a horizontal position, more dead than alive (the crucifixion) and returning almost a year later, driving his own car (the Resurrection). I'm sure this is one reason I had been attempting off and on for three days to retype the story of the great Visitation and the one concerning the Palm Springs 'Jerusalem' cycle, and accounts for the fact I had been 'weeping' inside.

I have the feeling of another layer lighter.

* * * * *

April 13, 1969—For three days (off and on) I have been editing and retyping your pages of the wonderful Visitation of the electronic configuration of the energy body of our Moderator. I should say, I have been attempting to do this, for the energy present was so powerful, it was like being plugged in to a high-voltage current, and as I typed, I would find my eyes closing and consciousness leaving, and so transcended, to continue the work was impossible.

379

Finally today, the typing is completed, and as I look back, great appreciation wells up within me for the most beneficent and life-changing, healing energies projected. It seemed like a wide, tight band around my head with electrodes attached, through which the energy flowed, and I was aware that the Light was penetrating the dark recesses of my psychic body, gathered from the dust of ages past, the negative wave forms changed to a more positive oscillation with the present.

This all must be, so that I may continue my humble part in the great Unarius Mission, to work compatibly with Ioshanna in her joining with the Infinite.

June 14, 1969—Dear Ioshanna: I wish there were words to tell you of my admiration and love for your great strength of purpose and steadfastness against all odds which you exemplify each day.

To all Unarius students you are a bulwark, a magnificent pillar of Light as you Channel with our Beloved Moderator, the beneficent and healing Rays to us all in our struggle with ourselves.

Thank you and with utmost gratitude,

Sanosun

In Closing

Thus, as we sit and pass in review the wondrous unfoldment of the continuation of this Mission which Jesus started two thousand years ago and long before, as well, it is with nostalgia we re-attune to these past lives which were expressed during times of a great wealth of culture; none have been so barren of true spiritual effects and expressions as this, the present. We cannot help but wonder, for the most part, just which way man shall travel, spiritually speaking.

In this quiet contemplation, our Spiritual Brothers come to us; they appear, flashing their Lights to let us know of their nearness; and it is doubtful with all the phenomena which has been my pleasure to witness during these fifteen years together, were there as many in numbers at any one time, and their brilliance so intense as that which I witnessed this very evening. Every few moments, in would pop one, then another, some brilliantly golden lights, then a huge, vivid, radiant fluorescent-appearing luminosity, seemingly two to three feet in diameter, a great infusion. On one occasion, He was voicing a few lines of his heavenly verse to me, one of which, as I jotted it down, was:

> "And so I'll look from out these iron bars
> I call my life,
> My soul escapes to where the summer sun
> becomes the golden alchemy,
> To weave my dreams into a rainbow fair."

And as He was voicing, there appeared a great cloud-like formation of an intense blue-white color, a haze effect, and in the center more than twice the size of our huge fireplace, flashed a brilliant, sparkling, diamond-looking light, a most luminous Being. Although we see no physical body, for they have long since ceased to wear the body of flesh, the brilliance of their energy bodies is a joy to behold. So continuously did They maintain this Visitation this evening that most of the time I spent in that glorious transcended state—out of the physical. (Their Presence does not so intensely transcend the Moderator. He has lived too long with them for it to 'change' His frequency!)

Such an experience just fills one's heart so full it brings about such a mellow sensation—one of great warmth and of Infinite Love, impossible to define or describe. I'm sure the many Brothers who made the contact this night were intimating that they were there with Him when e'er He decided to, as He says, "Step from out these prison bars," which He calls the fleshly body; and to such a Being so entrapped, it does indeed become as prison bars! It was He, Himself, however, who so volunteered unto this self-imprisonment in order that the earthman may learn of life. Would an earthman be so completely selfless? It is doubtful! That is the way when one becomes wise in the ways of the Infinite; his purpose and life become one of serving.

Yes, to know and to see our Beloved Ones so near and in such numbers is most gratifying and heartwarming, for they are, any more, the only ones with whom we can compatibly oscillate. Eartheans all, have become strangers to me (and always have been to Him), the former compatibility has all been changed; and this, dear friend, is progress—a road each one can take as he must so constantly make his choice; but compatible or no, there's nothing we would not do to help in any spiritual or psychic way for the betterment of any man. Serving becomes our way of life, yet each soul must learn the vital importance of self-responsibility, of the need to conceive these life principles that can and do create for him his infinite future!

And as you so travel your spiritual way, know that whether or not we two are in or out of the 'prison of flesh', we can and shall be working with you, aiding you, always commensurate to your individual efforts to learn—and to apply! Thus, may your endeavors to seek be consistent, that our spiritual aid with you may be continuous until such time that you, too, may have severed the many ties of the past and become wise in the ways of spirit, so that you shall oscillate more infinitely as you learn to integrate personal consciousness more and more with the Infinite.

Thus, as you 'tune in' through these lines and all of the Unarius works you, too, should sense and partake of this great Radiant Light which has been brought so abundantly into this dimension this night, as it will be imparted to you via your consciousness, for in such Visitations and with the countless numbers that made appearance this evening, even to the point of building up and materializing the great blue-mist cloud of energy substance, such radiating, oscillating manifestation does not disappear because we cease to be conscious of it, but rather, do these Energy projections regenerate and exist eternally, oscillating there to impart the infinite polarization to those so likewise attuned! May your times of attunement be frequent.

And so, dear friend, these various notations, recalls and experiences so recorded of my past herein have been done to show and to prove to anyone so likewise dedicated to his own overcoming and development, that man can make his peace, he can find that long-sought-after and often-talked-about security —a security much more realistic and important and far-reaching than any physical achievements or accomplishments—the true inner peace of consciousness. I do stand as living proof and testimonial that man can learn the way to attainment through the conceiving of the curriculum of Unarius, which teaches the true Infinite Creation—life here and hereafter, as well as of eons of past evolution—that he can learn through his effort to conceive and thereby putting into practice the principles taught, he can live in that completely different and higher state of consciousness which this entity has come to know, to experience and to express the Kingdom Within. This is the prime purpose and goal for man—to learn through his many lifetimes and evolving, to become more and more infinitely-minded, more in attunement with the Infinite, 'The Many Mansions'.

Nor is this higher way, the new life or change, for just some certain few; it is rather, the way for all men —those who choose to follow and to remain steadfast to their goal and purpose, who will continue to persist and pursue the higher way in spite of all odds (and there will be many obstacles, all of one's own past making), shall likewise find their Kingdom Within; and it is exactly as Jesus said it was—right within one's innermost being.

Thus it is as our workings out, our flashbacks or recalls form and become the bridge from our past, yet too, and even more important, as we learn and incept from the Unariun Principle does this Wisdom become our bridge into the future, to the Infinite, or if you prefer—'The Bridge to Heaven'.

Moreover, this bridge is ever reaching and extending in any and all directions; thus, it is up to us, to each one as individuals, to constantly choose through our selection of consciousness, by our every act, deed and thought, what direction the path upon which we step will take us.

May your ever-present choosing and selecting be those which will set your foot firmly upon the most direct and upward evolutionary pathway into Eternity —into that never-ceasing, constantly-oscillating, rising and regenerating cosmos.

In closing, it should be apparent from these various recalls and pointings up, that Unarius places within the hand of the sincere seeker of Truth, the Eternal Flame of Life—your torch to light your way into the future. This spark of Infinite Creation will regenerate within, and as the seeker adds to his storehouse of knowledge, so shall this spark be fanned into a brilliant flame—a flame which will grow until such time that Infinite Consciousness is reached, whereby you, too, can become a beacon in the night, shining out to those reaching toward the Light.

Guard ye well, this flame of life from the minions of astral forces who would seek to destroy, to waylay and to deter the aspirant from his true course of a more progressive evolution, the true pathway which ye have now found—that most narrow of all pathways, which will lead you into the infinite vistas of the Cosmic Creative Interdimensional Worlds of Light—those many mansions of which Jesus so often spoke. Yes, I have found this Inner Way—the 'Way' He has prepared for us.—So be it.

Ioshanna

Note: Ioshanna, a name the Higher Ones related, was the name I used in Atlantis. They said it meant "The Shining One".

An Unplanned Addition

It was May 1st 1969, that I was awakened at two A.M. hearing screams and cries of, "Help me! I'm bleeding to death—I'm dying!" Jumping quickly out of bed, running to where his voice came from, I found my angel-husband sitting on the bathroom floor, leaning over the stool with blood pouring from his nose and mouth, and within moments, this life blood also began spewing from the rectum. The pain he was experiencing was excruciating and soon an ambulance was on the way to remove him to a hospital.

Because we have had no family doctor (our need has so rarely existed) we simply had to go to the emergency hospital. After a superficial examination, a tranquilizer and pain killer, (an unknown shot), was given and I returned him home to await the morn when we could get lined up with a physician. This being done, and after a more proper examination, the M.D. ordered him to the hospital for further tests, X-rays, etc.

He was kept quite deep in sedation for nearly a week, then after the second week's stay, was dismissed to come home with the admonition to be very quiet, relaxed and calm, that two large ulcers were found and the blood vessels had burst, causing him to lose three-fourths of his entire supply. For some technical reasons, they stated afterwards, when asked why he could not have been given blood, due to cross-matching, it was impossible; and at the present time there exists some sort of embargo on permits for transfusions as they have recently found hepatitis is often brought on due to blood transfusions.

The doctors later told us they were quite sure he had cancer and didn't expect him to live the night through!

Continuing on with medication that could help one, such as tranquilizers, etc., he spent the following two days at home, only to find his fever rose and fell repeatedly, several points. Upon reaching a very high level, I became a bit frightened, and pushing the panic button, phoned the doctor after twelve midnight, awakening him from sleep. He dashed over from his neighboring town, and after giving an injection, left, telling him to return to the hospital as soon as possible. The cause we found of this trouble was, that when the orderly was performing a catheterization, he contaminated Ernest through an unclean procedure. Thus, quickly did the staphylococcus germs multiply, causing him to suffer another week, undergoing extremely strong hypo shots to try to get the blood balance back to normal. The negligence and poor care, etc., left its many psychic scars with him, as well as physical distress.

Now, just five weeks after the hemorrhage, although still being kept under sedation, He feels he shall recover, although the climb back shall be rough and slow. Eventually, and only through the help of the Brotherhood, He emerged from the staff infection victorious.

June 1st 1969—It was just one week ago that he was quite low, mentally, psychically and physically, as he struggled to overcome, even though, due to the sedation, the words were indistinct, he voiced, so you sincere students might better understand his position, the article, "Me, the Android", (now available to any student, gratis).

Just previous to this voicing, we both were mentally depressed. (We are not perfect!) As I tried in ways I best knew to lift his spirits, little success was attained, but when he finished the informal 'Android' letter, he said, "I feel better; I've had a healing within me."

Up to that point, the bleeding continued through the digestive tract, and via their stool testings, blood was still present. That was two A.M., Saturday. Monday, on our office visit and the next examination and test, the appearance of blood no longer existed. It was 'clear'.

So you see, even though our Beloved One was at death's door, our Brothers of Light were able once more to snatch him from the jaws of death to help him remain with the earth people a little longer, which is his wish, due to the added power, light and energies that he can and does, regardless of any physical depletion or inadequacy, channel into the world.

Although this particular chapter or cycle of his expression has not been completed, let it be known that there was a tremendous overcoming, an incredible miracle—a miracle even greater than can be factually conceived—because this Person does not have the same drive to live; the tie with the earth which the earthman possesses does not exist with him.

Although the rest of his days on earth, whether they are few, a few weeks, months, or that he decides to extend it on to a few years, must be spent in complete isolation, not bedridden but very quietly. Another week was supposed to have told the tale as to whether or not he would make it, but I'm writing this in advance, for I know inwardly he shall emerge victorious—emerge to go on with the work and mission he chose to express, although his books have all been delivered to the eartheans.

It should be related, too, that at one point, after the hospital attendant (a dark force) infected him with the 'staff' and the fever was at the highest point, he began fading fast, so much so he was unable to speak, slipping into unconsciousness. I could feel no pulse, and with my cheek upon his lips, no breath. It was at this point I personally did believe (knew for a few flash seconds), he was dead. Just before this took place, his last words were, "I'm going," and they faded to nothing.

Then another strong voice—a Superconscious voice—said to me, "You go forth with the work, all the powers shall be with you." I knew he had slipped over to the other side, and I again ran up the hall to phone the doctor. The doctor said, "Can he come to the phone?" Well, to be truthful, at that point, I was a bit confused. I ran back to his room and, shaking him, said, "You can't go; come quickly and talk to Dr. Mac!"

I shall never know how he ever climbed out of bed but his body was moved. He staggered up the long hallway, hitting both sides of the wall all the way and finally fell into the chair by the phone, muttering the best he could to the doctor. Dr. Mac said, "You don't sound very good, I'll be right there." While the moments seemed to pass slowly, the doctor sped hastily with his penicillin which started the lessening of the multiplying of the white corpuscles for, as you may know, with such a condition as staphylococcus in certain inner organs, this oversupply of white corpuscles can kill a man very quickly as they take over the red cells.

Thus it was, he actually died the second time. As he says, "I was hovering over my body, looking down at it!"

Now that this entire month has passed and with his analyzing, etc., he knows, as I too realized, the ulcerous holes in the lower stomach or intestinal tract were due to the sword thrust two thousand years ago. In fact, he states, " As I viewed the holes in the X-ray film, I was impressed with the fact they were the result of that sword thrust. The swords used at that time were not mere pointed steel shafts but had a large barb at the end so when the spear was removed, it snared the flesh even more.

As has been related previously by Him in his 'Red Box' relatings, as well as in the foregoing pages of this book, his earth cycle was actually concluded with the manifestation of the 'Jose' book and especially the short period later, the Red Box book, but this intervening time since is a representation or a symbolic repeat of the time He (Jesus) lived in Jerusalem after the crucifixion, after he healed himself, (such as it was), for if you remember in the 'Jose' book, Jesus did not convalesce sufficiently to permit complete healing and recovery, but instead went about continuing on his work healing and teaching before the infection (from his crucifixion wounds) was stopped. His mission and people were to Him far more important than was himself, or his health—even though those few who loved him begged him to refrain and rest, he heeded not—and it's exactly the same today! He wants to pour even more of himself, and his energies out to you Unariun students and is so doing!

But such a Being and Soul is not self-concerned; even now when He should be completely concerned with preserving his vitality and energy for recovery, whenever the opportunity presents itself, he gives of himself to those about him—the nurses, doctors, orderlies, cleanup people—yes, even the evil one who caused the infection that so nearly cost his life, did he teach to him, give to him his books and his very life forces!

This, too, was the reason why Jesus died when He did, six months after the crucifixion, due to infection which set in from his wounds; He was too disconcerned with the physical man.

Although at the time the situation did look most grave as I watched the color leave him, as his flesh receded and he lost two, three, and then five pounds a day. Still, I never for one moment (other than the few seconds He left (died), lost faith. I knew inwardly he would recover, and kept telling him so, and now I predict He shall overcome and again enter into an even higher and more beautiful phase of his cycle, mission, and purpose.

Several times during the day or evening of late, he makes the inner contact and the beautiful verse, heavenly beyond words, is voiced. Much is pertaining to myself; He expresses and conveys his love and appreciation of me in the most divine verse, and so I firmly believe and predict he shall, due to his great love for all mankind, completely overcome this ill and evil, the powers of Light shall be victorious and He shall, as proof, again give voice to his Infinite Message of Truth which shall, no doubt, be put into the form of superb, celestial verse—the likes of which man has never heard. This He says he wishes to do for me in his appreciation for my dedication and help to him, that I may hear these Poems, set to music in my car helping to retain His attunement, as He says, whereby there will be never a separation, when He does step from out the earth body.

Thus I know—so shall it be. And so, dear Unariun friend, when you hear his future Infinite Words of Wisdom on the tapes (and you shall) which He shall voice, know too, and truly so, He has again cast aside his opportunity to return to his people, the Brothers of Light, purely to bring to you a little more of Himself, of his Light and Love, to help lift you up a little further from the mire of the earthworld.

Greater Love hath no man.

June 10, 1969—And now my prediction has been made manifest: the six week allotted time over, and He has recovered. Our Brother, the Interplanetary Traveler, although his body may appear as the eartheans, is very, very different; the only similarity is in appearance—which had to be; His disguise, an excellent one. He and the Brothers of the Inner have repaired his vehicle he calls 'the Robot' to endure, that He may again come to you with his further Message of Truth.

The "Light of the World" shines on, and I know when the proper time comes when He does make the change, when he wishes to return to his Flame people, it will not be through or from some horrible bodily earth condition, but He shall simply step from out the prison of flesh painlessly, very possibly as He voices his Message of Light, and I, for one, shall be thankful—thankful that He no longer need remain in this flesh which is not of Him or of His world. I shall sing praises to the Infinite that another Bright Star shines in the firmament, and I expect to continue to sense his love which He radiates to all people in all worlds and all walks of life, "We love you, Beloved One!"

Note: As an added note of interest, the following could help the individual better understand this Super Being, the Moderator's Higher Self. During this entire time of three weeks in the hospital, although He is super-sensitive to all drugs (a single, ordinary aspirin can cause him much dizziness), it was utterly impossible to quiet or tranquilize his Higher Mind. Even after the full dosages of sedatives, his Mind functioned and raced rapidly. It was impossible to relax its incessant, rapid oscillation. Even in such drastic condition, He would be reciting beautiful poetry and voicing abstractions only the Higher Minds could conceive.

On one occasion, He was conscious (after realizing how very antiquated were the present-day hospitals) of complete plans and diagrams for the hospital of tomorrow the likes of which were remarkable, with many new inventions far in advance of those of today. He had the revelations of how to build a third-dimension X-ray machine where the body could be viewed as it really exists; saw precisely how the certain fre-

quencies could change and explode decayed cancer-
ous cells, leaving the healthy cells untouched.

He viewed the entire electronic brain of the 'hospi-
tal-of-tomorrow' and could relate how to build it—a
'brain' that would censor the patient instantly as he
lie comfortable in his bed and relay the entire report
electronically on tiny stored tapes that could be
checked or observed anytime; or by the same token,
the nurse in charge could, by means of button manip-
ulation at the relay station, dispense desired medication or necessary application—which were very often
specific frequency rays. All this would eliminate the
many nurses, much walking up and down the halls,
thus giving the patient far superior service.

This awareness and transpiring went on and on in
the great Mind of this genius, and of course, for Him
to be aware or conscious of something means He is
oscillating or relating it on to others! Here in the hospital where his physical body had temporarily broken
down and worn out, his true self, the 'Android', as he
terms it, with the Inner contact, was working mentally
with the doctors and nurses in charge. They may not
possibly, at the present time and place, be able to
carry out all He was relating but nevertheless, the
seeds were planted, and in time to come, possibly the
next lifetime—forty, fifty or so years into the future—
these persons will return, after a stay in the inner
worlds, to make use of this information, the know-
how, and thus, the world will be much richer in the
many new inventions; possibly the doctors and scientists will be called 'genius' and presented with Nobel
prizes because this dying 'android' had passed on to
them his great wisdom which He brought from the
Higher Spiritual Worlds.

Could it have been that He may have arranged for
(or caused) this robot-body to break down to the
point where He had to be hospitalized that He might
be put in physical contact or with these persons

whereby He could relay all this wonder to them—the hospital of the future? Very possibly! For such a being is not self-motivated nor concerned with the physical but rather, mainly concerned with "How much can I give them that they can use wisely?"

And now we learn the Staff of this very dilapidated and antiquated hospital has plans to build on the hills practically within a 'stone's throw' of our home—a fine, lovely, new, modern hospital, and through these people and their minds can He work with them in the future. Whether He is in or out of the fleshly body makes no difference—the seeds have been and are being planted. What could be more beneficial for mankind! (For one such place can be the means of many.)

It should be noted, too, that the hospitals of the future will not be as the butcher shops of today, where man is sliced and butchered, but his corrections will take place due to inconceivably high frequency beams, about which man knows nothing at present. The incredible laser beam of today will become child's play compared to the intensity of the frequencies used in the future when man begins to express this knowledge and know-how which the Moderator has, during this 'incarnation'—his present earth life visit—been teaching.

The foregoing may better help the reader understand the incredibility of this Being, the Soul we call the Unarius Moderator—the One who is bringing the wisdom of the ages unto man for his future. So never underestimate from any visible aspects, the accomplishments and expressions of this 'Contact'—the Moderator—for He is indeed a Contact with thousands of Infinite Minds, relaying intelligence that could (and shall in time) make of this earth world a far better place to live. Were it not for the self-erected pedestals of the eartheans, these things could all be done now, but man is not one to have his ego deflated; he believes he knows all, when frankly, he is very unlearned, unwise, and stupid, comparatively speaking.

And so, this relaying and relating must be done the only way possible—given unto man from the inner, in spite of himself! Thus it has been and is being accomplished, and future years will find and prove many of his relatings manifest on earth.

Thus, you, friend Unariun, could possibly return also in a subsequent lifetime with something of great value for posterity, for this is the way the wheels of time, the cycles of progress move and turn, and the way those of the Inner dimensions (Kingdoms) work —for the benefit of this and other earthworlds to help progress the planets and mankind in his evolutionary travel and which becomes a never-ending turning and changing of cycles.

Would any earthman be so selfless! No, He shall not die like a dog who must succumb to the various and countless diseases and ills he encounters. I have complete and full faith and realization in the great Spiritual Organization of Unarius that with Their and my help and that of his own Inner Self, no earthly condition shall bring about this termination but only when He simply steps out because He has totally completed that which He so planned and set up to bring. He could give worlds and worlds more of wisdom, but as has been related, this hell-earth-world is not ready to accept.

Also I am quite conscious of the wondrous powers that the Intellects from the Higher Worlds can project psychokinetically from their Minds, as well as the various ray machines, ejecting frequencies in the millions and millions of megacycles per second. Just as my car axle was held together to bring me safely down the long, steep mountainside, so surely could these frequencies weld or knit the broken blood vessels in his stomach, and which, evidently, is being accomplished. As the doctor, himself, said after only the first few days of hospitalization, "I am quite amazed at the amount of healing; we didn't expect you to last the night through!"

And so blame me not that I shall cherish and treasure every added hour He chooses to remain—and as I say, 'expect it to be for several years!'

In reply to those who'll wonder, "Why?" this breakthrough of the blood vessels—let it be repeated: the physical body (our Channel is using) was not formed and created as was yours (all eartheans) through eons of time, through thousands of years of evolution in these earth worlds but was rather, a mental creation for this one lifetime purpose only; thus it is not relative to all the elements, environments, etc., so common to earth people. And as has been said, the fact that he grew up at all is one constant miracle. Moreover, He actually, in a sense, (psychically) died at the manifestation of the Jose book (and The Red Box book) and additional hours, days, weeks, or time since then, (two years ago), was extended purely from his sheer will, determination to share with us a little more of his very being. Selfless?—doesn't begin to tell it!

Ernest's entire lifetime has been one of being met with the negative forces, the opposition was ever-present. He has constantly overcome again and again, and the forces of darkness shall not again win out, as happened in Jerusalem, for the Powers of Light and Truth shall be victorious! As one famous seer once said to Him, "You have encountered sufficient to kill one hundred men and shall still experience sufficient opposition to kill another thousand before you're through!" But overcome He has. He practices what He teaches; and for an interplanetary traveler, it's many times more difficult, as the world is so foreign to Him, who truly lives in the World of Light.

And now may we relate as it is engraved upon the loving cup a group of Unarius students presented to Him, years ago: (To) "The Light of the World—To honor our beloved teacher whose Infinite Wisdom and

Love shall live in our hearts and minds eternally. In gratitude, Your devoted students."

Ioshanna

June 12, 1969—And thus as I have so prophesied —even when the hours seemed darkest, yet hope had not flown, for I've learned well of the great and wondrous Powers this great Intellect, The Moderator, wields; and of the limitless help our Brothers of Light extend. Although such a Being is much too outgoing, far too selfless to be concerned with self sufficiently to turn the powers inwardly upon the self, and yet this night has fulfilled my prediction, our promise that this evil would be overcome and that The Channel of his Mind would again become The Way—an even greater portion of the Infinite beauty could be brought to the earth and mankind.

And so, as I sat by his bed last evening, although I'd not brought in a recorder—the time was not for that, He taught for more than two hours of greater Infinite truths, ending before sleep, with this lovely verse—and there shall be many more to come:

* * * * *

"If it could be that I could breathe
     forever
The breath of eternity
Then let it be that in each breath
I would find the greenness
     of growing things
The whispers of life — each
     in its time and place
This, my breath of life — of eternity
There would I hear the sighs
     of soft breezes
The chirps of fledglings
     in the nests
A new-born infant's wail
Eternity breaths its song of life
May I forever find
My life the issue of its song."

Letter from Sanosun

June 8, 1969—I was 'caught in the middle' again —which has been my story down through the ages, in many times and places.

I had been working in a small hospital for the last two years. This was my first experience in medical terminology and hospital procedures, and although I was puzzled at the time as to why I was there, the job came to me, I reasoned, for a purpose, and questioned no further.

Then just at the end of my second year, the Moderator was booked into the hospital for X-rays and various tests, and as He called it, incarcerated there for too many days to remember, for I was living again the Jerusalem life, with the emotional strain of the crucifixion. There were many incidents which tuned me back; unethical practices, medication error of careless employees, the lack of proper care where He was concerned seemed to snowball, but the last day particularly, the place was no longer a hospital but a court, a tribunal.

The Moderator was scheduled to go home that day, and later in the morning when He was ready, his doctor had not yet released him. The Moderator called me to expedite the matter—He could get no action from the nurses in charge. It happened that the Administrator was involved in an important meeting, and at the particular time of the call, I was busily gathering and copying necessary papers, for which he was waiting. Which way to turn? My mind was churning with the pressure of the past regenerating and my nerves were taut in the reliving.

I put down the papers—the Administrator could wait. I phoned the doctor to learn that he was in surgery. I broke the emergency rules and called Surgery and finally the doctor came to the phone. I explained that a patient of his was waiting to be checked out to go home. The doctor was a little taken aback that I had called him for that—but he couldn't know how very special was that patient—and he said he would be out in fifteen minutes. Those minutes seemed an eternity to me—but finally the Moderator was free of the place—and soon I had given notice to leave as well for I felt this place had served its purpose, I had worked out some more of the Jerusalem cycle.

P.S. June 12, 1969—And now this day brings fulfillment of Ioshanna's prediction when she related how on June 12th He will have overcome. I had need to stop at the Light House (their home) and soon was overjoyed to see Them driving in with the Moderator at the wheel!

My Erosean Visit

May 29, 1969—Only because the Unariun student —so engaged in making the master copy for this book (from which the many shall be duplicated) has been, during the very last few pages, held up or delayed, due to other pressing personal activities, am I able to include this notation. To some it may seem less important but when I related my recent revelation to the Moderator, it was, to him, the most important of all revealings. "Now," he said, "I know when I am finished with this created composite called physical body and return to my Flame (energy) people in the Spiritual Worlds, that you shall be thoroughly capable of my working through you, that you are now, indeed, one of us." This, of course, made me very happy but I, myself, was also quite aware thusly.

It was just yesterday, as I lie contemplating the many great wonders of the inner dimensions which I'd seen through past years that I suddenly was transported, visited and viewed a beautiful luminous home. The walls seemed made of some lovely, synthetic or plastic substance with swirling cloud-like patterns in pastel shades which were luminated from within. There seemed some substance was included in the material which created a soft, rosy luminosity. The floors were similar to beautiful marble, yet the material was not opaque but seemed translucent, and they, too, were illumined softly from underneath. Well I remember the gold strips or bands in a radial pattern meeting in the center radiating outwardly to the perimeter which formed a lovely pattern to walk upon, and in between each separation were glorious scenes depicted and which, too, could be changed at will! The feeling when walking over this lovely floor was that it gave off some energy radiation of an uplifting element, a sort of buoyancy, that made walking seem more like floating.

No lamps or lights were visible for there was no need for such, as the lighting element was evidently mixed in with the building material—such as a fluorescence.

Centermost in this elegant circular home was a beautiful mosaic alabaster fountain with levels of various graduated sizes. The dancing waters sprang into many varieties and patterns as multi-colored lights slowly and systematically played color upon the cascading, dancing waters as they continued through the many beautiful designs and effects.

Along with this colorful display of color and water was an accompaniment of soft, healing music, so muted that it seemed to influence the waters in its cadence or rising and falling as the tone colors rhythmically imbued their beauty to both eye and ear, as well as the soul. Some of the musical instruments being heard were strange to my ears and not of the earth-world instruments and which, in itself, carried radiant energy healing frequencies. This soft music seemed to create the mood for the dancing waters, all a most soothing and relaxing sight to behold and to breathe into one's very soul. Beauty indeed, beyond description. Also, I detected a delightfully faint fragrance being emitted, from where, I knew not.

The only partitions noted to separate the rooms were those of the sleeping areas and which were walls of very full rainbow-colored, sheer, chiffon material which hung softly and gracefully about for any desired seclusion.

Most vivid in my memory is the beautiful free-flowing staircase which seemed to have no supporting structures but rather, twisted gracefully in one complete turn and a half, then disappeared through the ceiling. I learned when one stepped upon this conversational stairway, it simply, automatically motivated or transported the person right up to the roof where existed a lovely, formal, sculptured garden filled with many glorious flowers and plants. There was a viewing platform where huge telescopes and viewing instruments were located that the owner might scan the heavens and other planets, from this heavenly abode.

The home was not cluttered as are most earth homes with many furnishings but was spacious and beautiful in its simplicity. About the sides of the circular room were located, here and there, long graceful lounges for sitting or reclining in relaxation. They seemed not to be placed upon the mosaic floor but were rather, suspended slightly in the air, and upon each such lounge were luxurious soft cushions of various soft, muted tones in pastel shades.

Outstanding in my memory of this Erosean home was a sort of television that filled one entire wall in color and was a three-dimensional project.

When one wished to go from one area to another, there were no frustrating door-knobs or locks, but the slight wave of the hand quickly slid the particular section open silently and back out of sight. Other details are not so prominent in my mind but the very peculiar part of it all was, I had the definite feeling and told my Beloved, "I'm going to build you a plastic house; I know just how," and I described what I've just written here. Then he knew I had visited Eros. It made him very happy, of course, but do you know the visitation still seems so real, as if it actually happened or will take place here in the physical. I know where I shall go when I leave this earth-world for I've just visited our spiritual home; one we have mentally and psychokinetically created on the inner and a delightful and elegant abode it is!

And so, dear reader—friend, such experiences as these can be your personal realizations, too, and are in store for you each one, some time and place as you travel your pathway—your bridge to Heaven.

The Moderator today again expressed his great joy and feeling of fulfillment that I, too, was able to bring back these memories of the transportation to the spiritual planet. The many visions related before were of a different nature—often they were mental projections from the Brothers of Light—the Flame People, but this 'trip' was an actual visitation such as He wrote in his 'Pulse of Creation' books, as He says, "Now I can go, when the time is right, knowing full well that the work will continue, that I shall be completely able to work through and with you as we travel on the Inner together in these Inner Mansions or dimensions." He feels, as He has related, that this is the most vital part of his cause, for now He knows His mission shall be carried on, even though his cycle has been completed, and that which He came to do, to express, and to help prepare this one, has been achieved. As He says, "My feeling of fulfillment is complete, I can now go on any time, knowing all things which I so set up to do have been accomplished in this present time on this, the earth plane," and as He continued, "Now this robot or android man can return to his people any time, for I can be satisfied that I can carry on from the Inner through you and with the compatible frequency which we have created as an oscillating polarity through eons of time in the future." So be it.

ALL THAT

WHICH IS IN HEAVEN

HAS MADE MY LIFE

COMPLETE.

Notes

And now, three days later (as I again pick up my notes), finds me still transcended, filled and overflowing with the Light so shared by our Beloved One, the ecstasy almost beyond the point of endurance!

*

Even now, as the days move on in procession, one to the next, the weeks find me with a need and way to interject still another word, a line, to relate how very much more prevalent have become our Heavenly Visitors since the earthly visit on Easter Sunday a few weeks past. The Lights of our Ascended Brothers have become far more numerous and frequent as They oscillate and project into our dimension and consciousness. Now, it seems, we are ever surrounded with Them—never alone. Further proof that the Master Jesus has returned—and with His Host of Angels—invisible to most persons but most discernable to we who are more compatible to Their frequency. The flashes of Their Presence, the Lights seem more brilliant, and there are many more of Them as They so frequently surround us; beautiful Beings projecting Their help, protection and love to us here and to all mankind. They are ever close and we know that even this, too, shall continue to be stepped up and up until we two become as One with Them in the abstract—in the Inner Worlds of Light, freed of the flesh.

*

Now, too within a couple of weeks after the last and greatest of all Visitations, comes a letter from my seventeen-year-old granddaughter Sandi, and who just never writes; (I believe I have had but one note from her previously) telling of her personal, psychic, transcending experience in Palm Springs during that Easter week. A sentence from her letter reads: "I went to Palm Springs with some other kids for a week, and Gram, in that quiet, still, lonely, desolate, barren desert late one night, I sat on a huge boulder and 'found' myself, my mind, and most important, my soul! Since, everything has such a beautiful hue to it now! . ."

Could it be that the power and Energies which were oscillated and brought into this dimension during our stay in Palm Springs helped polarize that area whereby others, too, shall be spiritually influenced and helped! I'm sure of it! This girl! has never previously had any such revelation, and what happened was: a Higher Being came to her, creating the wondrous feeling of, as she terms it, 'finding her soul', and that is just about the feeling one experiences in these times of attunement with or from such an Advanced Being—possibly either one of our Higher Selves, or any one of the Brothers. But one thing certain, Sandi —love her—will never be the same; she's been indoctrinated with the Light! An experience many strive for many lifetimes to undergo; and we here are most happy for her that she was so ready and receptive. 'Carry on', Sandi, there's a wonderful World of Light ahead! That was but one of the Many Mansions of which Jesus spoke!

No Separation In Spirit

Incidentally, a note of interest is found in the very wonderful guidance and promptings I experienced as I remodeled our home during Ernest's hospitalization. During the past few years he'd mentioned several large projects and changes he wished could be made in the home, such as removing the wall-to-wall carpeting and putting down parkay flooring, adding accoustical ceilings to dampen the noise, lessening the sound factor, etc., replacing carpeting in his sleeping areas, etc.

Thus, in my effort to do something whereby I could maintain the most positive state, I quickly got busy from the very first day of his absence, and although I made two and three trips daily, to the hospital to sit with him, along with as many or more phone calls from him, I still accomplished all the projects set forth to do; even to replacing the slate in the entrance hall with terrazzo (a stone cement element) I obtained new furnishings in the living room, new huge paintings, lamps, etc., so much so that it looked entirely different, and upon his first viewing as he returned, he said that he thought he had died and gone to heaven!

It was indeed all most miraculous workings—not a hitch in the entire endeavor; the inner knowing was ever-present and everything went off like clockwork, even though we had to be most time-conscious, for I never knew exactly when he might become too displeased with his 'incarceration' that he would call to be brought home before the doctors would dismiss him. But the joy of it all was as his eyes took it all in he'd say, "Oh, you found my favorite picture I've been looking at in the store," and, "there are my lamps that

I just couldn't keep away from," and on with several other objects d'art I had purchased and which were things he had polarized with his consciousness, as he viewed and liked them. I remember so well his first words (and which I recorded as he entered), "I don't believe it, I don't believe it—I can't stand it!" He became very weak having to sit down. Yes, it was quite a revelation to him to have the many things manifest which he, himself, had selected but saying nothing about it, for it was, in its entirety, quite a doing away with all the old and in with the new and which I felt would be a helpful adjutant in his recuperating, seeing the many long-wished-for projects all accomplished without his physical aid or contacts. He still sits in wonder and amazement, yet knows full well he, himself, on the Inner or other side helped, prompted, and worked so closely with me in and through the conclusion of all things.

The thing that made me happiest was when he said, "Now I know I shall be able to work with you completely after I leave the flesh, that we shall never again be separated in Consciousness and that the work shall be able to proceed through your mind, for this is a perfect demonstration and proof of the oneness we maintained."

Indeed it can be (and was) oneness of spirit, and I'm thankful.

Letters from Helen Moore

April 6, 1969—Ioshanna, while proofing your pages, I was dripping with perspiration and very warm; the subject matter was re-mention of Akhnaton. In your personal life incidents, Ioshanna, cited in your recalls, it would certainly seem that you were brought into contact with all levels of human development in the paths you followed up to the present; first hand experience and understanding instilled for your preparation, as so many of those crossing your path were in urgent need of help and of the Unariun Energies. Wherever you stepped and in the backtracking, all were aided whether they knew it or not. Fortunate they were to be in your company as you walked toward and in the Light.

In another vein and referring to the time you and the Moderator spent in Palm Springs, how graphic and subtle the sojourn there. You had mentioned to me how ill and inconsolable He was before the move there, that it was the only thing to do in hope of pulling him out of his very low ebb. Then to have Him formulate the landscape as His tomb! Surely it was the reliving of His near death as Jesus and the actual re-creation of the tomb, in effigy, in front of the house!

No wonder the cycle came to conclusion and you moved back home to Glendale! He did not, according to the 'Jose' book, remain in the tomb, but with the aid of His White Brotherhood, lived for some time afterwards and which He is now doing. (Surviving some years after rebuilding symbolically his tomb.) Yes, I saw the stone structure outside the cement wall and the guard beside it. Shades of my own miserable past, but I am now contributing constructively instead of the tearing down.

Still another thought comes to mind. It was Dr. Norman's need and it was He who found the Palm Springs house in the setting which you told me at the time, as I visited there, 'was like Jerusalem'. These things did not 'jell' in mind until doing your book—the total working of the very low ebb in His health and feelings, the move to Palm Springs was so very necessary—and His comeback as you returned to Glendale, it being no longer necessary to stay by the 'tomb' which you turned over, appropriately enough as you stated, to a Jewish family. So is the land of Jesus' tomb, in the here and now, again in Jewish hands!

Helen Moore

Note: Possibly needless to mention, Helen was one of the Roman soldiers who stood guard at the tomb, and although I was completely unconscious of the significance at the time, she was one of only four persons whom I had invited during our entire stay there—a note of interest, that she should also be represented as her (symbolical) statue guarded the tomb! Thinking back, two of the others (Sanosun and Louis) to visit there were Pilate and his secretary-counselor, who also had to do with the tomb affair! The other student who made the trip from an eastern state has now too dealt with or cancelled out that past experience. Often it is most difficult for one to accept his guilt-ridden past lifetimes, but 'tis the only way to free oneself from them and on to a more positive, progressive future. R.N.

April 15, 1969—Miracles? Like this morning when I slipped back into bed after getting husband off to work. I slipped off into another dimension of Light. And Light it was! The room was rather dark as the shades were drawn and the Light was observed when I closed my eyes. I dropped off and awakened in a great Light. I was seemingly in a great bath of completely surrounding energy and I observed that several layers were removed from the shell of self and the Light was tremendous. The feeling—pure and wonderfully relaxing and so very clean!

I dropped off again and felt each atom in the body physically shaking; they shook so hard I thought here was the expected earthquake the unlearned have been predicting will wipe out 'California'. But 'twasn't so. It was just little old me getting the zut zuts. I would relax into almost sleep and again it would recur. Over and over again and I very much liked it to happen. I do thank you All for the wonderful goings on with me and know the results will be all to my benefit.

Helen.

Note: Sounds like HM has sensed the Power brought through via the Beautiful Electronic Mechanism!

I was proofing last evening just before releasing the envelope to the mailbox and there you were—right beside my right cheek in all your glorious light! And I knew it was you, Ioshanna, so lovely and reassuring and assisting, your strength, and so very much needed and appreciated. It makes me cry to think of such beauty and your strength and assistance. Thank you, dearest Channel Ioshanna; and like you say, do come often!

After mailing the envelopes, I came back home and the rooms looked smaller and very different to me, I felt so tall and big! The house was no longer the same to me, all was different; and the atmosphere about me felt very different.

Note: Here Helen conveys the proof of a big step-up with herself as she completed this book for me. It was an initiation or new awareness, and indeed, a climb over one of her first bridges to Heaven; and of which there are many. We are glad for you, Helen, in your dedication to your overcoming and efforts to help, to grow, to become more infinitely conscious.

Addendum

Although for many persons the following may be completely foreign, some mention should be made that mankind shall come to know how it is that the Unarius Moderator is, has been, and shall continue, so long as He maintains consciousness with this earth body, to be actually giving his life for the earthean, for his Mission. Because He has created for this channel (called his physical body) from the energies of the few previous earth lives lived as namely, Anaxagoras, Spinoza, Akhnaton, Zoroaster and Jesus, this is the energy from which He draws to function in this dimension (so foreign to Him) and the only way such a Being can enter and exist in this world, for He has long since ceased to function as does the earthean, from a psychic anatomy created from the many hundreds of former lives, having the subconscious, etc.

The truth of the matter is, He has never been an earthean. He has come from a distant spiritual planet, not of the material or physical nature, and has, on rare occasions, descended into these earth hells to bring to man Wisdom that can begin to teach him the better and higher way of life; how to begin to pick himself up from the depths he has so deeply fallen into, for man as a whole is regressing spiritually!

Thus it is that He had created, while He was still in the Inner Worlds, this energy body from the energies of those few lives lived which were compatible to him; and as He extends himself outwardly to all students—which is constantly being expressed as the student studies and during his sleep—He is actually exerting and expending his very life forces, from which He, along with the Infinite Powers of the Brotherhood, created.

So it is true to say, He is dying for each one; for each student so in touch, a very part of Him goes out to you. This is the Infinite Creative Life Force which will regenerate with you eternally; it can even serve to be the Guiding Light for the many thousands who have merely read our invitations sent out!

When, as is now being experienced by Him, He begins to suffer in a psychic way due to too much outflow, He is again, just as He did in Jerusalem, giving his very life for mankind, and even though He is very conscious of this, would He cease in his efforts? Indeed not! If He knew the next second would be his last on earth, and someone needed his extended Consciousness, He would give it unstintingly! But this is the way with a truly developed Being; He is not concerned with Self.

Now, in his last cycle on earth, as each new student is added, it is another addition, another plug in the line which will (as He has so set it up) begin to draw on Him, and myself and upon his Infinite Life Force. This, his very purpose here on earth—his Mission. This cycle toward which we have been striving ever since the start of the Mission, was brought to a conclusion as the "Life of Jesus" book made its appearance. Then, as He 'found and repossessed' his long-lost red box (chest)—lost for nearly two thousand years—this did indeed bring things to a conclusion. Thus, any additional endeavors which He extends are entirely and strictly due to his sheer determination, willpower, and added extension of not only His Mind Forces but of His Very Being, and from which He created this Channel-Energy Projector Radiator (body). Thus, He is, in a sense, dying with each extension of Consciousness, but He dies not, as does the earthean, who will soon again reincarnate into the physical world, for He has finished with the use of the self-created psychic which served his purpose and was formed to appear like the earth-man. Appearance, however, is his only similarity to the earth-man, for He functions in a completely different manner and way, in fact, He is quite different in all respects.

As He says, soon He will step from this robot arrangement, and the Higher Self will ascend unto the Higher Worlds where It lives most of the time, and where his Brothers of Light await Him.

My effort here is being made to try to point up that He is again dying for the earthean, just as surely as He did in Jerusalem, the purpose mainly, He often says, to reach out to those who had to do with these destructive acts, to help them change about in their former negative, retrogressive direction, and to project the Light that can help lift mankind onto a higher plateau and, eventually, upon a more progressive evolution—another proof of this Mind being the greatest life ever lived.

Letter from Sanosun

April 7, 1969—Dear Ioshanna: Assuredly and with great intensity of energy projections do you pass on and share the awareness and the frequency of this great experience with us.

Since the time of your call at the office and all during the typing of your illumined experience I have been alive and completely energized. My face was wet and my knees like putty as I left my desk at the office to go to the lounge and be alone to oscillate with you in the radiant energies which you channeled; and since then and driving home and all through this evening, the top of my head has been heavy with the Ray-Beam projected.

And as you have been stepped up and become One with the Infinite we who share in your experience shall grow in expansion of consciousness.

My cup runneth over,

Sanosun

P.S. My love for You Two fills my whole being and that I am a Unariun and a part of this Great Mission overwhelms me. Eternal gratitude.

The Pulse-Throb of God
(or Creation In Action)

Monday, April 6, 1969—The experience being related here took place last night, Easter Sunday night,
2:30 A.M.:

Although the penning of my notes has been 'completed' and sent to Helen to typeset, I find there really
is no end—or a place to end such relatings! Wonder
of wonders appeared to me that truly no words exist
to even begin to describe, but as I told Ernest of my
wonderful night's vision He said, "Well, you'll just have
to try to describe it the best you can." Thus, an effort
here will be made, although words seem so flat, so
meaningless and crass for such a tremendous happening—indeed, body shaking!

As usual, we retire around twelve o'clock, last night
no exception, Ernest had gone to his bedroom. After
but a few moments sleep, I was suddenly awakened
with the feeling, "Well, my sleep is over," even though
the hands on the clock had scarcely moved. I thought,
"Since I'm so wide awake, I'll edit one of the lessons,"
which we are planning to put into book form—my
present new project. I propped myself up in bed and
read carefully through the thirty pages of His lecture.
Strangely enough, although reading the Unariun liturgies, with their great energy-Power usually causes me
to become drowsy and, before long, off to sleep I go,
here it was quite the opposite. Power and energy seemed to build up intensely, and after completing the
lesson in my searching for typo errors, found I was
even wider awake, alert; and a strong, loud, singing
frequency was present. The high-pitched hum of the
energies was far more pronounced than I'd ever sens-

ed it previously; in fact, the intensity of the energy-hum was so great, I tried to cover my ears to lessen its effect, yet this made no difference as it was an inner manifestation. I wondered, "What goes on, no one here ill, we both felt very well, so what is this power all about?" But I soon learned. I had, in my consciousness in reading, 'tuned in', as it were, unto the wonderful worlds of Light, of Energy—the Infinite.

At the time I did not think of it, but now I remember the Moderator's descriptions in the "Pulse of Creation" books how, just before the emergence of some Spiritual One into another dimension, They created from Their mind energies and caused to manifest, the sing-song chorus of the Energies—a necessary adjutant in these manifestations. The energy song, the intensely high, oscillating frequencies continued for many moments, and my thought, "Well, it looks as if there's no sleep for this one tonight," when above my head (seemingly) in the ceiling, suddenly appeared in consciousness the vision of all visions!

I had thought that I had seen a Higher Being in all His glory and that was the 'utmost', but this Spiritual One appeared many times larger, brighter, and remained longer than any previous visit. Even more wondrous was the detail which I could discern. The nearest I could relate the beautiful phenomena would be similar to lightning but in a pattern within its centermost area similar to a snowflake, so intricate in design, yet the electronic pattern was in all colors, gyrating and oscillating in all directions—oscillating the colors out into the room. So brilliant was this wonder that its radiance would dwarf the sun, yet in some way, I was able to view it without the glare, the reason being, in such a state and contact, one does not view with the physical eye, but it is rather, an inner and mental attunement or an oscillation with the psychic anatomy.

I've written previously of several most wondrous

psychic viewings, and most tremendous they were, but the experience of last night—just six hours ago—was incredible, magnificent beyond description! The Being, far larger in size, much more brilliant, and for the first time did I see the intricate and marvelous electronic mental workings, the central pulse, as it seemed, of this Higher One. As It remained in consciousness, It continued to seemingly 'operate' its mechanism; it was as if one were looking into the mechanical works of some huge, fantastic, electronic mechanism, the snow-flake-like patterns in all magnificent multi-colors, very busily operating and oscillating—so very, very, rapid, the brilliant energy bolt gyrating in the intricate patterns. It was the first time I had discerned the various and many radiant colors in this Being who has made contact in this manner—the Infinite Mind whom I have come to know to be our Moderator in His Higher Self. Yes, this Creative Mind was surely helping to create of me a better person, and I'm most grateful.

Significant, too, of this visitation was the nearness it seemed; it was as if it were within a very few feet of me and I became one with Him. I was instantly awed by the intense brilliance. Space and time were non-existent as I viewed and oscillated momentarily with our Heavenly Visitor—and Heaven!

The outstanding importance was that the entire situation seemed in an entirely different dimension than previously seen. Now it was there beside me—not in the distance to view. The Higher Ones must have prepared me especially for this advent, for I remember well how, when Ernest visited certain areas on Venus where the High Beings were gathered, they enclosed Him in a (seeming) plastic bubble so that his psychic would not become damaged from the high frequencies and He could view them minus the distraction; thus, the sing-song chant of the energies, no doubt, helped condition me for this magnificent display.

It was just a few days ago that our Moderator had mentioned to me as I was relating to Him another of these Visitations, "Oh, I wouldn't be surprised if one of these days They actually materialize to you (He, of course, is one of 'They')—that They project right down into the physical dimension unto you." And thus, this experience was just that; They did indeed materialize into this very dimension. I shall never be the same!

No doubt, were the average person to be so confronted, he would become quite frightened, for it would indeed be a most shaking and shocking experience unless one has been conditioned through eons of time and preparation; yet at the time the Visitor was present, it did seem quite natural and anything but shocking—rather, there was present a great and strong feeling of love outpouring; surely, this was His emanation unto this one. Earthman would be unable to conceive of such impersonal and infinite love feeling—a oneness with all creation, far removed from the personal attachments man experiences, which he terms love. But this is man's future— to be lived.

Thus it is and has happened—surely the most tremendous manifestation and wonder that has ever come to man on earth (other than via the body of flesh in which our Moderator in His Higher Self functions unto the earthman)—an actual Visitation of one of the Most High Infinite Beings. The impression sensed was that here was the Prime Source of Creative Energy—This Great Infinite Being—and countless others like Him (if we can place a gender with it—and which does not exist, as on earth). Infinite Creative Minds are factually the Creators—or, if you will, Gods. We could compare, and quite similarly, the central nucleus of the great configuration to a concentration of lightning bolts—expressing instead, rather than simply in jagged lines of light, in certain specific patterns which occupied possibly more than half the circular area of the entire formation. This luminous concentration of flashing light, remember, existed in many and various colors. Thus could one imagine my feelings as I was suddenly confronted with this Infinite Mind in action! There He was, actually projecting His very Infinite Intelligence unto me! And I could view it all. I felt this great and Infinite One was lifting me up unto His very Consciousness. Now I know what was meant as our Moderator spoke in the 'Joining' tape—to be 'Joined in Spirit' with the very Infinite.

To reiterate more completely, the picture—yet it cannot be called a picture, for it was more of an experience, a happening, an actuality: within the darkened room, there appeared a most glorious sight—a huge, luminous ball or phosphorous area of cloud-like energy, seemingly the size of nearly filling the room. Centermost was something like, if one could imagine, an energy bolt, similar to lightning in intensity and in patterns similar to those of snowflakes, gyrating, oscillating in incredible speeds, this would be in essence as near as I could describe our Visitor's workings, his manner of energy projection. Then inwardly from the outer edge, the configuration became more and more brilliant, and within the last approximate third of the great circular nebula was centered the very intricate, brilliantly colorful, oscillating pattern; we might term it the very Infinite Mind of God! I felt I had been shown wonders that man on earth had not before seen.

Yes, I feel I've been face to face with God—if God had a face—and which He certainly would not; but the Infinite in all its glory, in all its intensity and wonder did indeed pay visit to my humble self. The entire situation seems so vividly impressed within consciousness, the feeling is that it could be described from now until the end of time, yet no adequate defining could ever be given. The reason is these things

are of the Inner and Higher states of Consciousness—
not of this world, yet here in this hour of wonderment, this Being did practically materialize into this,
the earth dimension. Yes, I am unable to even begin to
relate to you my innermost feelings of just what this
tremendous experience has done for me, but upper-
most in consciousness is the sensation that my arms
are not sufficiently long to encircle the world, the Infinite Love is still present—the very 'Presence of God'
feeling. And I trust it lingers eternally! Now, with the
several intervening hours, I still sit atop my 'cloud
nine' with the desire of just wanting to remain quiet
so not to lose 'awareness' of this most 'Blessed Event'.

As I again spoke to our Beloved One about this
transforming happening, in my attempt to describe to
Him how He looked on the Inner in His True Self,
saying, "It actually seemed as if I had been, for eons of
time, watching and wondering about a very wonderful, electronically-manipulated robot—one who could
perform numerous wondrous feats, when suddenly
the entire casing or front of his mechanism dropped
open that I could view the complete operation that
enabled him to function as he did. I could see and
understand now how this very intricate network
within functioned as it flashed about, projecting its
pyrotechnics in living color." His reply was, "No doubt,
that is just about what happened as Truth was manifest." These words may sound strange but that is exactly the feeling I have as I reiterate in consciousness
this body-shaking event.

The star the Wise Men (supposedly) saw in the
East, the burning bush of Moses, the golden plates of
Joseph Smith, the many other historical visions and
events of the past of this spiritual nature are all
dwarfed completely by this one great happening just
related; they are but child's play in comparison. And I
say this to simply point up how it has great significance for the future betterment of mankind; for well I

know that it is, in effect, ushering in a new and greater, more spiritual cycle for mankind in general. This is the reason why I'm stressing in effort to convey to you the unique and tremendous revelation. It is far more meaningful than any personal evaluation. Thus, it should be understandable why I now reaffirm my dedication and service to the cause of Unarius.

Most pronounced and remarkable, too, was the particular type or manner of what we call color that was expressed at the core of the configuration of pyrotechnics; the colors were so radiant and seemingly 'alive' and breathing or pulsating. This incredible and incomprehensible nucleus of color could be likened (I'd imagine) to, for instance, a huge IBM space computer blowing all its fuses simultaneously, the amassment of sparks colorful patterns they would form, etc., yet, this viewing of infinitely intelligent energy was, we know, the very Infinite Mind with which I was then in attunement—and a Fourth of July fireworks display would be completely dwarfed by the luminous display of our visiting Erosean. How I wish it were possible to obtain a picture of this Infinite Being who came so near and gave of Himself unto this one. Oh, do come again! I'm very aware, too, of the great 'step up' this experience brings about. Another bridge has been crossed!

As the Presence started to change dimensions, I noted that the entire room had been phosphorescent, but I could not view it after the Visitor had left, for He had taken me out with Him and I remember nothing after the presentation of Himself in the deliverance of His great energy projection. Much work was accomplished with this one, for again, all physical things are even more foreign to me.

Yes, this Easter night, 1969, was indeed the most tremendous and exceeded by far, all previous experiences, and my feeling is "How, just how, after all that beauty and wonder could there be anything else—to top It!" Oh, such a feeling of inner peace, of satisfaction and joy, of love and upliftment exists! I just want never to lose consciousness (sight) of that divine, heavenly experience; and I wish to pass the 'awareness', the frequency of it all unto you, each one who reads these lines. Still I float in that glorious, indescribable sea of infinite bliss and wish to share it, in part, with all. To speak or write of it brings another rivulet down the cheeks, so overwhelmed am I—so filled, my cup truly runneth over.

Quite a time I had to get down to mundane things this morn, such as preparing breakfast for our Beloved, for I had indeed 'crossed over the bridge' unto Heaven (the Infinite).

Selah.

Ruth E. Norman

AND SO BECOMES MY GOLDEN HOUR
BECOMES MY FLEETING MOMENT
LIVED IN MEMORY
TRANSCENDENT NOW BECOMES MY SOUL
AND WEDDED THERE FOREVER
MY EARTH WITH HEAVEN
AND ETERNAL IS MY LIFE

(E.L.N.)